Praise for Wilbur Smith

'A memoir as vividly thrilling as his novels'   *Daily Mail*

'He is lyrical when writing about Africa'   *Daily Express*

'Wilbur Smith's enthralling account of a life well lived is the equal of any of his great adventure novels'
                              Lord Renwick of Clifton

'A thundering good read is virtually the only way of describing Wilbur Smith's books'   *The Irish Times*

'Wilbur Smith . . . writes as forcefully as his tough characters act'   *Evening Standard*

'Wilbur has arguably the best sense of place of any adventure writer since John Buchan'   *The Guardian*

'Wilbur Smith is one of those benchmarks against whom others are compared'   *The Times*

'Best Historical Novelist – I say Wilbur Smith, with his swashbuckling novels of Africa. The bodices rip and the blood ⸻ ⸻ d misplace all of ⸻ *phen King*

Wilbur Smith is a global phenomenon: a distinguished author with an established readership built up over fifty-five years of writing with sales of over 130 million novels worldwide.

Born in Central Africa in 1933, Wilbur became a full-time writer in 1964 following the success of *When the Lion Feeds*. He has since published over forty global best-sellers, including the Courtney Series, the Ballantyne Series, the Egyptian Series, the Hector Cross Series and many successful standalone novels, all meticulously researched on his numerous expeditions worldwide. His books have now been translated into twenty-six languages.

The establishment of the Wilbur & Niso Smith Foundation in 2015 cemented Wilbur's passion for empowering writers, promoting literacy and advancing adventure writing as a genre. The foundation's flagship programme is the Wilbur Smith Adventure Writing Prize.

For all the latest information on Wilbur visit www.wilbur smithbooks.com or facebook.com/WilburSmith

WILBUR SMITH

On Leopard Rock

A Life of Adventures

ZAFFRE

First published in Great Britain in 2018 by

ZAFFRE PUBLISHING
80-81 Wimpole St, London W1G 9RE
www.zaffrebooks.co.uk

A CIP catalogue record for this book is
available from the British Library.

ISBN (Hardback): 978-1-78576-530-8
ISBN (B Format Paperback): 978-1-78576-535-3

also available as an ebook

1 3 5 7 9 10 8 6 4 2

Typeset by Palimpsest Book Production Limited, Falkirk, Stirlingshire
Printed and bound by Clays Ltd, Elcograf S.p.A.

Zaffre Publishing is an imprint of Bonnier Zaffre,
part of Bonnier Books UK
www.bonnierzaffre.co.uk
www.bonnierbooks.co.uk

Contents

The book is for you, My NisoJon,
with my undying token of eternal love.

Your husband

Wilbur

'There is no such things as magic, though there is such a thing as knowledge of the hidden ways of Nature'

H. Rider Haggard, *She*

1

TWILIGHT

Africa is ancient, vast, monumental, a land of death and renewal. We may think man is the dominant species, but on these everlasting plains with the blue sky hazed by a searing sun, the rhythms of life are indifferent to us. Here we are allowed freedom, our spirit its release, but only if in return we offer respect, loyalty and humility.

In the midday sun my wife and I seek shade, and, with my back resting against a tree, I'm as still as I can be to conserve energy. I take a mouthful of water. The grass is sharp and dry, gilded with dust, and I can hear the slow rush of life in the air, in the bushes, in the soil, a mechanical murmur like the stirring of blood with the pulse of my heartbeat. The wilderness is as beautiful as love and as deadly as heartbreak. I turn to my wife, and she looks at me and smiles, but sometimes I think there is pity in her eyes for this driven man, condemned to never-ending wandering, in pursuit of something he cannot define, that will probably always be beyond his grasp. What sort of man has she committed herself to? What is this journey she decided to embark upon?

A week ago, she sat with me in a crude grass hide, staring through its eye-slit down a narrow tunnel that had been beaten out of the dense bush by the gun bearers, for a bullet travelling at 3000 feet a second could be deflected by even the smallest twig. The tunnel had been paced out to precisely sixty yards so that the rifle could be zeroed in with pinpoint accuracy.

My rifle was resting in the vee of a branch in front of me and I only had to lift it an inch or two to be ready to aim and fire. The rifle was a .416 Rigby, a tenth anniversary present from my wife.

Before we had left camp, we had showered using unscented soap so that the big cats would be less likely to pick up our smell; otherwise they could sniff us out downwind for two miles.

We had baited the site with the carcass of a buffalo cow and the stench was wafting into our hide as we sat below the prevailing wind. The cow I'd selected was well past its breeding prime and one of a herd of several hundred of the muscular black animals. A shot low on the shoulder and through the heart dropped her dead before she hit the ground. The heavy rifle crash had echoed across the plain and sent the herd scattering as blood surged from the wound in the harsh sunlight, the cow's deep death roar as always inspiring in me an electric shock of exhilaration and regret.

The trackers had cut up the animal and hoisted her into a tree at a height that would allow a lion stretching on its back legs to feed, but not to take the bait whole. It wasn't long before the blowflies appeared like shiny round ballbearings to a strong magnet and hastened the putrefaction.

The smell of death contains its own unique primordial fear, and as we waited for the cats to come alive to the prey, the sun slipped slowly in the sky and lent the bush an apricot glow, allowing the colours to become saturated, heavy with their own beauty. The dusk encouraged the birds to emerge, fighting for their territory and staking their claim with raucous abandon, the parrots swooping like fragments of rainbow. There was a pair of sunbirds, anxious and flighty in their rich-sheen plumage, siphoning nectar from yellow flowers.

Suddenly there was tension. An animal padded into the hunting area beneath the buffalo carcass. I lifted my gun, gently easing off the safety while I strained to see what was about to feed on the bait. Its golden pelt caught the dying sun, the light illuminating its cream throat, its soft black-tipped ears, and its yellow ever-vigilant eyes stared, the black pupils like the tips of two cold steel daggers as it looked down the tunnel at me sighting behind the barrel of my rifle.

It was a big cat, sleek and supple and majestic. There is no finer wild animal. It's at moments like these that I consider the deadly calculations that go through a lion's brain as it considers the danger or opportunity ahead of it. Man has the upper hand, but not always. A squeeze on the trigger, as Hemingway put it, like the last turn of the key opening a sardine can, and it would be all over. I beaded the lion's skull. It had no mane; it was a lioness. I would not shoot. She's too precious as a life-giver and besides there are hefty fines for the hunting of a female, even a prison sentence. Legal safari hunting is well managed, it's one of the most effective means of conservation in Africa, and I have my own principles from which I never deviate. If you are loyal to the land it will embrace you; if you kill indiscriminately your soul will eventually reside in hell.

The lioness climbed onto her back legs and began tearing at the buffalo carcass with a savage, violent hunger.

We were mute spectators, my wife and I, witnessing raw power, something that never failed to send a shiver down my spine.

We returned for many days, repeating the vigil in the hide, but the big old male lion never showed up. Perhaps he was wise to our tricks, not ready to concede the fight, and would rage until the dying of his day.

This morning we had seen kudu and reedbuck on the grassy glades that intersected the forest. On the sandy track were spoor of the animals that had crossed in the night. There were elephant droppings, still steaming in the cold air of dawn, a pile knee-high. They came from an old elephant, his teeth at the end of their days, because the dung was full of twigs and leaves that were almost whole. He couldn't chew his food. In the dust were large round footprints, the size of hubcaps. They were smooth imprints from the pads of his feet which were worn down like car tyres stripped of their tread. He was a big old elephant and he was close.

We climbed the kopje, reaching the summit just as the sun broke out from behind the forest, and all about us the land shimmered with the radiance of daylight, new life unfolding in a blaze of colour. The tracker pointed to a far-off clump of forest, perhaps two miles away. There was something grey, impossible to distinguish from a lump of rock, until it moved. We set off down the side of the kopje and onto the golden grass plain. We followed the spoor in the spongy earth, and we could see where the elephant had ripped branches and bark from trees as he fed.

Now, leaning against the tree for a brief rest, cross-legged with the Rigby across my lap, I considered the elephant. A bull of this size could have tusks that weigh up to a hundred pounds each. Like humans who are either left- or right-handed, an elephant will have a dominant tusk, which means that one tusk might be shorter than the other, or even broken. In my grandfather's day, the prize of ivory was always the quest, and the nobler the animal, the greater the desire to capture the trophy. But I also knew that the chase is everything; once you kill, it's only dead meat. The hunting impulse is part of every man's soul; some supress it, some disguise it in behaviour that appears strange and unknowable, some start wars. I choose to constantly move forward, never looking back, and hunting is what I have always done. And writing: I put my heart and soul into every book I write.

• • •

I was eight years old when my father, Herbert Smith, gave me my first rifle, a .22 Remington. I shot my first animal shortly afterwards and my father ritually smeared the animal's blood on my face. I was a new hunter, the blood the mark of emerging manhood. I refused to bathe for days afterwards.

The rifle had 122 notches carved on it, one for every animal that had been hunted with it. 'It's yours now, Wilbur,' my father said, 'but there's a code that goes with it. A system of honour. You fire safely. You shoot clean. You only kill that which you're going to eat.'

The Remington had belonged to my father and before that to my grandfather, Courtney James Smith. Grandpa Courtney had been a transport rider during the Witwatersrand gold rush in the late 1880s, and before that he had led a Maxim gun team in the Zulu War, decimating the enemy with 600 rounds a minute. He was a tough guy, full of burly opinions and apocryphal, self-aggrandising stories.

Hunting was in his blood. I had sat at my grandfather's knee listening to stories of his great elephant hunts, which provided sport and meat to sustain his family. 'You don't hunt an elephant with a gun, you kill him with your feet,' he said. He would walk the elephant down, there were no four-wheel drive vehicles in the 1900s. He always hunted the old bull cleanly, before the animal even knew it was being stalked.

In those days, the big game hunter was revered. My grandfather's heroes were men like Karamojo Bell, a Scottish adventurer who plied his trade in East Africa and was famous for being one of the most successful ivory hunters of all time, and for perfecting the difficult diagonal shot from behind the elephant, known as the Bell shot, which produced an instant kill. There was also Frederick Selous, explorer, hunter and conservationist whose real-life exploits inspired H. Rider Haggard's fictional character Allan Quatermain. Between 1874 and 1876 Selous shot seventy-eight elephants with a short-barrelled musket that fired a quarter-pound bullet. He was an Indiana Jones character, a Victorian gentleman with a wild, untameable streak.

That age is gone, just as my father and grandfather have passed away. The spirit of the times has changed and we have different heroes now, media icons, celebrities, perhaps not so real as the gods of the past.

I rest, I dream, my grandfather is alive in my imagination. I hear his voice:

'The sun's heat was lessening from its midday intensity so we resumed our pursuit. The lead tracker's eye could see the disturbance in the grass, the small scuffs on rocks where the elephant's pads had scraped off the lichen. In a ravine between two hills there was water that was brackish and foul-smelling, but the bull had drunk, leaving behind a pile of his yellow dung. Further on he had eaten the fruit from a cluster of marula trees; as legend has it, the fruit that drives elephants mad with intoxication if the fruit has been left to ferment on the ground.

'Wilbur, a bull elephant needs to eat over a ton of vegetation every day and will have to stop moving to feed. This is when it's at its most vulnerable. Its eyesight is poor and with eyes positioned towards the back of the skull, its forward vision is compromised and its massive ears can impede vision behind him. His hearing is acute and he can sense movement with uncanny precision.

'There was a grumble like a loud purr that echoed across the still plains, the sound of an elephant at ease, feeding contentedly. We pushed forward into the bush and suddenly there was an explosion of twigs breaking, branches being stripped from trees and there he was, his enormous ears gently flapping, and I could see his eye, grey with age and weeping as if he was sentient of his decline and the end of his life. There was sadness in that moment, a melancholy that seemed to rush in like the tide, demolishing all resolve before it.

'His huge tusks were a heavy burden, each day they

would be less supportable. His joints would ache with every step and, if he was in his seventieth year, his sixth set of molars would be worn away and slow starvation would be his fate as soft grasses and fruit, his only manageable diet, would not sustain him. His skin sagged with wrinkles like deep fissures. And yet he was defiant, unbending, purposeful.

'A brain shot would kill the bull instantly. I lifted my rifle, trusting experience and instinct. I took a deep breath but I could not still my heart.

'The old bull elephant in my sights, no more than twenty yards away, was coming to the end of its life, but it still stood proud amongst the trees, feeding on the grass of its homeland, the ragged curves of its bulk an assertion of its massive presence, of nature's mysterious will. Not so many years ago I would have already pulled the trigger of my rifle in an unthinking instant, but now, in my own twilight years I felt an affinity for its life, its struggling, stoic soul that would never give up the chase.

'I had to decide quickly or the bull would sense my presence and charge.

'As the day began its final descent into the half-light of evening, there was a stillness and silence as if the birds themselves had paused before a moment of departure and I lowered my rifle, stepping backwards, taking care to leave with only the slightest disturbance.'

2

LIONS IN THE NIGHT

My father, Herbert, meant everything to me. He was my god, I loved him with every inch of my being. He could be a cussed old bastard, and his values were strictly from the Victorian age, but every boy has a hero in his life and my father was that man. Sometimes I think the world was too small a space to contain his soaring, rebellious spirit and perhaps that was why he was so obsessed with aviation. He loved to join 'the tumbling mirth of sun-split clouds' as RAF pilot John Gillespie Magee put it in 'High Flight', one of my favourite poems. My father named me after one of the Wright Brothers, Wilbur, who, with his brother Orville built the first controllable aircraft.

I don't know whether I ever reached the heights he expected from his son; he thought reading books was a waste of time and writing them even more puzzling. He was a practical, active man, a do-er; a problem was something to be solved, not reflected upon.

I remember the time as if it was yesterday when I first saw what my father was capable of when confronted by danger. He became a real hero to me then and my respect for him was sealed. It was a terrifying experience and it took place at night-time. I was sleeping and woke to roaring.

Wrapped in my sleeping bag, I opened my eyes. Beside me, my sister was already awake, staring nervously at the sliver of firelight between the canvas flaps of our tent. We were used to the ordinary sounds of the bush at night – the whoop of hyena, the chorus of cicadas, the distant growl of a leopard hunting in the dark – but this was tumult beyond all my imagining. I crawled along the stretcher bed and moved to peer out of the tent.

I was eight years old, my sister only six. In the darkness around us lay the wild country of the Zambezi Valley. This was the untamed land, yet to be touched by road or rail, that my father had led us into two weeks before, at the start of the long dry season. These annual safaris had become the highlight of my year, the trips into the countryside around which my young life was built. Sometimes we would venture north from our home in Northern Rhodesia, as far as Kolwezi in the Congo – but this year we had remained closer to home, making camp in the heart of the Luangwa Valley itself.

The Luangwa Valley, even now, is an unspoilt wilderness teeming with wildlife. Over thousands of square miles, the valley is fed by the Luangwa River, one of the tributaries of the Zambesi River, and its many oxbow lakes and abandoned river lagoons provide broad expanses of drinking water. When the rainy season arrives in November, the golden-brown, dusty dry landscape turns to vivid emerald green, and the fresh clean scent of the first rains is a fabulous portent of nature's rebirth. There are more hippopotami splashing in the mudflats of the Luangwa Valley than anywhere else in the world, as well as huge numbers of leopards, elephants, crocodiles and lions who live in prides of up to twenty animals. The lions are dominant and fierce, as if emboldened by the absence of man, and, unique to the area, are known to kill hippos. The birdlife is spectacular and I never tire of seeing the crowned crane roosting in trees, with its halo of straw-yellow feathers, white cheeks and red throat pouch; or the jewel-like carmine bee-eaters, the setting sun magnifying their pinkish-red and blue colouring as they gather chaotically to nest on the river banks. The Luangwa Valley is a place of extravagant beauty and abundance.

Every year our voyage would begin the same way, with my father's tiny Tiger Moth biplane disappearing north to reconnoitre the best hunting grounds – before a group of labourers from the ranch would be dispatched, on bicycle, to burn back the bush and prepare for our coming. Once the new growth had sprouted in the clearing, tempting the game down to lush green shoots, our journey would begin. My father's three big Ford trucks would be packed with tents and camping gear, folding chairs and beds, pots and pans for my mother's outdoor kitchen, rifles and axes and racks for hanging meat. Then, as my father clambered into the cab of the lead truck and gave the traditional cry of *Kwenda Safari!*, we would set out. Travelling with my mother, my father and sister would be twenty or thirty of the best men from the ranch. Crowded into the open backs of the trucks, laughing at the prospect of endless fresh meat grilled on the coals or blackening on the drying racks, their hunting songs filled the air.

We had come for the buffalo, the sable and reedbuck, and the elephants whose meat was crucial to the survival of the local villages. Little did we know that, before the expedition was out, it was we who would become the hunted.

• • •

'Is it them?' my sister asked.

I hesitated on the edge of the stretcher bed, not daring to leave the tent. The thought had entered my head as well. Four days ago, a runner from the District Commissioner's Headquarters, fifty miles away, had arrived in camp and presented my father with a letter warning us that a pride of lions was on rampage through the district. Turned man-eater, they had already killed over twenty villagers, women and children among them. My father's reputation as a good shot and hunter was well known, and the District Commissioner had written to ask him to eradicate this menace if he could.

My father was about to get his chance to confront predators with a taste for human blood.

Outside, our camp was encircled by a *boma* of branches which had been harvested from the bush. In the middle of the protective enclosure sat our two canvas tents – one for my parents, and one I shared with my sister. On the edge of the barricade, our camp retainers – labourers from our family ranch – slept out in the open, the darkness lit only by the faltering light of their fire. Through the sleeping men moved a monster in silhouette: a lion with a mane of black, his luminescent eyes focused on the rack of meat we had butchered that day hanging out to dry.

As I watched, the alpha lion hesitated. Something else had caught his attention. He turned, eyes dazzling in the firelight, and approached the camp retainers. This lion was not interested in meat left out to dry. It wanted the meat of man. It wanted to kill.

The lion was almost on top of Peter, my father's foreman. Lesser men might have faltered, but in an instant Peter reached for the axe that lay at his side. I held my breath, unable to picture what might come next. The lion roared as it sprang forward. Peter raised the axe high above his head and for a second the lion's jaws loomed above him, ready to savage him to pieces, but when they clamped shut, the demon had sunk its fangs into the heft of the axe itself, missing Peter's arm.

Pandemonium broke out. As the camp took flight and screams drowned out the sounds of the bush, two other colossal silhouettes appeared. The lion pride had arrived in force, and we were trapped inside the *boma* walls. I slunk back into the tent, fear overcoming my excitement for the very first time.

Then my father appeared.

From the opening of his tent, my father staggered half-asleep out into the night, wearing only the shirt of his pyjamas. With one hand he seized his rifle, with the other his torch, but as he took his first stride his face smashed into the tent pole and his proud, imperial nose – already broken in some long-ago boxing bout – scythed open, split to the gristle and showering blood. If anything could wake him properly, this was it. Blinking back pouring blood, he turned towards the chaos. The alpha lion, Peter's axe still lodged in his jaws, lifted its head to meet his gaze. There was a grunting, a furious roar, and then the lion charged.

Beside me, my sister panicked. Fear is an infectious emotion. Only seconds ago, this had been an adventure, one of the most thrilling episodes of my young life, but now the enormity of the moment took hold of me and would not let go. Clouds of dust rose to obscure my view. The shrieking of thirty men was dwarfed only by the cavernous roars of all three lions. Tears suddenly poured from my eyes. They say that time slows down, but that is not how it felt; instantly the alpha lion had crossed the camp, ready to tear my beloved father apart.

In these situations, heroes show their true worth. Without trousers, displaying his masculinity to the world, blood streaming from his ruptured nose, my father stood his ground.

In a heartbeat, he turned his torch on the charging lion. Holding his rifle in his other hand, he aimed it like a pistol along the beam of bright light – and fired.

The deranged animal was arrested, mid-leap. The bullet had found the centre of its chest, cleaved through muscle and bone, and buried itself deep in the beast's heart. I watched, incredulous, as the great carcass dropped and, in a whirlwind of dust, rolled to my father's feet. There it lay still, blood pumping out of the hole in its breast.

Dad dropped the torch to reload. The torch's beam tumbled, cutting arcs over the campsite, and fleetingly picked out the faces of the other two lions. Before it had come to a rest, my father lifted the rifle and released another two shots. At each, a lion dropped dead. Silence settled on the camp. The distant sound of the bush returned, the screaming of the camp retainers ebbed away, and I wiped the last tears from my eyes.

I was about to tell my sister it was over, that we could venture out and see my father's prized kills for ourselves, when I heard another sound. My father was kicking his naked feet fiercely into the air and uttering a series of terrible cries. His face caked in blood, stark naked from the waist down, he whirled like a dervish, bellowing what seemed like a triumphant battle cry. Was this some kind of ritual? Or had my dad lost his mind?

'What's he doing?' my sister asked, creeping to my side.

My eyes lifted from the fallen lions to my frenzied father. This was his celebration of the great victory he had achieved, maybe.

It was only as his war dance ended, and my mother came running out to make sure he was alive, that we dared creep over to the lions – and finally realised what he had been doing. As they tore through the camp, the lions had destroyed the camp fire, scattering hot coals across the open ground. It was not triumph my father had been chanting; it was pain. He was kicking to keep the burning coals from scorching his feet.

I looked between the lions and my father then realised how close we had come to being the beasts' next victims. As I marvelled at the beautiful man-eaters spread out beneath me, I was hit by the feeling that there had been only one person standing between them and my sister and me becoming their next meal: my father, my hero, my god.

I stared up at him. He was grinning, proud not only to have survived but to have bested these beasts. He would never know how long that moment would last across the years of my life.

Even now, more than seventy years later, I can remember that night vividly. As I write, on my desk is a faded photograph taken the next morning with my mother's old *Box Brownie* camera. My father and I are kneeling side by side, each holding the head of one of the lions. In the background, Peter stands beside one of the Ford trucks, wrapped in a blanket. Although my father is wearing his pyjama bottoms, his nose remains swollen and lacerated. In the foreground, I am wearing one of my father's hats, copying his style, trying to be him, grinning into the camera as if to say: *these are my lions* . . .

Many lives were saved that night, and the local villagers would never forget it. Nor would I. The memory of it would echo across all the novels of my life, through the Courtneys, the Ballantynes and beyond. Literature throws many great heroes at us, but real life invariably outdoes them. That night I truly understood – my own father was a hero for the ages. And, looking back – across the years, across my novels, into the depths of this faded yellow photograph – I know it was my father who would be the inspiration for the heroes who eventually graced the pages of my books.

The human need to seek out heroes is deep-seated and it's been recognised by storytellers ever since Homer wrote his epic of the Trojan War, the *Iliad*, nearly three thousand years ago. My passion is to bring to life those heroes – and, if ever I need a model for one, all I have to do is remember that night when I was eight years old: my father, his Remington rifle, and three man-eating lions, rampaging in the night.

3

THIS CHILD'S LIFE

'That is a stupid idea!' my father had said. 'You'll starve to death. Go and get a real job!'

From an early age, I wanted to be a writer. I loved telling stories. It was a skill I had been honing from the moment I could read, a way of escaping into distant, imagined lands. My father always had a deep-seated distrust of stories. He was a man who built workshops, buildings, factories, who raised cattle and laid down new roads, but I had discovered the joy to be found in books when I was very young. It was something I inherited from my mother, whose passion for art found fertile ground in me, and slowly the pleasure of losing myself in the visions of my favourite writers – Rider Haggard, C. S. Forester, Ernest Hemingway and more – had transformed into the dream of one day standing alongside all the great writers who had turned life's base metal into the gold of thrilling narrative.

Now, those dreams seemed to have come to nothing. In 1962 I was twenty-nine years old and, sitting in the bedroom of the bachelor's mess where I lived, I stared at the twentieth rejection letter I had received for the novel I considered was my masterwork, *The Gods First Make Mad*. As I screwed it in my fist and prepared to tell my agent to stop submitting the novel any more widely, I faced a troubling thought: my father might have been right.

I do not know where the urge to tell stories comes from. All I know is that it was in me from the time I could compose my first sentence. Books comforted me through the dreaded days of boarding school, when I would rather have been anywhere else. When I was twenty-five, I had to take a dead-end job for Her Majesty's Inland Revenue Service in Southern Rhodesia, and writing was my escape. I had moved to Salisbury to work for my father – who, upon retiring as a cattle rancher, had come here to found a new business, manufacturing and selling sheet metal. Business, however, had not been good – and, with Dad unable to keep me, I'd had to move on. I felt like an abject failure. By that point I was divorced, a single dad with two kids, and just about penniless. Working as a tax assessor was soul destroying, and the evenings were long and lonely. The only good aspect was that the job came with an almost unlimited supply of paper, albeit adorned with Her Majesty's crest, along with pens and plenty of spare time.

I turned to my first love that had got me through the darkest times in my life: my love for the written word. For a year, I had whiled away the nights, pen in hand, as my first attempt at a novel poured out of me. Characters and events seemed to spring fully-formed into my mind, the imagined world opening in front of me on the page. I had taken solace in my imagination, dispelled my loneliness by spending nights with the characters I created, enjoyed on paper what I couldn't do in real life – the adventuring, the carousing, the fighting. And, by the end of it, I was convinced of my abilities as an author.

As the pile of rejection letters, sent by telegram from London, grew taller in front of me, I began to realise what I had, until now, neglected to see. *The Gods First Make Mad* wasn't the landmark of fiction I thought it would be. It was an atrociously pretentious title for an even worse book. I had made all the mistakes of a first-time novelist, walked blindly into every narrative trap, thought myself more talented than I was – and now it was plain to see. In those pages, I had contrived more characters than in *War and Peace*. By attempting to confront the reality of modern Africa I had gone too far, pontificating on politics, racial tension and women as if I was an expert. Even by the standard of those days, *The Gods First Make Mad* was racist. The book was apologetic for the sins of the white man in Africa, making them all out to be heroes without giving voice to Africa's native inhabitants. The sex in it was coarsely written, the stuff of a young man's crudely conceived fantasies, and it was cringeworthy to read. My life skills as far as women were concerned consisted of stolen sex on the tennis court, fumbles in the back of a Model T Ford, and one cata-strophically failed marriage. My novel had not one redeeming feature, and I had been a fool to send it out.

It was a shock that bruised my confidence. Rejection is a harsh taskmaster and failure was becoming a nagging burden. I recommitted to the daily grind of life as a tax inspector. From now on, my only writing would be the endless reams of assessments I sent out.

And there this story might have ended: just one more man whose dreams had been sacrificed on the altar of real life; the drudgery of rent and bills to pay, of work that dismantles one's being, of ambition cast aside as impossible, unrealistic, no longer worth trying. Perhaps I would have gone on as a tax assessor for the decades to come – because, for a year, I heard nothing from London and London heard nothing from me.

When I was twenty-seven, a telegram arrived from London. It was from my agent, Ursula Winant, asking me where my new novel was. I stared at those words, sitting in the same stark bedroom where my dreams had been shattered. It seemed incredible that Ursula might have expected me to write another novel after my first attempt had been turned down by publishers from all over the world. And yet, here was a telegram encouraging me to try again. I should not give up, Ursula was saying.

I had shown potential and I was – or so she said – at the start of a very long road.

For a while, I tried to put it out of my mind. I remembered my father's words of discouragement: life, he had said, is not to be lived in the pages of a book. But I had a rebellious streak, and maybe it was time to show my father what I was made of. Disappointment can be an incredible spur, if it doesn't kill you. I'd never backed down when faced with a challenge and I wasn't going to start now. My father had encountered numerous knockdowns in his life and he'd risen to fight again another day. Slowly, over the next days and weeks, ideas began to unfold inside me, story and character leading me on.

This time, I knew, had to be different. If this did not work, it would surely be my last attempt; bouncing back from failure is exhilarating and validating, but persisting in doing something for which you are not made is foolish beyond measure. I began to look around me for material, within myself and back in time, searching for the shreds of potential that *The Gods First Make Mad* had shown.

The Gods First Make Mad was not my first work of fiction – and I had already, fleetingly, had a taste of success. I knew, on some rational level, that I was not without talent. Sometime before embarking on that ill-fated novel, I had made my debut with a piece of writing called 'On Flinders' Face'. In those days, there were more magazines which concentrated on publishing new fiction – magazines like the *New Yorker* and *Argosy*, both based in America

– and, beyond all my expectations, *Argosy* had chosen to run one of my earliest attempts at a short story.

Seeing my work in print for the first time was one of the most uplifting experiences of my life. It wasn't published under the name 'Wilbur Smith' – I was convinced that Smith was a common and unromantic name that would scupper my bid before it had even begun. I'd submitted it under the pseudonym 'Steven Lawrence', after my mother's maiden name and because I'd just finished reading T. E. Lawrence's *Seven Pillars of Wisdom* for the third time. Acceptance lit me up in ways I could not describe. *Argosy* paid me £70 for the story which was an incredible sum of money at the time, twice my monthly salary, and even more important for someone forced to depend on his parents for hand-outs to get through each month. But what mattered more was the effect it had on my confidence. My story was published alongside S. J. Perelman, Lawrence Durrell and the American science fiction genius Ray Bradbury, and the magazine had featured my hero C. S. Forester, and even printed some of Edgar Rice Burroughs' first instalments of *Tarzan*. *Argosy* also published one of my great literary heroes, Graham Greene.

I was proud of 'On Flinders' Face' in a way I could never be about *The Gods First Make Mad*. What I needed to do was recapture that moment, the joy of a successful creation, the essence that had made 'On Flinders' Face' come alive while *The Gods First Make Mad* had not.

'On Flinders' Face' was the tale of a man going mountain-climbing with two friends, one of whom had been cuckolding the other by sleeping with his wife. In the months before writing it, I had myself discovered rock climbing with a group of friends. On the weekends, we would head out into the veld around Salisbury and scale the granite koppies which are so typical of the landscape there. I had had my share of close scrapes on the ranch where I had grown up, but this was a different challenge – and a daunting introduction to a world of terror-infused adrenaline that I had not quite anticipated. The cliff faces of Rhodesia's heartland were sheer and smooth, offering few handholds, even for a seasoned climber, but I had given myself to them with gusto, displaying a confidence to which I had no real claim. Soon, my confidence got the better of me – I reached too far, committed myself too early, and the granite slipped out of my grasp. One petrified instant later, I was plunging downwards, the cliff face rushing into the sky, the whole world a blur of colour and churning air. I fell for what seemed like an age but it could only have been seconds, and suddenly I was swinging helplessly from the end of my rope, several hundred feet above the ground.

As I dangled there, reflecting on how easily lives could end, the plot of 'On Flinders' Face' flowed into my mind. It was a moment of pure inspiration in which story and characters simply materialised in front of my eyes. I knew that, if I survived, I would have to write it down. This was a story and world that I understood. I was living it, every heartbeat of the moment, after all. I knew about the terror and thrill of rock climbing from personal experience. I knew how the hard granite felt beneath a climber's fingers, how the challenge of pitting yourself against a mountain could come to dominate the mind. And now I had first-hand knowledge of the fear all mountaineers, professional or amateur, will one day come to know: the sensation of freefall, as the mountain betrays you at last.

I was lucky. My good friend Colin Butler was belaying me; a bull of a man, with the strength of ten, he dragged me single-handedly back to the ledge from which I had just slipped. Later that week, once the shakes had worn off, I sat down in the Salisbury office and, ignoring the pressing demands of income tax assessments, began to write the story in longhand, because I couldn't type. A young secretary in the office offered to help and even though I didn't have a cent to pay her, she helped me anyway. Perhaps she could see how desperate I was to capture the moment, to hone my craft.

Now, faced with the idea of beginning a new novel, I sat down with my copy of *Argosy* and stared at 'On Flinders' Face'. There was magic in my hands. There was alchemy. And, suddenly, I realised why. I had been writing about what I knew. I had recreated the sensations of being on that mountainside, translated it to the page, captured the real feelings of that dreadful moment. 'On Flinders' Face' had been true.

I was determined to do the same again. I had my life to draw on. I had vivid memories of my childhood, living half-feral on my father's cattle ranch. I would write about my adventures on that ranch. I would write about the people I had known, the black and the white, about hunting and gold mining and carousing and women. I would write about love and being loved, about hate and being hated. I would leave out all the immature philosophy, radical politics and rebellious posturing that had been the backbone of my past work, and only write about the subjects and people I knew.

At the age of 29 in 1962, I picked up my pen to begin, and an old memory returned. It was a story I had thought of often over many years, one that made me marvel even to this day. It was the memory of the time I had woken in the night and, crawling out of my tent, watched my father shoot three man-eating lions without breaking a sweat.

I looked down. My pen was already moving over the page. *When the Lion Feeds* were the words I had written. I had a title. At last, I was on my way to eternal freedom.

. . .

I was born on 9 January 1933, in what is today Zambia in Central Africa. In those days independence was still thirty-one years away, and Northern Rhodesia, as the country was then known, was a protectorate of the British

Empire. The first air I breathed was the air of the Copperbelt, in a tiny maternity ward in Ndola. Eighteen months later I was fighting for my life, after contracting cerebral malaria. The doctors warned my parents that it might be better if I died. They worried that if I came through, I could be brain damaged. I survived of course, and it probably helped me because I think you have to be slightly crazy to try to earn a living from writing.

My father had been drawn to this remote country as a journeyman metal-sheet worker, having completed his apprenticeship in Pietermaritzburg, South Africa, and it was here he had made his first fortune. The Kafue River, a tributary of the great Zambezi, had long ago drawn investors to the rich copper deposits along its banks, and for a time a thriving mining industry had existed – but, by the time I was born, the Great Depression had taken its toll, reaching even this remote place in the heart of Africa, and the mines sat stagnant, an underworld museum waiting for a new beginning.

When the mines were closed, most of the workers had been sent back to England with just enough money to give them a chance of finding their feet when the ship made port. My father, however, was not a man to make that bargain, and stayed on in Rhodesia determined to find a way to survive. He was resourceful, he could see opportunities. I was born the son of a hunter and trader, a man who built and sold what he could.

Life was hard and my father used his wits and sometimes

his rifle to provide for his family. He set up a chain of fourteen stores, simple corrugated tin huts perched precariously on the edges of Rhodesia's roads, from which local men in his pay would sell whatever wares he could provide. Mostly, it was day-to-day goods – blankets and tools, animal skins and clothes – but sometimes he would disappear deep into the bush, coming back with buffalo hides and butchered meat to sell. My sister, two years younger than me, and I lived like natives as, little by little, he built his empire. By the time the effects of the Depression began to ebb away, my father had decided he did not want to live his life working for somebody else. There was a visceral thrill in pitting yourself against the world, in relying on nobody but you. It was a lesson I would one day learn for myself, though in a very different sphere to my father.

When the mines were reopened in the late 1930s, my father was contacted by the authorities running the Copperbelt, and asked to repurpose the dilapidated houses so that the miners could return. Sensing the chance to find some stability for his family, he led us back to the mines – but soon he had decided to break free and, in 1938, we finally moved into a ranch of our own.

My father's ranch was 25,000 acres of forest, hills and savannah near the town of Mazabuka, nestled in the banks of the Kafue River, which ran for more than a thousand kilometres, down from the Copperbelt to join the mighty Zambezi. The land had once been a succession of separate farms, each allotted to returning soldiers after the First World War, but my father had painstakingly bought them all – and now everything I could see, from the miombo woodlands in the north, to the lush grasses of the Kafue flood plain, was ours.

At the age of twenty-eight, in 1961, I stood outside the traditional thatched Rhodesian farmhouse my father had built, a polished red veranda running all the way round its white-washed walls, and watched him approach. I had always thought of my father as the master of all he surveyed, a semi-mythical figure hewn out of the wilderness and bending the world to his own shape. He was not a huge man, but sun-burnished and fair, with forearms grown immense by his years of working with sheet metal and ventilation pipes, and a head that had been bald since his early twenties. His eyes were piercing blue, his nose misaligned from the time it was broken in a boxing match – and, as he veered off to talk to his foreman, I took my chance. This was time for some secret reading.

My father didn't hate books. In a lot of ways, he too was a bookish man – and, late at night, he could often be found under the lantern light of the ranch house, poring through his mechanical books and manuals, absorbing all the factual, technical knowledge he could find. My father did not distrust books; it was *stories* he was highly suspicious of. He was convinced stories could infect a young mind. Stories were flights of fancy, ways of escape, imaginative confections that took you away from the real world of taming and conquering the wild, laying roads and raising empires out of the dust. To my father, stories represented a distraction from the proper business of life, they were unmanly. He had no love for them and would have preferred it if I had none either.

In my early teens, while back at the ranch for long summer holidays, when I was sure he wasn't looking, I scrambled around the side of the ranch house and crossed the scrub land. There, by a koppie of brown stone – on which sat the vast water tank that fed into the ranch house – I made my way down to the outhouse. Inside lay the long-drop latrine. Once I had made certain the bolt was dropped, I unearthed my secret cache from the hiding place I had burrowed out many months before. Here were the prized possessions of my young life: *Biggles in the Baltic*, *The Black Peril*, *Just William* – and, my current favourite, *King Solomon's Mines*. Certain that I would not be discovered for a while, I settled down in my hiding place to read. I used to spend so long in the outhouse latrine reading books that my father was convinced I had a stomach problem and ordered my mother to force me to swallow copious doses of castor oil. It was a small price to pay.

At other times my father would send me to collect wood for heating and cooking and I'd head off with the tractor and trailer and a gang of workers. Before we set off I'd sneak a book down the front of my shirt. As our men worked up a sweat chopping wood, I'd be perched on the tractor, reading my book out in the open with this big sun hat on. My father never caught me because I could hear his car coming. And when the car did come tearing down the road spitting dust, I'd leap off the tractor, shove the book back up my shirt and pretend to make myself useful. The men didn't mind; I was too small to wield an axe and they made sure to keep my secret. Sometimes they'd point to their head and make a small circle with their index finger to indicate that I was a smart, brainy chap because I read books, but more likely they thought I was a bit mad.

It was my mother who had introduced me to the magic of the written word. Her love of reading touched me deeply. She was ten years younger than my father, and she had met and fallen in love with him on the Copperbelt, at one of the dances to which the locals from many miles around would descend every month. If my father was my god, my mother was my guardian angel. She shielded me from my father's rage, until it cooled. She ignited my interest in the wonders of nature, trees, plants, species of flower and their exotic classifications. Together they made me who I am. Her name was Elfreda, and she balanced my father in a way that made them perfectly matched. Where my father was headstrong and single-minded, my mother was gentle and artistic. With dark hair and almond eyes, she was English by birth but embraced the wilds of Africa without breaking her stride. When she wasn't sitting at her easel with her watercolours, painting this dramatic landscape, she was cantering across the veld on horseback, equally at home under the endless African sky as she had ever been in an English city or town.

For as long as I could remember, my mother had led me into the fantastic worlds lying inside the pages of her books. After a long day following my father around the ranch, bedtime would bring adventures of its own. I would curl up in bed and listen to my mother reading from books just like the ones I now had hidden in the long-drop latrine. One room in the ranch house was dominated by her library, with shelves of books lining every wall. I could never understand why this was not an object of awe to my father. There may have been a real life out there offering its own unique experiences, but in my mother's library there were hundreds of other worlds as well, all of them waiting to be explored. The hour before I went to sleep was the greatest pleasure I could remember. As I lay in my bed, letting her words wash over me and staring at the book in her hands, every night I would think, 'She's not making it up! It's all coming from those pages. That book . . .' Those were the first moments I knew books would always play a central part in my life.

As soon as I was able, I started to read books myself, starting with *Biggles* and *Just William*, and no longer was it a pleasure reserved for night times alone. Soon I was lost in the worlds of C. S. Forester, with his exquisite Horatio Hornblower tales of adventure on the high seas, or John Buchan and his thrillers set in the wild places of the distant north. My mother struck up a friendship with a public librarian in Bulawayo, almost eight hundred miles to the south, and every month a package of new adventures would arrive on the freighter trains that were then spreading across the continent. From that moment onwards I always had a well-thumbed novel in my pocket. I could dive into books where I found gripping tales of death and danger, the heroism and savagery of this continent we called home. I loved the romance of Africa, the mysticism of its lost tribe and the sorceress, She Who Must Be Obeyed. H. Rider Haggard, one of my favourite authors at the time, showed me that Africa was a vast repository of stories – and, better yet, that I was close to those stories. Hidden in the long-drop latrine, I got to thinking that Haggard's hero, Allan Quatermain, was in some way a reflection of my father and his own African adventures. Quatermain was English-born, the same as my father – and, like my father, he too was a professional game hunter and trader. Haggard's love for Africa and its people was so deep he too learned the languages of the natives and supported their affairs. It was from these men that I learned to look at Africa as a continent filled with heroes and heroines, a place of infinite adventure.

I was reading about the jungles of Africa's dark heart, journeying in my imagination with Quatermain, when I heard my father bellowing my name from the back of the ranch. Fumbling to hide the books, I emerged from the outhouse in time to see him descending from the veranda.

He looked at me with the same scrutinising expression I can still remember, even though he has been gone from this world for over thirty years. It was a look that said: *What were you doing in there, boy?* He wanted me to be like him, and in many ways, I was. I just had another facet to my personality, a love for imaginative invention that maybe he thought was some kind of affliction. My father was not an unimaginative man; he simply never had time to indulge in solitary abstract pursuits. There was constant physical work to be done.

'Wood,' my father said, and I nodded. It was time for my chores to begin.

Once, when I was hurling firewood into the tractor's trailer, the book I'd hidden up my shirt bounced out into the dust. As luck would have it my father had joined us to keep an eye on the workmen as they cut down the bush. I hastily rammed the book back up into my shirt and continued as if nothing had happened. I heard the crunch of footsteps as my father came up behind me and put his big hand on my shoulder. I turned around. I don't know if it was the sun glancing off his face, but I'm sure I saw the briefest of winks in his eye. Nothing more was said.

• • •

I was so proud when I held my grandfather's rifle for the first time. My father handed it to me without a word, and of course I knew what it meant to him and to me. I had marvelled at this rifle on many occasions, known its long and storied history. The old Remington was cared for and in perfect condition, and I ran my fingers along the notches and tried to breathe in the hunts, each one a story in my mind which I loved to hear again and again.

The sportsman's code that my father taught me was an order that brought decency to killing, an unspoken line across which a true hunter never stepped. Hunting, for my father and grandfather, had never been an indiscriminate practice, done for joy. Hunting was a way of life, a skill by which you provided for your people or helped the natural world retain its balance. Those were lessons to which I would stay true throughout my life, but in that moment, I could think of nothing but the legendary rifle in my hands.

The fact that my father had trusted me with this rifle was a privilege and an honour. We did not see my grandfather often, only when we took long journeys south to his home in Natal. He lived alone in a twenty-acre plot outside town, surrounded by the guns, spears and fishing rods of his life, a pack of dogs his only company. If my father was a god to me, then Grandpa Courtney was a god to my father. To me he was Methuselah, an ancient man from a different age. With his dazzling blue eyes and a pair of magnificent moustaches lightened by tobacco juice, he could hit a spittoon at five paces without spilling a drop. He appeared like some vision from the storybooks I loved – and was himself a fountain of stories. I used his name for the hero of my first novel *When the Lion Feeds* but in truth he inspired both Sean Courtney, and Sean's father, Waite.

I remember the day he told me the story of the sjambok, which is a long, stiff whip originally made of rhinoceros hide. Grandpa Courtney must have been 55 or 60 years old, but to my mind he was ancient, mythological, an icon carved out of stone but still animate. He had been an inspector of roads in what was then Zululand, riding the highways, and then a lieutenant in the Natal Mounted Rifles, one of the finest cavalry units in African history. Our trips to Natal were lit up by tales from him which stunned me; they left me breathless and gave me bad dreams for about a week afterwards.

'My boy, let me tell you the story of the Black Mamba!' he said one day.

'It was after the war,' he began, 'when I came to the Witwatersrand. Those were the days of the gold rush, when there were fortunes to be made . . .' He spat into the spittoon emphatically. 'But the gold fields weren't for me. For ten years, I was a transport rider along the Delagoa Bay route, all the way from the coast to the Witwatersrand goldfields. It would take three months for the wagons to ride that route, ferrying everything from blankets to champagne and dynamite to ore crushers, a 1200-mile round trip. And I'd be riding out ahead of the ox-wagon train, hunting and bartering with the African native tribes as we went . . .'

It was just like *Jock of the Bushveld*, the book by James Percy Fitzpatrick which told the story of an ox-wagon transport rider and his dog in the Transvaal of the 1880s.

'One time, before we set out from Delagoa Bay, I won a dog in a game of poker. It was the biggest, dumbest boarhound you ever saw. Four foot high at the shoulder, a big jowly brute. That dog was the most stupid dog I ever owned in my life. It was totally untrainable . . . I called him Brainless. So Brainless rode the trail with us. Along the way, I tried to train him – but it never did take. All that dog did was hang around the camp, or lope after my horse with this dopey expression on its face. One night, we were camped in the Lowveld; it was dark that night, though the stars were out. I was laid out to sleep in the cot in the back of one of the wagons – but that dog, that dog just kept barking, on and on, keeping us all awake. I groped around beside the cot and I found my sjambok, and I slipped from the wagon, the sjambok in my hand, and strode out of the camp, into the darkness where he was standing. I clobbered that dog until, suddenly, on the fourth or fifth strike, the dog started acting in a different way. It made a new sound, a sound it never made before. I was a bit taken aback. I reached into my pocket, struck one of my matches and held up the light. Right where Brainless the boarhound should have been was a fully grown male lion, its eyes mad with fury, its mane matted with blood. It had eaten my dog! I froze. Because there I was, giving this beast the hiding of its life with the sjambok . . . I turned and ran back to the cabin, jumped inside, closed the curtains and stood there panting with horror and relief. And then I felt the sjambok twitching in my hand! I lit another match . . . It was no sjambok I was holding. It was a snake. I'd been beating that lion with a Black Mamba!'

It wasn't only the story that thrilled me. It was the way Grandpa Courtney hollered with laughter, his guffaws echoing around the room. Man versus beast; he'd survived this close encounter with death.

The Black Mamba has a reputation for being the most dangerous snake in the world. Its bite is known as the 'kiss of death'. It can exceed two metres in length and it likes to live on the ground, waiting to ambush its prey. When under threat it rears up high with its black mouth open, spreading its neck flap and hissing. It strikes faster than the human eye can see and from long distance, often biting many times very quickly. Its poison is highly toxic and will incapacitate a man in less than twenty minutes with a single bite. Many myths surround the snake, such as its ability to bite its tail and roll down a hill then straighten out like a spear to attack at great speed, or that it can ambush a car by coiling itself around a wheel to spring at the driver when he stops and gets out. It is a killer but I always found in it a sinister beauty with its sleek, slender olive-brown or grey body and gun metal eyes. Despite its cold scaliness, it's not hard to imagine how Grandpa Courtney could have mistaken its long, whippy, dark length for his sjambok.

I'd had my own run-ins with the Black Mamba. Sometime before Grandpa told me that story, I'd taken to climbing the koppie behind the ranch house to the reservoir that lay on top, a big tank filled with water pumped up from a bore-hole. The water attracted flocks of doves and pigeons every evening, and I used to go up the hill with my pellet gun and bring back some birds for the barbecue. One evening, when I'd reached the water tank, there were no doves or pigeons to be seen at all. The place was deserted. It should have been a warning, but I paid it no mind. Instead, I started walking up to take a closer look in the reservoir – and suddenly, out of the knee-high grass in front of me, appeared this horror: grey-black, glistening in the sunlight, with two beady eyes! It was a Black Mamba, known by the locals as the 'lights-out snake', because if it taps you, your lights go out pretty quickly. It was an enormous snake, as thick as my wrist around the neck, and its head was a whispering menace, its little black tongue slipping in and out. Its eyes mesmerised me, shiny black, as pitch as coal, as hard as death. It rose, and kept on rising until it was at my eye level, and then beyond. The snake was over the top of me, staring down. Slowly, I raised my pellet gun and took aim at its head. As my finger hovered over the trigger a small voice whispered to me: *Don't be a damn fool, Smith. Get the hell out of there!* With meticulous precision, I lowered the gun. I knew better than to run, the Black Mamba is a fast mover, so I took two short steps backwards and the snake dropped down a couple of inches. I backed off two further steps and the snake bobbed down two more inches. It was following my every move, its eyes on me all the time as if it was trying to hypnotise its victim before striking. By now it was all or nothing, I turned tail and ran down the hill like a terrified gazelle, jumping and kicking my heels, panting and squealing as the air burst out of my lungs with sprinting. By the time I reached home I was a trembling mass of giggles and nervous laughter. I had lost my appetite for barbecued doves and pigeons. That was the last time I ever went hunting at the reservoir.

• • •

Grandpa Courtney had been a hunter on the Delagoa Bay trail, my father had been a hunter in the Witwatersrand, and it was imperative that I turn to hunting of my own. In those days, it was the measure of a man, as well as a way of providing meat for the table. I wanted nothing more than to prove myself capable of surviving the demands of the wilderness.

I didn't have normal friends. My childhood was bordered by the bounds of the ranch, and my only real friends were the children of the farm labourers, who shared the same interests as me: getting out from under the feet of our elders and living free, hunting all manner of prey with our slingshots and pack of mangy farm dogs. My first and best mate was a lad named Peter Matoka, whose dad,

Peter senior, was my father's foreman back when he worked on the mine. My friend would go on to become Minister for Information in Kenneth Kaunda's government when Zambia became independent in 1964.

The other friend I had was Barry, the son of one of our neighbouring ranchers, and it was with Barry that I spent many of my longest, most hair-raising days.

I did not need an excuse to go after adventure and Barry was the perfect partner in crime, each of us egging the other on to wilder extremes. It was with Barry that I had my second run-in with the dreaded Black Mamba. There was an abandoned tobacco barn on our ranch with a pair of beautiful Lanner falcons nesting in its eaves. The Lanner falcon is a medium-sized bird of prey, with dark grey-bluish plumage on its back and a lighter brown mottled underside. It has a reddish head and distinctive dark streaks down both cheeks, like a pair of raffish moustaches. It really is a most handsome, dignified bird, and we should have treated this nesting pair with more respect. I knew the mother had laid her eggs, and, after consulting his manual of falconry, Barry and I determined to get ourselves a chick each and train them to hunt. This, we were convinced, would make us real hunters – to go out with a falcon at our command. It was a terrifying climb to reach the nest in the rafters, not just because of the height and precariousness of the ascent, but because I was constantly being dive bombed by the angry parents. The Lanner falcon hunts with its partner, forming a coordinated attack from two angles, so I was being given a proper going over – their talons are very sharp. Yet, with Barry urging me on, somehow I reached the rafters and counted three little fledglings in the nest.

Barry's book had said the chicks would be ready to train in six weeks – so, four weeks later, this time with a pith helmet jammed squarely on my head and the strap cinched under my chin, I made the daunting climb again, finally ready to rob the nest. As I got closer, I became aware of a terrible silence. The mother and father falcon did not shriek nor dive at me from above; the baby birds were not crying out for their mother, neither hungry nor in fear. With a growing sense of unease, I reached the nest and peered into it. The three chicks were stone dead and looking straight at me was a snake! It was a Black Mamba and it was very angry. Immediately it struck at my face. I ducked and it smashed into my helmet like someone had punched me in the head. I dropped and crash-fell the thirty feet to the floor of the barn, picked myself up, and ran like hell. Barry followed, sprinting behind me, shouting, 'What is it? What is it?' He must have feared I'd unlocked the gates of hell. We didn't stop running until the barn was out of sight. With our hands on our knees, catching our breath, Barry suddenly looked at me in horror. He pointed at my head. I removed my pith helmet and, right at the level where my forehead would have been, were two puncture marks in the cork, the cloth soaked with the snake's pale yellow venom.

I almost threw up in relief. Neither Barry nor I ever went back to the barn.

I had shot my first animal soon after my eighth birthday, with the Remington rifle handed down from my Grandpa. I had stalked that reedbuck by drawing on every lesson and piece of wisdom my father had given me, keeping low and silent in the bush until I got the chance and took aim. When I brought my first meat to the farm, my father shook my hand, and for that moment I felt ten feet tall, immutably connected to this vast and beautiful African landscape, its history and the long reach of my family and their ancestors. My small hand almost disappeared in his. He squeezed tightly and I shook his hand vigorously in return, sealing the bond as the adrenaline coursed through my veins.

After that, Barry and I would roam the trails from one corner of the ranch to another, sometimes crossing the Kafue into his own family lands, sometimes straying even further afield, deep into the untamed bush. The animals we didn't shoot, we would trap – laying down snares for birds and other small creatures, anything we could roast to eat above an open fire. Then we would return home, long after the sun had gone down, to avoid that most dreaded punishment for all wild boys: the bathtub. My legs would be scratched and scored from the vicious *wag 'n bietjie* thorns, I would have blood-sucking ticks in places I could not show my mother, I would stink of wood smoke and dried sweat – but none of it mattered. I was as happy as I ever could be.

For a time, we hunted only small game: reedbuck and impala, bushpig and the puku. But, as in every young hunter's life, our ambition soon turned to bigger animals such as antelopes or bushbucks. On a bright summer's day when we were no more than fifteen years old, beneath an unending expanse of stark blue sky, Barry directed my gaze to the mountains that marked the horizon beyond the churning Kafue, and whispered of a rumour he'd heard.

'There's a kudu bull, roaming in the lowlands of that hill. Wilbur,' he said, 'we're going to hunt him.'

Kudus are a tall woodland antelope, with narrow bodies and long legs, their coats marked by vertical white stripes stretching down from their pronounced, curved spines. To my young mind there was no more elegant antelope to hunt; its two large spiral horns were coveted trophies. Bulls, I knew, sometimes moved in small bachelor herds – but more often they lived solitary lives. Barry had heard of this fine specimen from the labourers on his farm: a legend of a bull, with horns bigger than any they'd ever seen.

Barry and I set out, borrowing my father's old Willy's Jeep from the back of the farmhouse, fording the river and journeying into the forested hills. I had driven this way before, but soon the roads petered out and we rolled, instead, through deepening scrub. When the jeep could go no further, we jumped out and went on foot. It took an hour for us to spot the bull's spoor, finding evidence of his passing in the tracks he'd left behind, the familiar diagonal walk and prints of his cloven hoofs – but it took longer to discover the beast himself. The sun was already sinking by the time we first saw him. Even from five hundred yards away, he was as regal and dominant as I'd imagined. I marvelled at his size, he was a big bull, his proud head adorned with two magnificent horns.

We tracked him down the valley, along forest trail and empty scrub, but by the time the sunlight was paling to dusk we still hadn't come close enough to take our shot. We turned to the skies. The last glimpses of sunlight were hovering over the mountaintops; soon they would be gone, plunging the land into impenetrable night. Neither Barry nor I wanted to be the first to admit defeat, but we would have to head back to the jeep, and get home, soon.

We had found the bull and we'd find him again; I shouldered my rifle and began to tramp away.

It was some time before I realised Barry hadn't followed. When I turned back, he was walking in the opposite direction.

'This way, Smith,' he said.

'*This* way,' I said, trying to draw him to me.

The realisation hit us both at the same time: we didn't know where we had left the jeep.

Too obsessed by our prey, we'd made the same mistake that has signalled the end for reckless outdoorsmen since time immemorial: we'd allowed the wilderness to turn us around. We'd stopped paying attention to the shape of the koppies, the types of tree, the ground beneath our feet, all the markers an experienced bushman would note.

Worse still, we hadn't plotted our route back. Intent on taking the kudu before nightfall, we'd pushed on without a thought to the trail we were leaving behind.

We set off in one direction, but soon the bush grew entangled and we knew this was not the way. We took off in another, only to find ourselves climbing unfamiliar gullies that we had not come down. Up above, the last rays of the sun disappeared from the horizon, and the stars appeared in the inky canvas – and, as the chill of night descended, we stared at each other and silently acknowledged that the day had gone badly wrong. We were lost. We were not going home that night. Before long, our families would know we were missing, and chaos would break out across our respective ranches.

'We're screwed,' said Barry.

'It will look different in the morning,' I said, only half-believing it. First, there was enduring a night in the bush, without fire, food, or water.

The sounds of the bush at night are magical when you are safely under canvas, or warmed by the touch of a flickering campfire. But the distant growl of a leopard, the shriek and whoop of hyena – these sounds have a different effect on two boys cloaked only by the dark. Sleep did not come that night. We clung to our rifles, backs braced against an outcrop of cold stone, and waited for the black sky to pale.

When morning came, two hungry, bedraggled boys tried to follow their own spoor, hoping they could backtrack and find the place they had left their jeep. But it was hopeless. By the time the sun was at its zenith, we had turned ourselves in yet more circles. Desperation had long ago set in. I did not speak to Barry and Barry did not speak to me. The hunger in the pit of my stomach had turned into a fist of hard rock, and the scabrous sensation at the back of my throat was only the first of many signs that we were dangerously dehydrated.

When I heard a noise overhead, I couldn't be certain it wasn't the roar of anxiety in my febrile mind. I squinted into the cruel afternoon sun and saw a shape that lifted my heart. It was my father's little Tiger Moth biplane, sailing out of the blue.

Adrenaline pumped through us. With energy I had not known we still had, we leapt up to grab his attention, screamed crazily and waved. I would have recognised the sputter and whirr of that aeroplane anywhere; it was in the cockpit, alongside my father, that I had first taken to the skies, wrapped up in hat and goggles as we glided over the contours of the ranch.

The plane banked overhead. There was a moment when I thought he had seen us. Then, he flew on.

I yelled until I was hoarse, my throat raw. It was as if an invisible tow rope had snapped and we were left drifting, buffeted by thermals, abandoned. I had never felt so alone and helpless.

Barry shrugged his shoulders. There was a fixed expression on his face, a thousand-yard stare.

We collapsed onto the naked red earth and, for the longest time, sat there, being baked by the unrelenting sun.

We had given up finding our own way back to the jeep. The thought of the kudu bull was so distant it was another lifetime. Now, our only focus was the tormenting hunger in our stomachs, the way our bodies were screaming out for something to drink. Thirst can be all-consuming. It drives men to the brink of madness and beyond. We stumbled on, and only when we came across a lot of spoor heading in the same direction did we begin to hope. There was a waterhole somewhere. With our last reserves of strength, we started to follow.

Sometime later, we staggered down a steep, scrubby escarpment – and stretched out before us was the watering hole. Like madmen, we reeled down to the edge and dropped our heads to drink. Barry was the first to taste that sweet water, with all its promises of life. Moments later, he recoiled, retching.

'What is it?'

'Elephants,' he spluttered. 'There have been elephants here . . .'

I scanned the watering hole, but there were no signs of elephants, no signs of any living creatures but two boys, desperate to drink. I cupped my hands, filled them with water, and bent my head to take my first mouthful. Only now did I know what Barry meant. The water tasted stagnant, with the faintest hint of ammonia. Elephants have a habit of finding a watering hole, submerging themselves and emptying their enormous bladders in the fresh water. What we had hoped was water was mostly dilute elephant pee.

You would have to be dying of thirst, really craving liquid, to consider drinking it. I dropped my head and drank and drank.

Soon, night had returned. Barry and I found shelter in the bush and lay awake until morning brought us back to our senses. It was as dawn broke on the third day that I heard the Tiger Moth again. This would be our final chance. Ripping off our shirts, Barry and I scrambled for higher ground and began waving them furiously back and forth. Then came the signal we had been praying for. Far above, my father tipped the aeroplane's wings back and forth to acknowledge us, extended his hand from the cockpit in an instruction I understood immediately to mean '*stay where you are!*' and banked around. There was no place for him to land in bush this thick, but he had located us and he knew we were alive. Barry and I settled down for a long wait.

Time went by and another sound reached us through the bush. It was my father's truck, grinding its way towards us. At long last, it materialised out of the scrub. My father sat impassively behind the wheel and motioned for us to climb into the back. Relieved at our rescue, it wasn't until I saw the stony set of his face that I knew how much trouble we were in. The truck wheeled around and, at last, we were on our way home.

We dropped Barry at his house first, to face the wrath of his parents. Then, we made the long, jarring drive back to our own ranch. Outside the farmhouse, my father climbed out of the cab and came around to face me. The bigger part of him, I knew, was grateful I was alive. Only now did I think of the panicked nights my mother had spent, the terrible calamities she must have imagined had happened to me. I watched as my father pulled the belt out of his pants to give me a well-deserved thrashing. What we had done was reckless and foolish, and the guilt I felt at putting them through such worrisome times was overwhelming – but there was another part of me that revelled in the adventure. Lost in the wilderness. Two nights without food or fire. Only a rifle to keep the wild world at bay. This was a tale of survival to rank with the best of them, and one of my own. Experience was beginning to shape me, to show me what I was made of and if I could stand up after a fall.

That night my father came into my room. I was wide awake, unable to sleep after the terrors of the last few days and my father's anger. He sat on the bed next to me. I was expecting a stern talk about lessons to be learned, cautions to be taken, but he didn't say a word. He stared beyond me for a while, as if considering a difficult problem. Then he touched my forehead briefly and left the room.

• • •

I had another near-death experience in my late teens when I was the budding hunter determined to prove myself and shoot a buffalo. The African or Cape buffalo is one of the 'Big Five' group of animals and is a sought-after trophy for hunters. It is known as 'the Black Death' or 'widowmaker' because it's a very dangerous animal, reportedly goring and killing over two hundred people every year. Hunting the buffalo demands considerable skill and vigilance because they have a devious habit of circling back on their pursuers and counter-attacking, especially when wounded. It's a stocky beast with the stance of a sumo wrestler, all pumped-up muscular menace and aggression. They are black or charcoal grey with short, coarse hair. Their formidable horns curve downwards and then upwards and outwards and have fused bases forming a continuous bone shield across the top of the head known as a 'boss'. When two 800kg African buffalo bulls charge each other head on, the collision is equivalent to a car hitting a wall at 50 kmph. I'll never forget my first attempt at hunting a buffalo because it was very nearly my last.

Barry was once again my co-conspirator in impetuous bravado. My father was away at the time, so without asking permission I borrowed his rifle and we headed into the bush. In those days, you could hunt wherever you liked and we roamed for miles without seeing a single buffalo before we came upon an African village. The locals didn't particularly welcome a couple of dusty, exhausted teenagers toting an enormous gun, but I flashed some cash and they let us camp overnight. The next morning, we asked them if there were any buffalo around and they said, 'Ja, there are buffalo down on the river.' I asked one of the men if he would take us there if I gave him five pounds and he jumped at the chance.

Two hours later I was crawling through thick *kasakasaka* bush, which is so dense you can only see a few yards ahead of you. Suddenly our guide froze. He pointed: 'There it is.' I peered into the bush but my spectacles were so streaked with sweat that everything was blurred. I carefully took them off and wiped them but that only made it worse. Squinting, I thought I could see four hooves, but I had no idea which way the animal was facing. I calculated that the buffalo must be going towards the water so its head would be on the left side. I fired a shot and the beast thundered off like a runaway express train. I said to the guide in Fanakalo: 'His head was definitely on the left.' He replied, '*Aikona* (no), his head was on the right.'

I'd shot the buffalo in the hip.

We followed the blood trail for about an hour. There was blood spoor all over the place but no sign of the animal. I suddenly remembered what my grandfather had told me: the buffalo will always circle and come up behind you. I started walking with my head askew, constantly looking over my shoulder like I was anticipating a jump scare in a horror movie.

I looked. Nothing. I looked again, and there he was behind me, several hundred kilos of red rage intent on pulverising me, extracting their revenge. As soon as I made eye-contact, he charged. I fired and I fired but he just kept coming, I didn't know where to shoot him properly, and when he was almost within touching distance I knew it was all over, I was never going to be a famous hunter and my father would kill me anyway if he found out, and then Barry shot him in the brain and the animal dropped instantly. You could hear my heartbeat from a mile away and my ears rang with all the shooting, but when I stopped shaking I took one step forward and touched the buffalo on the nose with the barrel of my rifle. It was a small gesture of respect. Despite my cack-handedness, I got my buffalo but he'd almost got me.

• • •

Life and stories are inextricably intertwined. We create narratives to make sense of the world, rebuild it to bring joy and wonder. My writing instincts were being honed. In my nondescript bachelor's mess in Salisbury, I had lost sight of the fact that my life was already storied, full and rich with history, peopled by characters more exciting than a novice writer could ever pluck out of their imagination. My father, my mother, my grandfather, all the countless people of my own corner of Africa. In them were the key to writing my first successful novel.

• • •

I put down my pen. *When the Lion Feeds* was written, its fate for the first time out of my hands. In those pages, I had chronicled the stories of Sean and Garrick Courtney. The brothers had inherited my grandfather's name, and their father Waite was modelled on my grandfather himself. Their tale of growing up on a cattle ranch in Natal at the end of the nineteenth century was inspired by my own wild boyhood. Garrick's disability, first as a result of a hunting accident, and later because of his inadvertent heroism in the Zulu War, was a reflection of my boyhood polio, which would forever leave me with a weak right leg. Sean's adventures in the gold rush of the Witwatersrand, his journey as an ivory hunter in the Bushveld, even the dramatic highs and lows of his love life – these all emerged directly from my own past. The genesis of the two boys came from deep within my own personality; they are the two contrasting sides of me: Sean with his robust, driven, heroic ambitions, and Garrick, who is more reflective, sensitive, someone who understands his own fallibility.

I thought it was a good novel – it was real and grounded and true – but, as I sent it off to my agent in London, the doubts every young writer faces began to creep inside.

In the weeks that followed I was determined to forget about it. I tried not to imagine my novel's journey into the world: my agent composing a killer submission letter to accompany the novel, the pitch phone calls. I tried not to think of it sitting on the desks of commissioning editors in London or New York, the bulky manuscript a tower of expectation among so many other hopeful first novels. I tried not to picture the editors in their arm-chairs reading it, frowning, dismissing it. And when, at last, a telegram arrived from London, I did not want to open it.

I was trembling. Get it over with, I said to myself. I opened the telegram. Inside were the words that would change my life. *When the Lion Feeds* had found a publisher. Charles Pick, who had recently joined the prestigious London publishing house William Heinemann as Deputy MD, had made a bid to acquire the novel. This was a man who had accompanied John Steinbeck to his Nobel Prize dinner, a man who drank vermouths with Graham Greene in Antibes. Now, he wanted to publish an unknown writer named Wilbur Smith.

It felt like I was falling again, the granite of the koppie slipping out of my grasp, leaving me dangling three hundred feet above the ground. It was the defining moment of my young life.

When the Lion Feeds would go on to be a bestseller, to ensnare readers across the world, and begin the career that would bring me so many adventures in my long life.

4

THIS BOY'S LIFE

Schooldays leave an indelible mark on any young boy, lessons learned can shape a destiny or distort a growing mind, and one can spend a lifetime repairing the damage a school can inflict on you. I made some great friends at school and had experiences I'll never forget, but when I recall those days I'm reminded of Woody Allen's line: 'My education was dismal. I went to a series of schools for mentally disturbed teachers.'

I was eight years old when my idyll on an African farm came to an abrupt end. My friend, Barry, had been sent south to boarding school and I thought I should follow him. He was, after all, my brother-in-arms on my adventures, my loyal lieutenant during our reckless escapades, so I asked my parents if I could go too. My mother burst into tears at the prospect of her boy leaving home, which confused me. What did she know that was so upsetting that I had no conception of? My father had no doubts; he had learned his trade in Maritzburg and, though no bookworm, he knew the kind of education he wanted for his son. Stories may have meant nothing to my father, but knowledge was the key to success. 'I think that's a good idea!' he said. I was duly enrolled at Cordwalles boarding school in Pietermaritzburg in Natal, South Africa, a preparatory school for that little 'Eton on the Veld', Michaelhouse in the Natal Midlands.

The Cordwalles school motto was *'courage builds character'*, which I thought was pretty good. The buildings were attractive redbrick and there were extensive playing fields and forested grounds to get lost in. The first week was exciting, but the novelty soon wore off. The cold showers, the discipline, the terrible food and interminable church services soon dampened my youthful enthusiasm. And then, in the parlance of South African boarding schools, I got *jacked*, given three 'cuts' across the backside with a Malacca cane for the unforgivable crime of talking after lights out. My father would never have been so unjust. He administered tough justice but it was fair.

I asked to see the headmaster. When I was finally granted a meeting in his office I explained that it would be a good idea if I returned home to the family ranch; the school didn't appear to be fulfilling my needs. The headmaster peered over his spectacles and explained that he didn't share my opinion. I left the office disconsolate.

There was no turning back, I would have to serve out my full sentence of five years here, in drudgery and misery.

The train trip from Zambia back to school after every holiday became purgatory. My mother would be fighting back the tears as I said goodbye, and the dread in the pit of my stomach would feel like lead as I boarded at Lusaka. I would change trains at Bulawayo in what is now Zimbabwe, and then again at Johannesburg to catch the train to Natal. It was a journey of two nights and three days, and I would spend that time staring out of the window, yearning to be free as I watched the countryside I loved disappear into the distance. The school was a constant torment. It was maybe a small thing, but before the first year was out, my prized Joseph Rodgers clasp knife had been stolen, a theft that left me inconsolable. Grandpa Courtney had given me that knife when I turned seven. I'd watched him slaughter pigs with it, he'd used it with astonishing expertise, and it was my link to home, that rough, tough devil-may-care world I'd left behind. Now it belonged to somebody else, just another stolen item, and I would never see it again. I was homesick, I would cry myself to sleep every night, burying my tears in the pillow because if you were caught blubbing, you were an outcast. You could never show weakness, admit to feeling hurt or missing the warm embrace of your family. I learnt stoicism and endurance, hardening my heart by trying to cauterise the small parts inside that bled. My escape became books, and at boarding school stories were my only companions through those long days and nights. They gave me new worlds to explore, characters I could befriend and love, adventures that had meaning and purpose, places that were exotic, exciting and full of wonder. They gave me hours of release from the austere dormitories, the bellowing classrooms, the frigid lavatories or punishing gymnasiums. Getting lost in stories became an essential survival skill – and they have stayed that way ever since.

I wasn't a good pupil. If you had no interest in swinging a cricket bat or kicking a rugby ball, and if you hated Latin and mathematics, you were considered a 'slacker'. This was not a good thing to be. It turned you into a social pariah. But I didn't care, I had my books. The school library had a special section in the upstairs gallery devoted to fiction. There were over a thousand titles. They may have once been organised alphabetically, but now it was a lucky dip of discovery. I started at one end and worked my way through them. In bed, I read under the blankets because it was lights-out at nine, no talking, silence strictly enforced, only the occasional squeak from our sagging, ancient bedsprings as we shivered into the night. I would read by torchlight which probably ruined my eyesight, but not enough to affect my shooting. The first book I ever read under the covers was *Forever Amber* by Kathleen Winsor, a risqué historical set in seventeenth-century England that was banned by the Catholic Church for indecency in its day, which did wonders for its popularity. It was a highly rewarding experience.

My English master was a man I'll call Mr Forbes, which isn't his real name. He had a register in which we were required each week to list the books we had read. The average for our class was zero to one per head while in a good week, I would notch up six or seven. My voracious appetite for books caught Mr Forbes's attention. He made me his protégé, and would discuss the books I had read that week with me. He encouraged me to think that being a bookworm was praiseworthy, rather than something to be deeply ashamed of. He told me that my essays showed great promise, and we talked about how to achieve dramatic effects, to develop characters and to keep a story moving forward. He pointed out authors who I would enjoy and books I should read.

And, unheard of in those days, he called me 'Wilbur' rather than 'Smith', as though I was actually a member of the human race. Fifty years later, I can look back on a career as a best-selling author and it all started under the blankets in a dorm at Cordwalles.

I developed a religious fervour for reading and for the written word, the beauty of the English language, its rhythms and sounds, the music of it. Once I had my mind opened to the richness of language, I could make the first step into my own writing. It started with English class writing projects like 'My last holiday', or 'My dog'. Once I'd mastered them, I moved into fiction and let my imagination run free. And after a while, I was achieving A's, and AA's and AAA's for my essays, while my marks for other subjects plummeted through lack of interest and I was getting B's and C's for the likes of maths and science.

At the end of the year, I won the form prize for best English essay selected by Mr Forbes. I'd written a story called 'The Monarch of the Ilungu' – the adventure of a wounded bull elephant who, upon defeating his hunter, returns to wrest back control of his herd from a young interloper. I wrote it when I was twelve years old. (You can read it yourself in an appendix at the end of this book.)

It was the first accolade my writing had ever received. The book I was given as a prize was chosen by Mr Forbes in person. I still have it: W. Somerset Maugham's *Introduction to Modern English and American Literature*. It sits on the shelf next to C. S. Forester. It is a collection of the great writing of the time, and one of the stories is by Ernest Hemingway: 'The Short Happy Life of Francis Macomber'. I'd never read Hemingway, but I loved this story so much that I immediately tracked down and read *The Old Man and the Sea*. Ever since I have respected Hemingway as one of the all-time great writers.

Hemingway became my literary god and writing seemed to be the occupation of the gods, the noblest calling, the highest aspiration, the tallest mountain to climb. I recalled Hemingway's comment that to write well was a 'perpetual challenge', the most difficult thing he had ever done, and yet, how happy it made him when he succeeded.

This was the first time that it entered my head that one day I might join the pantheon of writers, and live on Olympus amongst them. Then at the beginning of one new term I was distraught to learn that Mr Forbes had left the school staff, hurriedly and unexpectedly. I never learned why.

Mr Forbes was my first teacher in the art of storytelling and it was many years before I met another man who inspired me in the same way. In the meantime, my only teachers were the writers whose work I devoured.

. . .

The next year, in 1946, just after the Second World War, I moved on to senior school, Michaelhouse, in what is now KwaZulu-Natal Midlands in South Africa. It was established as a boarding school for boys in 1896, with a strong Christian ethos. The original school buildings are constructed using local Pietermaritzburg red brick and have an English gothic feel about them. The school is arranged in a series of interlinked quadrangles and you can walk from one end to the other without stepping outdoors, which was very handy on rainy days. Michaelhouse is one of the most prestigious schools in South Africa nowadays, with an international reputation for excellence.

In my day, it liked to call itself St Michael's Academy for Young Gentlemen. This was a manifest misnomer as there was not a single gentleman amongst us. The school's founder, Anglican priest Canon James Cameron Todd, had declared: 'Our aim is to make, not accountants, not clerks, not doctors, not clergymen, but men of under-standing, thought and culture.' He was either deluded or just downright mischievous. It was very much the same school routine as before, only worse. The food was ined-ible and the beatings for no reason were more frequent. There was the same obsession with team sports and science subjects. Situated on the foothills of the Drakensberg mountains, the winters were arctic. We never seemed to have enough blankets on the bed. We had to get up to shower at some numbingly early hour of the morning, when it was still dark, and the limited amount of hot water was reserved for the seniors; us little guys had to dash into a dribble of icy water and come out blue on the other side.

I was in Founders, the school house immortalised by South African actor and playwright John van de Ruit's *Spud* series, but my days within those walls were nothing like Spud's or even Tom Brown's schooldays. The first-year boys were called *kaks*, from the Afrikaans word for turds. We little *kaks* were at the bottom of the food chain and we had to fag or serve the house prefects, be at their beck and call. The new boys would line up and the prefects would make their selection – it was like a slave market. We'd be standing in one long line shivering in the cold, red-faced, kicking our heels, expecting the worst. I was lucky. My prefect was Chick Henderson, the Transvaal and Scotland rugby international, best remembered today for his work with the Barbarian Rugby Club and as the South African English-language TV commentator in the 1980s. He treated me with disdain, but never unfairly. I had to polish his shoes, iron his clothes and, in the morning, go into the bogs and warm the toilet seat for him, while my co-*kak* made him his tea and his toast.

Michaelhouse was a debilitating experience. There was no respect for the pupils. The teachers were brutal, the prefects beat us and the senior boys bullied us. It was a cycle of violence that kept perpetuating itself. The cane was a constant presence in everything we did, a dark shadow of malevolence. The beatings had their own routine and weren't administered at the time of the offence – beatings were scheduled on a Saturday night, and they accumulated. So, if you whispered in chapel on Sunday and were late for roll call on Monday, touched your cutlery in the dining hall before grace on Tuesday, or spoke after lights out on Wednesday, you would sit in the prep room on Saturday night waiting to be summoned to the prefects' common room. Once summoned, you would be lashed for the first offence and then sent back to the prep room to be called for the next offence and so on. You might take four or five beatings in one go. It was very painful. And when the last set of cuts was laid down, you would have to stand up straight and thank the prefects for the punishment without showing any sign of discomfort or anger – you couldn't even rub your backside in front of them. It was arbitrary, irrational and capricious, the maintenance of discipline through fear.

Some masters were experts at caning. They used to chalk the cane so the first stripe left a line, an aiming point, and they were very proud if they could lay their strokes all on top of one another so you had a very nice bruise afterwards, or else they cut through the skin. I remember the first time I returned home for the holidays, and my mother came into the bathroom while I was bathing and saw my backside which was all shades of purple. She was distraught. 'I'm going to see the headmaster immediately,' she said. I pleaded with her not to. 'Mother, you can't do that. You don't understand, if you complain to the rector he'll call in the prefects and I'll be marked as a squealer, a blubberer.'

My father wouldn't have done anything. He would have shrugged his shoulders and said: 'Well, that's just how the system works. It'll toughen you up.'

I learnt to accept punishment without complaint. It was a badge of toughness to be able to withstand a beating, but I was miserable at the time. My English master here was also my science master, and he had little wit or imagination. There was no poetry in his soul. There were no more form prizes for me.

Reading remained my safe refuge, my exclusion zone, and creative writing was becoming a drug. I excelled at school in essay writing. I was better able to express myself on paper than I could in conversation. But I had no idea how to exploit this to my advantage. How do you get noticed as a writer? How do you become a published author? I ended up starting a school magazine for which I wrote the entire content, except for the sports pages.

My weekly satirical column became mildly famous, and was circulated as far afield as Wykham Collegiate in Pietermaritzburg and St Anne's in Hilton village, the two girls' schools known for having the prettiest girls for hundreds of miles. It was my sole achievement of any note.

At the end of the year the school awarded the prize for achievement to the boy who operated the Roneo machine to print the school magazine. I was devastated. The head-master called me into his office and explained that he had decided to award him the prize as a symbolic gesture on behalf of all the magazine staff, choosing to overlook the fact that I was the *only* member of staff. He also failed to mention, though I was fully aware, that this boy was also the captain of the second eleven school cricket team.

My other achievement of note at Michaelhouse was to start smoking, in the school bogs of all places. I failed at this as well, got caught and was given six of the best. The upside of my schooling was that I managed to shake off all my vices at a relatively early age. I finally stopped smoking thirty cigarettes a day in my mid-thirties, after *When the Lion Feeds* became a bestseller.

By the time I left Michaelhouse I'm sure I'd read every book in the library. C. S. Forester and his Horatio Hornblower series remained a particular favourite. I read every one of them. Much later, when I could afford it, I searched for his first editions and had them bound in calfskin. Today they have pride of place on my bookshelves.

Hornblower was my perfect hero. He was a man of many parts – gentle, diffident and a staunch friend; he was plagued by self-doubt until he stood on the quarter deck of His Majesty's Man o' War. Then he became a gallant and intrepid leader of men. Hornblower played an important role in my life at school, giving me confidence to face the constant flak, because school felt like warfare at times, and the reassurance that the decent, loyal, good man would triumph no matter what the odds. Even today, I will take down one of those leather-bound books from the shelf and open it at random. When I read one of Forester's paragraphs, the goose bumps rise on my forearms as I speak the words aloud. They're like a fine old claret on my tongue.

. . .

Our only encounters with the opposite sex consisted of the once-a-term dance, or 'socials', with girls bussed in from sister schools. They were awful. We'd all line the walls, watching and whispering as the girls filed in. Then the lights would dim, the music would begin and everyone would try their damnedest to grope each other to death by the end of the night.

My own sexual awakening occurred on the Durban

beaches where we would spend our Christmas holidays when my family came down from the Copperbelt. I didn't go all the way, the girl led with her mouth, so successfully that it was years before I realised that sex could involve going below a girl's belt.

Our family would stay at the old Imperial Hotel, and spend most of the holiday fishing off the Natal beaches. It was pure bliss and sparked a lifelong love for fishing – sea and freshwater – that continues to this day. Once Dad had made his money, he moved with my mom down to Kloof, outside Durban where they bought a house.

But at the end of every holiday, feeling full of dread, I would have to embark on the long tortuous journey back to Michaelhouse in the Midlands. I remained a rebel to the end, not a good attitude if you want to fit in. I never made prefect, I wasn't interested. I was captain of the shooting team however, and captain of the rugby second eleven, playing number 8, a lazy, predatory position, which suited me fine.

Then my life took an unexpected turn. I contracted polio. I was sixteen, there was an epidemic and some children I knew didn't recover – their lungs collapsed. Polio was one of the most devastating public health problems in the world at the time, and most of its victims were children. It wasn't until 1955 that American virologist Dr Jonas Salk developed the first ever polio vaccine. My right leg was badly affected, it became weak and withered, but my left leg compensated for the rest of my life, and the right only started to protest when I turned eighty.

Finally, in December 1950, I was free. Many pupils from Michaelhouse distinguished themselves at sport – 157 Old Michaelhousians have represented seventy countries in forty-eight different sports, and some have gone on to be leaders in their field, admirably propping up the establishment. As for me, a full-time writer, I've been unemployed since the age of thirty, and, alongside the good reviews and loyal readers, what has given me the most happiness in my life has been the freedom to do anything I like.

I have driven past the school many times since I left, but I've never been in. It's like passing a haunted house. My time at Michaelhouse was the worst of my life. In 2001, responding to an article that I had written in Durban's *Sunday Tribune* about my schooldays at Michaelhouse, the then rector, Dudley Forde, himself an old boy, albeit seven years below me, acknowledged that bullying had been a factor in the 1950s, not just at Michaelhouse but at all South African boarding schools of the era. Corporal punishment by prefects, he said, had been abandoned in the early 1970s and phased out by staff before the passing of South Africa's new constitution (which outlawed it in any case) in the mid-1990s. 'Mr Smith's article is a forceful reminder to all of us in education,' said Forde, 'of the lasting damage that the practices he describes can have on a developing young man. The bitterness that he so obviously feels about his education remains untempered by any desire to have anything further to do with the school. From what can be gathered from reading his novels, there is a strong theme of compassion for those who are disadvantaged, a heroic sense of justice and a lifelong distaste for the arrogant, haughty and brutal. The present leadership of this school, staff and boys, share these views. Michaelhouse of today is a different school and gives all boys the opportunity to develop their talents to the fullest extent in a happy, caring environment.'

5

THIS STUDENT'S LIFE

After four years of misery and endurance, I moved on to Rhodes University, in Grahamstown, in the Eastern Cape Province of South Africa. The university's motto is *Where Leaders Learn*, and another Smith alumnus, Ian, put this maxim into practice by becoming Prime Minister of Rhodesia in 1964. I directed my energies in a very different way however, as paradise opened before me. Suddenly there were girls who did not wear gym slips and walk primly to church in crocodile formation. Up until that moment I had never dreamt of how soft and warm these gorgeous creatures were, or how sweet they smelled. 'Whoever loved that loved not at first sight?' as Shakespeare put it in *As You Like It*.

I was in Matthews, part of Founders Hall, and I soon found my way to the leading women's Residence, Oriel, named after Oxford's Oriel College. I fell for a girl who was in her second year. Her boyfriend was a lawyer in Port Elizabeth but she took a shine to me, a bumbling first year, naive and eager to please, but longing for adventure and new experiences. Within a week I discovered, to my joy, that the mouth wasn't the only way to give pleasure during sex. She was beautiful and we became lovers, unable to resist the commingling of our bodies, such wildly liberating tenderness. She needed to have a pass to be out late from Res but, typically in those days, I didn't need one because it didn't apply to male students. One night we went up past the tennis courts to a secluded spot and after the fun was over, we both fell blissfully asleep under the stars. We got back to Oriel well past midnight and, because she didn't have a pass, the senior girls nailed her. They turned her in. She mentioned my name and we were both sent up to the Vice Chancellor, Dr Thomas Alty, to explain ourselves.

There was no mitigation for the girl as far as he was concerned, so he rusticated her. Then it was my turn. He called me into his office and I thought I'd had it, that I was going to be sent down. 'Smith,' the Vice Chancellor said, looking me over, 'this is a very serious offence.'

'Yes, it is, sir,' I replied, looking at the floor, trying to appear contrite. There was silence, he seemed to be taking time to consider my sentence, or else he wanted to see me squirm, or perhaps he was simply imagining our sinful coupling, assessing its full weight and heated consequence.

Then he said: 'The young lady you were with, she's a pretty young thing, but she already has a reputation for being a bad girl.' I nodded and inwardly smiled, remembering our delicious cavorting and her enthusiasm. The Vice Chancellor continued: 'I think you were the innocent party in this, so we're going to give you a dispensation this time. Don't let it happen again.'

I didn't, because I never got caught again, but I felt sorry for the girl. She took all the blame and that was wrong. However, from then on, I dreamed of very little else but the opposite sex. Even books were forgotten in the feverish excitement of this new discovery. I became an expert at scaling the drainpipes at the various girls' Residential halls. I was a bit of a wild boy from the bush and girls seemed to like my derring-do, my disregard for rules and regulations which I thought were antiquated and joyless. I worked during the long university holidays and bought a Model T Ford, for £7 10s. The car was painted pink with sky blue mudguards and it had a sign on the back that said, 'Peaches, this is your can.' Yes, I know, I cringe now, but that was then when the floodgates had opened for the first time. The car had no seats in the back so we filled the space with mattresses. I had money left over from my vacation jobs, I had wheels and could travel, and my amorous experimentations went into overdrive.

I never saw my lover again after the meeting with the Vice Chancellor. But one day, at the end of 1999, I was driving through Kenilworth in Cape Town and stopped at a robot (traffic lights). Something made me turn my head and there, in the car next to me, was the girl I had loved at university, now a rather matronly woman. The encounter sent a sensuous shiver down my spine, but it was also like seeing a ghost, a spirit calling to me from so many years ago. She said nothing, just looked at me and mouthed, 'Wilbur', smiled, and drove off as the lights turned green.

Being sent down was just one of the risks in those days. We didn't have to contend with HIV and AIDS like today, but there was the age-old worry of getting a girl pregnant. We were very nervous about our contraceptives. The girl would say: 'It's okay, I've just had my period,' or something along those lines, and peace of mind would be restored. Sometimes we would take the condoms and wash them to save money. We'd put talcum powder on them to dry them out. Some of them we used three or four times, some half a dozen times. We'd blow them up and put them to our ears to check they weren't leaking. This is not a means of using contraceptives I'm recommending in any way! Even recalling our exploits as I'm doing now brings the colour to my cheeks at how reckless and disrespectful we were, but back then, needs must.

Consuming large amounts of alcohol, getting smashed and testing one's drinking limits are rites of passage at university. Competitive drinking was something of a sport, and great fun, but brought with it the obvious hazards of bad behaviour, falling over, and general stupidity. I was accomplished at the general stupidity, but I could also hold my drink. I had had my first taste of alcohol at the age of thirteen after one of my parents' parties during my summer holidays when I sampled the dregs of the leftovers. They tasted vile and I couldn't understand the appeal of drinking so I kept on drinking the leavings to see what it was that adults enjoyed so much. After a brief flash of euphoria, I threw up at the back of the house and then wobbled into my bed thinking my brain was about to explode. Strangely I didn't have a hangover in the morning; perhaps I hadn't drunk so much after all? The pleasures of alcohol remained an obscure mystery until I went to Rhodes and developed a taste for Castle Special. It was nine pence a quart and one quart would do you! In fact, my first hangover was at university, after a rugby match. I made my own cocktail – the most disgusting concoction ever, no one else would drink it. It consisted of Castle beer mixed with tomato juice, a sort of health shandy but with high alcohol content, years ahead of its time. I should have patented it.

Another bad habit I acquired at university was gambling, but my best friend's father, a highly-respected headmaster, told me that gambling is no fun unless you play it for stakes you can't afford. I thought about that and gave it up in an instant.

• • •

All too soon, my four years at Rhodes were up. It was time to go out, learn about real life and get a job. I'd wanted to be a journalist, following my love for writing, or become a big game hunter. But my father had told me straight to get a proper job.

I'd taken his advice and was now an accountant with a degree – something that still surprised me. On graduation, I didn't head home first, I went down to Port Elizabeth where I'd got a job as an executive trainee at Goodyear Tyre and Rubber. My first salary was £27 a month; it was OK, I lived well on it. I ran a car and was able to romance a few ladies, buy a few drinks. I was having a good time. Such a good time in fact, that within six months of adult life I was married – and I wasn't even twenty-four.

I might have moved to Port Elizabeth, but it was only 110kms away from Grahamstown and I hadn't really left my student days behind. I still had an impetuous sense of adventure.

That Easter, I headed up to Johannesburg to spend time with a dear old varsity mate of mine called Larry King, who was 5'2", Jewish and a natural comic. He was hysterically funny. We were at the Rand Easter Show, bellied up to the bar in the tent. Also attending the event was an American wrestler who had entered the tent and was looking around for a drink. His name was Sky-High Lee and he stood 7'2" in his socks.

Larry and I were talking about a trick where you slip behind a chap when he's not expecting it. You stand back to back and grab him by the seat of the pants and start walking forwards. He ends up off balance and you can take him anywhere you want.

Sky-High Lee wandered over to the bar and I whispered to Larry, who had already had a couple of jars, to do the trick on him. Larry eyed Sky-High Lee, craning his neck as he looked up, and said: 'You're joking.'

'No, nonsense, of course you can do it, don't be all talk,' I said.

Larry considered, then said: 'You know, come to think of it, I could do it!'

'Well don't tell us, show us!'

Larry put his drink on the bar counter and began backing up to Sky-High. He couldn't reach high enough to get him by the seat of his pants so he grabbed the back of his coat. He then started walking. Sky-High was just lifting his glass to his lips, when he felt the tugging behind him. He slowly put his glass down and nonchalantly turned around to see this strange little man, flushed in the face, standing there plaintively apologising: 'Sorry, Mr Lee, sorry, Mr Lee.'

Sky-High bent down, took Larry by the lapels of his coat and lifted him up in the air. He held him aloft, with Larry's feet dangling about a foot off the ground, and looked at him with amazement, like he'd discovered a new species of insect. Then he shook his head and dropped Larry right onto his feet and turned back to his beer.

I'll never forget that. I wanted to applaud. It was the

perfect put-down. He didn't punch him. He just couldn't believe that this little guy had tried to intimidate him.

Larry and I had some memorable times together, pranking each other, drinking too much; we were unleashed and carefree, refusing to accept we were no longer students. Tragically Larry would later die in a car crash. I miss him.

6

THIS UNDERWORLD LIFE

I stood on the precipice, staring into the swirling blackness of the mine below. In the world beneath the surface, miners were following rich veins in the earth, toiling in their cramped, poisonous tunnels to bring out the stone which has filled man with lust and envy since the dawn of time: gold. Up on the surface, I had been following my own rich vein. I had moved to Cape Town and was spending a lot of time on the gold mines of Johannesburg, going underground with the miners, diligently researching my latest novel *Gold Mine*. I wanted it to be real, authentic, to show respect for the truth of the miners' lives I was chronicling. Suddenly I lost my footing, the handwritten manuscript slipped out of my grasp and 150 pages, the only copy I had, fell down the mineshaft, the pages scissoring apart into the darkness. They spiralled down past the point where the mine bosses climbed in; past the level where the white mine overseers began their descent; and past the level where the black workers joined the skip to make the final descent to the heart of the mine. The pages returned to the earth, becoming dark matter. Those pages were my first attempt at telling the story of Rodney Ironsides, the ambitious and hard-living mining expert who compromises his career by agreeing to flood his own mine as a stock exchange scam. As I listened to the last whisper of the pages fluttering down the shaft, I thought about the special moments of character and plot that would be lost forever. I would have to rewrite it, but it could never be quite the same again.

It was the summer of 1969, five years after *When the Lion Feeds* had become a runaway success. That morning in Salisbury, reading the telegram from London with disbelief, had been the first in a succession of golden moments, each one of them more surreal than the last. Two days later, the postman had pedalled up the drive of the house which I shared in squalor with four other bachelors, and asked me to sign for yet another buff telegram form. He presented me with an envelope that changed my life forever. Inside was a cheque from William Heinemann, my first advance payment for my first published novel. It was equivalent to just under three years' salary. My life was taking an exciting new direction.

A week later, the postman returned with another telegram. *Reader's Digest* had taken my novel as one of their

Condensed Books. In uncontrolled excitement, I tipped the postman a pound. During the weeks that followed, he came more and more regularly. He arrived with letters of notification of a sale of film rights in Hollywood, of a Book Society Choice, of acceptance by Viking Press in New York for an eye-rolling sum of dollars – relative to my then financial situation – of new publishers in Germany and France, of a paperback sale to Pan Books in England. Soon, the postman and I became fast friends. He would holler outside my door – 'Another one, *Bwana*!' – and, when I opened the door, he was already holding out his hand for a tip.

The Courtneys had changed my life irrevocably, and I was determined that now I was going to do nothing but write. On my return from England in 1964, where I met my publishers and finally held a copy of the novel in my hands, I had officially resigned my job. I had not taken leave from the Tax Department for three years – I had never been able to afford the luxury of a holiday. Now was the time to cash in all that leave. Between that and the money coming in from *When the Lion Feeds*, I had enough to live on for a few years. I gave up being employed as an accountant. The success of *When the Lion Feeds* was enough that Heinemann wanted more, and I secluded myself far away from the distractions and everyday chaos of Salisbury to commit more stories to the page.

I borrowed Dad's caravan and headed out for the Inyanga Mountains in the east, a magical space of mountains, waterfalls, rolling grasslands and trout dams. I parked at a caravan park and started writing with a vengeance. I would occasionally drive back into Salisbury to see my family and relax a little with friends.

It was during one of those trips home that I bumped into a young prosecutor, John Gordon Davis. Gordon Davis and I were at Rhodes University together, but we hadn't really been friends.

He asked me what I was doing, so I told him about *When the Lion Feeds* and being out at Inyanga. About twenty years later, Gordon Davis, in an interview with a reporter, mentioned how I had inspired him to start writing.

Gordon Davis, who was then a junior public prosecutor in Bulawayo, was coming down the main road in Salisbury when he saw me and waved. After hearty handshakes, or as he put it to the reporter, 'we fell on each other's necks', we made for the nearest bar.

Over large, cool beers, he said he had just come back from Canada where he had gone looking for adventure but hadn't found it, and was now working in Bulawayo at the magistrates' court. He was bored and restless, with that feral look in his eye I've seen many times in frustrated creative people. 'And you, what are you up to, Smith?' he asked. There was a scepticism in his voice as if I was the last person he thought would be successful with any enterprises. 'I'm living off the royalties from my first novel which has sold 10,000 copies in the US and 25,000 in the

UK, and the film rights advances,' I said, genuinely not meaning to boast, just stating the facts. I could see Gordon Davis's eyes open wide in astonishment; he didn't think anyone could make a living out of writing, especially in Africa.

He became even more attentive when I told him that after I'd sent *When the Lion Feeds* to the publishers, they'd asked me for more work.

He said: 'Well if a jerk like you can do it, so can I.' His language was slightly more choice. What he actually said was: 'Jesus, if an arsehole like you can publish a book, imagine what I could do.'

'Well, Gordon Davis,' I replied, 'don't tell me about it, go and do it.' And to his credit, he did just that, writing what would become *Hold My Hand I'm Dying*, a bestselling novel based on his work as a native commissioner up near Kariba, and then as a prosecutor during the turbulence in Rhodesia, when Prime Minister Ian Smith and his Rhodesian Front government decided to issue their Unilateral Declaration of Independence from Britain. Gordon Davis would leave Rhodesia and work as a crown prosecutor in Hong Kong, writing all the time, until eventually retiring to Andalucia in Spain where he ran very successful writing courses for aspiring and published authors. Sadly he passed away in 2014.

Returning to the subject of my writing 'office': the beautiful Inyanga mountains sit on the eastern border of what was then Rhodesia, forming a natural barrier of sheer cliff faces, gullies wreathed in mist, and dense upland forest with Portuguese East Africa on the other side. Here, banked by black wattle and pine, listening to the holler and cry of Samango monkeys somewhere out in the forest, I lived and worked in the caravan, and soon I had written my second novel, *The Dark of the Sun*. It was about Bruce Curry, a thirty-year-old Rhodesian lawyer turned mercenary, seeking redemption in the bloodbath of the Congo's diamond-rich Katanga province while civil war erupted all around him. The solitude of the Inyanga was the perfect backdrop to lose myself in these imaginary vistas, to truly inhabit the characters on the page. Soon after finishing, I was writing my third novel, *The Sound of Thunder*, and in it returning to the world of the Courtneys. *The Sound of Thunder* found Sean and his brother Garrick resuming their fraternal battle, this time set against the theatre of the Second Boer War at the turn of the twentieth century. Next had come *Shout at the Devil*, the story of two freebooters making their living hunting in German East Africa, and the implacable Commissioner whose land they are poaching. These were novels set under the endless African skies – but, for my next story, I had been planning something a little different. I was going to take readers to a part of Africa few of them would ever have seen – the world underneath the surface.

· · ·

I had spent the early years of my life around the mines of the Copperbelt, in a place much the same as these gold mines. Those had been days spent following my father as he marshalled his men and dropped ventilation pipes deep into the earth, but I was here on the Witwatersrand as a guest of the Western Deep Levels Gold Mine Company. Being a successful novelist was opening doors that had until now remained closed, allowing me to get closer to my source material.

I had first written about the South African gold rush in *When the Lion Feeds*, as Sean Courtney and his partner, Duff Charleywood, joined the stampede to exploit the goldfields of the Witwatersrand. Gold had been discovered on this vast escarpment in 1886, and the sudden influx of fortune hunters from all over the world had given rise to the dusty mining village of Ferreira's Camp, which grew into the city of Johannesburg. As I stood here, now, the gold rush had been over for almost a hundred years, but there was still gold in these hills, and the men tramping into the tunnel ahead of me were here to bring it out. My new novel, *Gold Mine*, was going to be about men just like these and, if I was to get inside their heads, I needed to know the workings of the mines as intimately as any miner. I needed to live with their rhythms, learn their speech patterns, their attitudes, the tiny details only a seasoned mine worker could know. The Western Deep Levels Gold Mine Company had allowed me to join them for an extended period – so I climbed into the skip that would take me to the mine's lowest levels and prepared to descend.

Up on the surface the mine was its own world – a closed town of thousands of workers, with many more in the outlying villages run by the mine. Married miners often lived in those local villages with their families, but even they could not escape the control of the all-powerful mine itself. Single miners shared boarding houses closer in and I lived in these quarters, in between bouts of publicity for *Shout at the Devil*. They were pretty basic buildings, but they were leagues better than the traditional huts most of the miners had grown up in. In an age of apartheid, black workers had separate accommodation to the whites, but that did not impact on the sense of community in the complex. I had been here for several days already and was planning on staying a full two months. In the evenings, when the work was done, the miners congregated to play cards, sports and, in the single quarters, to drink. I sat among them each evening, listening to the talk.

Western Deep No. 3 Shaft plummeted more than a mile into the ground. As we rattled down, the air around us seeming to harden as the pressure built up, I was reminded of the first time I had gone underground. The unpleasant feeling in the pit of my stomach was frighteningly familiar from the days I had accompanied my father down a mine shaft much the same as this, and the long, tiresome hours I had spent trailing after him as he made his rounds. Those networks of tunnels, shorn up with wooden props, and the suffocating heat which the miners endured, had been no place for a boy. Yet, later – when we had moved to my father's ranch and the prospect of what lay beneath the surface no longer seemed so dull – I had joined a caving club and gone on pot-holing expeditions with companions from school, exploring natural crevices and tunnels in the rock. It had been on one of those first trips that my eyes had been opened to the fascination of the depths.

At last, we reached the bottom of the mine shaft. The skip gates clattered and came apart. The miners who had been crowded in with me trudged out into a narrow tunnel and, one after another, disappeared into the darkness, the lights on their helmets fading to points. It was eerie and strange, an unreal world of blackness, shadows and unexpected glaring illumination. When they were gone, there were only two figures left in the cavern: me and the mine overseer who had been given the responsibility of showing me around the tunnels.

George Orwell wrote about English coal mines in *The Road to Wigan Pier* and his words were ringing in my ears: 'The place is like hell, or at any rate like my own mental picture of hell. Most of the things one imagines in hell are there – heat, noise, confusion, darkness, foul air and above all, unbearably cramped space.'

'Stay close,' the overseer said. 'There are five hundred miles of tunnel down here. Some of those boys will have to walk two miles before they even start work.'

We began our tour of the mine. It was baking hot, and the walls themselves seemed to be perspiring as if they too were gripped with the effort of extraction. Water was sprayed liberally throughout the mine, not just for its cooling effects, but to damp down the clouds of dust that billowed through the tunnels. That dust could be cancerous to the miners who might spend long days breathing it in. The atmosphere was muggy, but that was something the miners were acclimatised to. Coming in from the bush, many of the untrained mine workers would have to spend long periods in the compound's steam rooms, so that their bodies became attuned to conditions this far underground. The pressure of the rock overhead could amount to as much as 12,000 pounds on a single square inch, and the risk of cave-in was something miners lived with daily.

The gold mine was a honeycomb, its cells and tunnels spreading out in every direction. We set out following the signposted tracks where ore was being transported back to the surface. On occasion the tunnels resounded with explosions from even deeper inside the mountain, the after-effects of dynamite being laid and set off, all part of the mine's never-ending quest to expand. The mine around us seemed alive, organic, constantly looking for places to infiltrate, always growing with new shafts and tunnels. As soon as a mine like this stood still it would grind to a halt. Only by going deeper, wider and richer could it continue to exist. It was a hungry beast with no sating its appetite, much like the gold market it was supplying. Today, Western Deep Levels are working the earth more than two-and-a-half miles beneath the surface, one of the deepest complexes in the world. In the years to come, they will plunge deeper and deeper still.

Most of the men working these tunnels were black workers from the rural homelands of South Africa. Although South Africa's racial tensions would soon explode with fire and blood in the world up above, in these tunnels there seemed to be no enmity between black and white. A miner was a miner, and that eclipsed the racial divide. The workers we encountered had come from all over: they were Zulu and Matebele, Sotho and Shona, Portuguese, Poles and Europeans from even further afield. Often the overseers were the educated white miners, and the men from the different African tribes seemed to have gravitated together so that gangs of Matebele men would work on the mine face, while a cohort of Zulu boys transported the ore.

After tramping through endless cramped, claustrophobic tunnels, the overseer and I reached the mine face, where more tunnels were being advanced into solid rock. This was dangerous work. There was no natural oxygen, it was pumped down through ventilation pipes of the kind my father built to make his fortune, and the air hung thick and heavy around us. The lights strung up from the wooden rafters flickered and strobed, sometimes short-circuiting and sending the world into a darkness more absolute than any I'd ever experienced on the surface.

Down in these depths, the water leaching up through the rock was coppery and poisonous, laced with natural arsenic from the minerals in the earth. And there was the constant fear of tunnel collapse lurking around every corner.

The men seemed heedless to the everyday hazards. The mines attracted a hard breed of man, capable and uncomplaining, bolstered by the relative riches of their wages. The true gold rush might have been over for generations, the land now monopolised and controlled by companies like Western Deep Levels, but the rewards for the miners were compensation for hardships in a gruelling world.

New recruits were brought in by Teba, the Employment Bureau of Africa, and Wenela, the Witwatersrand Native Labour Association. They would come from the deep bush, be signed up and brought in on lorries. Once in the mine compound, they were assessed by the trained mine captains who gauged their various abilities before allocating them to suitable teams. They were often under-nourished and weak when they arrived. Most would have to be trained before the captains would send them underground. As well as submitting to the steam rooms, they would be introduced to a healthy, rich diet, full of corn meal and meat, very different to the diets they were used to. Doctors would oversee them as they worked on treadmills and in group exercises until they reached a good level of fitness and were ready for the mine.

For the first time in their lives, they would be educated. Some of the mine captains saw this as a civilising process, taking men who had lived their entire lives in the bush and helping them face up to the demands of the modern world. They learned how to use tools and mine machinery, and also new languages. Fanakalo was a fascinating *lingua franca* that I heard echoing throughout the mine, a pidgin language I already knew from my days on my father's ranch, where he used it to communicate to his labourers. These days it is fashionable to decry Fanakalo as racist and colonial, but it is still being used on the South African mines because the people who use it trust it with their lives. The men came from all over sub-Saharan Africa – from what is today Malawi, Mozambique, Zambia, Namibia and Lesotho, to say nothing of the Eastern Cape and the rest of the South African hinterland – but, by the end of the induction phase, they were able to communicate and work together using a common language in a close, highly specialised, dangerous environment.

Most of the workers would spend two or three years on the mine before going back to their villages with enough capital to acquire wives, buy fifteen head of cattle, and become important men in their communities. They would return as educated men of the world, having learned skills from machinery operation to catching trains, and having been exposed to different people from all over Africa and the wider world. The lessons they brought back with them would contribute to the welfare of their native communities.

Gold Mine was a thriller, and the mine overseer who

was leading me through this subterranean world was to become the model for Rodney Ironsides, the underground manager – thirty-eight years old, divorced and desperate to succeed – who had got where he was on the strength of his natural ability and his work ethic. Like the man who was allowing me to shadow him, Ironsides had reached the top of his profession but he could go no further because he wasn't a university graduate, and the holy grail of running his own mine was out of reach. Soon he would be offered a break but it would lead him into crime. Along the way, he would fall in love with the managing director's young wife, while somehow keeping on top of the everyday stresses of controlling tens of thousands of staff. It would be a lean, claustrophobic novel – the only one I ever wrote that would unfold solely in one location, in the cramped tunnels of the mine. To conjure the world realistically, I would spend another two months there, walking the deep level tunnels for up to eight hours a day, going to an inordinate amount of trouble to get certain facts right and to pick up the prevailing attitudes of the mine. I had a tin hat and overalls and I walked around looking officious, but I don't think anyone even knew who I was. At nights, I lived in the mine's single quarters, drinking and carousing with the miners, listening to their stories, and I read voraciously, anything that I could lay my hands on about gold mining.

. . .

The lessons I had learnt in writing *Gold Mine* would stay with me across the novels of the next ten years. I had known, from early on, that if my novels were to be successful, they would have to be rooted in hard-won personal experiences. That had been as true for 'On Flinders' Face' as it had been for *When the Lion Feeds*. But *Gold Mine* taught me that I could go out there and have new experiences on which to build novels, that research did not have to be conducted inside an encyclopaedia or library. Later, when it came to composing *The Diamond Hunters*, the novel I wrote in 1971, I took my research just as seriously. Growing up in southern Africa had left me with a fascination for precious metals and stones and the rich stories that our obsession with them conjures up. My fascination with gold had been explored in *Gold Mine*, and now I turned my attention to Africa's other glittering resource: the diamond. *The Diamond Hunters* was to take more than eighteen months to produce – one of the longest periods I have ever spent involved in a single project. As part of my research I travelled to Luderitz in present-day Namibia, what was then South West Africa, and went onto the diamond barges which were recovering diamonds off shore. I spent a lot of time talking to the men and to absorb the atmosphere I ventured in a Land Rover into the surrounding desert that is rich in diamonds. I walked along the beaches to watch the miners conducting beach recovery, and I was allowed to touch and feel the diamonds. It's always such a thrill to have a real diamond in the palm of your hand and to think that it was produced by the immense temperatures and pressure typically found at depths of 87 to 118 miles below the Earth's crust, and over a period of time from one billion to 3.3 billion years. Diamonds are brought near to the earth's surface in a blaze of glory when volcanoes erupt and the magma that contains the diamonds cools into igneous rocks such as kimberlite, named after the town of Kimberley in South Africa where the Star of South Africa, an 83.5 carat diamond, was discovered in 1869. It set off a diamond rush and the creation of the enormous open-pit mine, the Big Hole, which 50,000 miners dug by hand using picks and shovels. The Star of South Africa was found by a Griqua shepherd boy on the banks of the Orange River. He sold the stone to a neighbouring farmer for 500 sheep, 10 oxen and a horse.

I'll never forget the excitement when the miners brought out a pint of recovered diamonds in a container and let me run my fingers through them – nor the incredible moment whenever a 'wild' diamond was captured. Recovered diamonds are small diamonds extracted from the kimberlite host rock, which is crushed, mixed with water to create a slurry, often known as a 'puddle', and then subjected to centrifugal forces which cause the heavier diamonds to sink to the bottom of the mix. A 'wild' diamond is a rare find, an individual, large gemstone glinting in the sun, prompting huge celebrations. Combining the details I gleaned from these expeditions with book research, I built up a picture of the broader diamond market, the international cartels involved and the ethics of the trade in what would ultimately become known as 'blood diamonds' – sometimes called 'conflict diamonds', rough diamonds used by rebels to fund military action against legitimate governments.

Both *The Diamond Hunters* and *Gold Mine* would go on to have second lives on the silver screen – but, first, *Gold Mine* had another, more unusual honour: it was the first novel I had written not to fall prey to the South African Board of Censors. Until this fifth novel was published, none of my work had been readily available in the country I had called home for so long. My novels were considered too incendiary to be safely enjoyed by what the Board thought was a prudish, easily offended South African readership. They were banned.

7

THE LAW IS AN ASS

By September 1964, I was married (for a second time) and living the life of a writer in Onrus in the Western Cape.

When the Lion Feeds had been published ten months before in the US and the UK, but was yet to be published in South Africa.

I had come down to Johannesburg in April 1964 to launch the book. I was jubilant at its success. US bookshops had ordered another 1,500 copies, Heinemann in the UK had sold another 20,000 around the world, I'd just signed translation rights for nine countries, the BBC was serialising it and *Reader's Digest* was condensing it – but South Africa's Publications Control Board was banning it, although not before a brisk 10,000 copies were sold.

The problem seemed to be about 1,000 words of the 160,000 total word count. Booksellers themselves were puzzled and even the reviewer of *The Star*, South Africa's daily newspaper, noted: 'There is one minor sex incident near the beginning and even that, in modern literature, cannot be termed offensive except by a prude.'

The Board had catholic taste and so *When the Lion Feeds* had company. At the same time the Board banned all editions of *Fanny Hill*, all future issues of *Playboy* magazine, Brian Bunting's *The Rise of The South African Reich* and Patrick Duncan's *Volume 2*.

Brian Bunting was a lifelong communist. A former journalist on the *Rand Daily Mail* and the *Sunday Times*, he edited no fewer than six political newspapers in South Africa, all subsequently banned, before going into exile in Britain and becoming a correspondent for *Tass*, the Soviet Union's news agency. Patrick Duncan was the son of a former governor-general of South Africa, a former national organiser of the soon to be banned Liberal Party and the first white member of the Pan Africanist Congress (PAC), a South African political party campaigning against apartheid. *Fanny Hill* was an erotic novel by English novelist John Cleland, first published in London in 1748 and widely regarded as the first of its kind in the world, while *Playboy* was paradoxically acclaimed not for its nudes but the quality of its journalism.

It was typical of South Africa at the time though, as an increasingly confident National Party government had weathered the storm of the PAC-organised pass law boycott – the pass laws were an internal passport system designed to control the movement of Africans under apartheid – which had led to the Sharpeville massacre in 1960 when police opened fire on protesters at a peaceful anti-pass campaign. The government had then begun clamping down on the African National Congress, the anti-apartheid political party, and the PAC with every tool at its disposal, legal and otherwise. In June 1964, Nelson Mandela, the leader of the ANC's new uMkhonto we Sizwe or Spear of the Nation liberation army, the military wing of the ANC, had already started serving what would be a twenty-seven-year sentence on the notorious Robben Island, on his way to becoming the most famous political prisoner in the world.

Heinemann took the case on appeal to the Cape Division of South Africa's Supreme Court in Cape Town. It was a test case, the first of its kind to examine just what constituted 'indecent, objectionable or obscene' grounds.

The Publications Board said in its papers to court that *When the Lion Feeds* had the 'tendency to deprave or corrupt the minds of persons who are likely to be exposed to the effect or influence thereof. It is offensive and harmful to public morals. It is likely to be outrageous or disgusting to persons who are likely to read it. It dealt in an improper manner with promiscuity, passionate love scenes, lust, sexual intercourse, obscene language, blasphemous language, sadism and cruelty.'

The case had to be heard twice. At the first attempt the two-judge bench of Mr Justice Van Zijl and Mr Justice Diemont couldn't agree, so the whole process had to be repeated, this time with the division's Judge President, Mr Justice Beyers, sitting in. After the second hearing, the decision went our way 2:1 with Judge Diemont still dissenting.

There were moments of levity and humour, as there always are in court cases of high tension. Advocate G. Duncan QC, appearing for the Board, had a battle on his hands with Judge Beyers grilling him on the issue of morals. 'Times change,' he put it to Duncan. 'There was a time when table legs were covered with all sorts of drapes, because they gave people all sorts of ideas. I live at Clifton [a well-known Cape Town beach] and I see a lot more than table legs.' To which Duncan replied that there were two extreme points of view: from the one that claimed table legs should be covered, all the way through to total nudity. The judge retorted: 'It is very difficult for me, I am a Bachelor's Cove man. You see what I mean? It depends entirely on the judge you get.' Duncan diplomatically responded that perhaps the solution would be to take a middle course. He objected to statements that the frank treatment of sex was customary in contemporary society. Judge Beyers, on hearing this, turned to his fellow judges and said, 'I don't know why he says "contemporary". Has it not been discussed ever since literature was born?'

Delivering the majority judgment Judge Van Zijl found that no part could be singled out from a book and given extra weight because it suited the complainant: 'The impact of the part – its effect or influence – on people must in a large measure depend upon the impact of the whole, the part's relationship to the whole and its relationship to the other parts making up the whole. It is the weight of this impact upon certain specified matters that determines whether the book should or should not be declared to be an undesirable publication.'

Apart from taking a dig at me for the 'poor literary quality' of *When the Lion Feeds*, and for 'the falseness of ascribing to two children the sophisticated love passage, that is described at pages 71-72 as taking place between them', Judge Van Zijl found that these were not grounds for either the Board or the court to find the book undesirable.

'The first passage concerns an incident in which Anna, a girl of about 17, seduces the hero of the book, Sean, a boy of about the same age. The tale tells of how Anna forces her company upon Sean who is going fishing; of how when they get to the fishing spot, she became bored, dives naked into the pool and entices Sean into the pool and now, after a brief physical encounter in the water, she goes out onto the bank, and of how they sit naked next to each other and she asks him to have intercourse with her.'

Sean and Anna then chat about what has just happened

and Sean confides to his brother Garrick when he gets home. Judge Van Zijl found there was nothing in these four pages that would tend to corrupt or deprave the minds of those likely to read it. There was nothing, he said, that the elder teenager could not have thought of for him or herself. The passage, the judge found, had been written with restraint and could not be said to advocate immorality.

The second passage covered a page and a half, but the piece that had riled the Board was barely ten lines long. This piece, said the judge, described sexual behaviour which in all probability deviated from the normal. But the knowledge imparted in the passage could be gained from any standard work on sex or sexual behaviour and Judge Van Zijl could not see any ground on which it could be contended that the passage could in anyway be held to 'corrupt or deprave the mind of an adult'.

We had won, but it was a pyrrhic victory because Judge Van Zijl granted the Board leave to appeal to the apex court (the supreme court) at the time, the Appellate Division in Bloemfontein, and banned any sale of copies of *When the Lion Feeds* until the appeal was heard. It was a double blow because I had funded the legal suit not wanting to burden my publishers with the case. Charles Pick had said Heinemann would foot the bill, but I was adamant. It was a small price to pay to reinforce the deep mutual respect Charles and I already had for one another.

My second novel, *The Dark of the Sun*, published in

January 1965, was also banned. A year later, the Board would ban *The Train from Katanga*, which was the American version of *The Dark of the Sun*. The good news though was that Metro Goldwyn Mayer had already paid £26,250 to buy the film rights when the book was published in the UK. Ironically the book wasn't banned in Rhodesia, where it clearly hadn't offended anyone.

The Appellate Division announced its finding on *When the Lion Feeds* on 26 August 1965. The country's most senior judges weren't as sanguine as their brothers in Cape Town. A full bench consisting of five judges, led by Chief Justice L.C. Steyn, heard the appeal.

The chief justice lashed my writing style. *When the Lion Feeds*, he said, was not 'a publication for any select circle of mature literary connoisseurs'. He continued witheringly: 'Making due allowances for the trends of our time, there are passages which I consider calculated to incite lustful thoughts and to stimulate sexual desire in at least a substantial number of persons: ordinary men and women, of normal mind and reactions, including some of the younger generation, who will be the probable readers of this book.

'However much fashionable sophistries obscure the simple truth, the plain fact remains that the sexual urge is much too powerful to be so dulled and blunted by exposure to the more indirect daily stimulants of our times that there is no longer a substantial number of ordinary men and women who are liable to be appreciably stirred by descriptions such as these of matters so directly, closely and intimately associated with actual consummation.'

Two of the judges, F. Rumpff and A. Faure Williamson, dissented. In his dissenting judgment, Judge Rumpff managed to pull back a small victory for common sense. As far as he was concerned, the book taken as a whole could not possibly be said to have the tendency to corrupt or deprave. In fact, if the average modern reader with a healthy mind, said the learned judge, wanted to read about sex in a manner which left little to the imagination, it was not for the court to say that he should not do so.

The decision had been political. Charles had no doubt of the outcome before the court had even reconvened. 'Of the five judges, two came out in our favour and the other three served their judgment for the recess. I was told by a South African ex-judge living in England that this was going to be a political decision and that there was little chance of the three judges coming down on our side.

'By chance, I met the South African ambassador at a private cocktail party in London and couldn't resist mentioning the subject to him,' wrote Charles in his unpublished memoirs. 'I was immediately up against a brick wall. He went on about how he wouldn't allow his daughter to walk through the streets of London because the bookshops were so full of filth and pornography and that the South Africans had the right idea in banning books. I came away from that party very despondent.

'Sure enough, the three judges voted against us and there was no appeal against this decision until a further ten years had elapsed.

'By then the relaxation of the Censorship Board was such that the book was allowed. After these years, the number of copies in South Africa of *When the Lion Feeds* was considerable, as everybody who travelled came back with one or more copies. This shows the folly of censorship; the moment you draw attention to something, rightly or wrongly, it only enhances its popularity and people will move heaven and earth to get copies.'

Charles was right. I had my own personal epiphany a little later. I was incensed when I read a review of *When the Lion Feeds* in the *Los Angeles Times*. It was a full two pages and it was savage, along the lines of 'this guy should be locked up, and prevented from writing about all his racist crap'.

At the time, I had become friends with Stuart Cloete, the blockbuster South African novelist of his time, who was living in Hermanus, a seaside town south east of Cape Town. He lived just down the road from me and he liked hot curry, which his wife, Tiny, used to cook, and I would be invited to eat with him.

His first novel, *Turning Wheels*, about the Great Trek which was published in 1937 – a year after the centenary celebrations of the Afrikaners leaving their farms in the Cape and travelling by ox wagon into the hinterland to escape British colonial rule – sold more than two million copies. It too was banned. Stuart was born in Paris to an Afrikaner father and a French mother, went to a British public school, became a second lieutenant at the age of seventeen, during the First World War, before returning as a very young husband to farm in South Africa. He divorced, found the love of his life and started writing. He would write fourteen novels in all, several volumes of short stories, three biographies, and even poetry, between 1937 and his death in 1976 at the age of seventy-eight. I liked him a lot, he was a lovely gentleman, but it went further than that. When I signed the contract with Heinemann for *When the Lion Feeds*, their Johannesburg representative described me to journalists as 'the Stuart Cloete of Rhodesia'.

I went down to Stuart brandishing the offending review and said: 'Look what they've done to me!' And he replied: 'That's wonderful, Wilbur, that's one of the best reviews I've ever seen for a first-time author.' Puzzled, I said: 'But you haven't read it.' He said, 'Wilbur, you don't read the stuff, you weigh it. If you're important enough for people to want to write two full pages about your novel in a big-selling publication like that, then it's worthwhile.'

Stuart was, like Charles Pick, one of my first mentors. His rough-hewn, unpretentious wisdom was a great source of inspiration. Both Stuart and I had the dubious honour of being banned authors in South Africa. It reflected the uncertainty of the times and how progress is invariably a many-sided thing. Stuart's novels would remain banished until 1974, while the first work of mine that pleased the gimlet eye of the censors was *Gold Mine* in 1970.

The courts finally unbanned *When the Lion Feeds* in South Africa eleven years after it had been published, following this up with the unbanning of my second novel, *The Dark of the Sun* ten months later, but it wouldn't be the last time my books were banned in South Africa, or elsewhere.

In 1977, I published *A Sparrow Falls*, the final instalment in the trilogy that had begun with *When the Lion Feeds*. It starred Sean Courtney, returning as a general from the First World War to build up his country, put down the Rand Revolt of 1922 and then die because of the perfidy of his awful and evil son, Dirk. In perfect symmetry, the Directorate of Publications, the successor to the Publications Board, promptly banned it – for being indecent and obscene.

Heinemann South Africa's managing director Andrew Stewart went out to bat for me, telling the Directorate's appeals board that the average person was unlikely to buy a 650-page book just to read three pages of sex. Andrew told the court the sex scenes were no more graphic than in any of my previous books, for which there had been no complaints. *A Sparrow Falls* was my eleventh novel.

'People will buy the book because it is an adventure story and because Wilbur Smith is a well-known novelist. They will not buy it for the sex scenes,' said Andrew.

Bizarrely, the Directorate briefed counsel to appeal its

own committee's decision – only the third time in history that this had happened. Quintus Pelser, who was appearing for the Directorate, told the court that the book had 'great literary merit' and 'that the sex scenes were functional'.

'They form an integral part of the plot and help the reader to a better understanding of the characters. The book would not have the same impact if the sex scenes were left out.'

The appeals board reserved its judgment in the same week as *A Sparrow Falls* and *Cry Wolf*, my novel published the year before, achieved the unique double of topping the British hardback and paperback bestseller lists respectively. By now I was getting sacks of fan mail from international readers, particularly in America following the breakthrough of *Eagle in the Sky* (1974), thanking me for writing about South Africa, clarifying the country's complex and tumultuous history, highlighting the issues and dramatising the nation in an entertaining and accessible way.

The decision of the South African board underscored that they had exiled me just as the rest of the western world was welcoming me. The people I felt sorriest for were the local booksellers. They were already buckling under the pressure of the new nationwide television service introduced in South Africa the year before, in 1976. But I didn't regret a word I'd written – and nor did the readers. *A Sparrow Falls* was one of my most successful novels.

A South African returning to his country felt the full

force of the ban. He was on his way home from London and had bought a copy of *A Sparrow Falls* to pass the time during the flight. With nothing to declare on arrival at Jan Smuts Airport (today Oliver Tambo International Airport) he casually went down the green aisle only to be stopped by a zealous customs official and told the book was banned.

'Some twenty minutes later,' he wrote to the *Star* newspaper, 'I was still filling in forms, having my name and address taken, my passport examined and being rather officiously lectured to about my contravention of the Act.'

The paper took up his case in the editorial column the next day:

'You have arrived at Jan Smuts Airport,' as the old joke would have it. 'Would passengers please put their watches back 25 years.' The experience, which a reader described in a letter to the Star, made the apocryphal story ring uncomfortably true . . . The undesirability of the novel A Sparrow Falls *is highly arguable to say the least. Last year a committee of the Publications Directorate found it indecent and obscene. However, the Directorate itself joined the publishers in a successful appeal against the ban. Then the Publications Appeal Board re-banned it citing eleven passages where sexual description was too explicit. Certainly it is no Kama Sutra or* Das Kapital. *It is a typical modern adventure tale in which an occasional dash of sex is almost an*

*obligatory part of the formula and very much subsidiary
to the main action. Are such books really worth making
such a fuss over? Doesn't banning them simply serve as
a needless irritant to unknowing South Africans and
make the country look petty rather than prim in the
eyes of the outside world?*

The Publication Appeal Board lifted the ban on *A
Sparrow Falls* in 1981. As always, they couldn't resist taking
a swipe at me. The descriptions it found were not
'blatantly shameless and not so crude to taint the whole
book with undesirability'. That was the good part. The
book had no literary merit, the good burghers harrumphed,
'but it will have a wide probable readership – it can be
described as escapist fiction.'

It was necessary to adopt a realistic approach in this
respect, the Board said, because 'escapist fiction has a
place in the South African community and forms an integral part of many South Africans' relaxation'. It would be
absurd therefore to expect such fiction to be without
sexual descriptions.

Just why its committee could not have come to the
same conclusion four years earlier and before the expenditure of tens of thousands of rands in legal fees, only it
would know, but we would have the last laugh. *A Sparrow
Falls* was to win me my first golden Pan award in 1982.
Pan Books, the publishers who I had moved to after
Heinemann, had created the award to recognise authors

in their stable who had sold more than a million copies of any particular title. Standing 25cm high, it was a golden statuette of an original bronze Pan figurine dating from between 1BC and 1AD held by the British Museum.

There was one final twist in this strange saga of censorship. In 1980, I started writing what would become the four-part Ballantyne series. The novels chronicled the lives of the Ballantyne family from the 1860s to the 1980s against the background of the bitter struggle between black and white in Rhodesia's (now Zimbabwe) brief history. The series ended with *The Leopard Hunts in Darkness* (1984) which the Zimbabwean government promptly banned.

8

THIS SEAFARING LIFE

I had known Hillary Currey nearly all my life. We had first become friends at Michaelhouse, where Hillary, a popular boy who made a good fist of appearing responsible, rose to become Head Boy while I did everything I could to buck the system. Later, Hillary and I had gone to Rhodes University together. He was the sort of friend who proposed wild adventures in which I would become a more than willing participant. In the long varsity holidays, I would work, and on one Christmas vacation, Hillary suggested how we could make more than £60 a week. It would be easy, he said, we'll get a job on the fishing boats.

Now, somewhere in the middle of the Namib desert, this did not seem like such a good idea. I looked at Hillary, encrusted in the sand and grime of the sun-blasted landscape, and wondered if he was thinking the same.

It was approaching Christmas, 1953. The bushmen of the Namibian interior called this place 'The Land God Made in Anger'. The Portuguese sailors who once made landfall at the port where we were heading had called it 'The Gates of Hell'. We were bound for the fishing town of Walvis Bay, sitting at the head of the newly christened Skeleton Coast, but between us and the water there was endless, unchanging desert. It was a journey of 1500 miles and would take us six days and we had now been two days without a lift. Until then we had cadged rides with local farmers and travelling salesmen, but good fortune had deserted us. We tramped in silence along the Trans Namib railway line that stretched all the way from the Namibian capital Windhoek to the coast, lost in our own thoughts of incipient despair and the folly of youth.

From behind us came the creaking of something approaching along the rails. At first, I could see nothing in the heat haze – but slowly the sound grew louder, and an image began to coalesce out of the rippling air. It was a maintenance buggy, rattling its way along the tracks by means of a pump worked by a red-faced engineer.

We flagged it down, gesticulating wildly. No doubt perturbed by the sight of two twenty-year-old white men tramping through the midday heat, the engineer slowed the buggy.

'What's happened here, boys?'

'Room up there for two more?' Hillary asked.

The engineer looked at us like we were about to steal his lunch.

'Are you bedol [mad]?'

Nobody hitch-hiked on the railways.

Then Hillary fished out a couple of notes from his pocket, and the driver took them.

'Climb up back,' he said, 'you're going to die out here else.'

And that was how we arrived, exhausted and stinking of the desert, into the fishing port of Walvis Bay.

• • •

Walvis Bay was a natural deep water harbour where the seas were alive with pilchards, plankton and the whales after which the settlement was first named. There had been a town here since the fifteenth century, when the harbour was a valuable haven for European ships sailing around the perilous Cape of Good Hope. Out on the seafront lay half a mile of jetties, and at dusk the waters of the harbour thronged with more than a hundred fishing trawlers, each fit for seven or eight men. We wanted a job on one of the pilchard boats.

We spent two days walking up and down the docks asking for work. But no matter how hard we tried, we couldn't find a captain to take us on. Naturally, the first thing the skippers asked was how much experience we had. The answer was simple: none. I was used to boats, that much was true – we had spent long childhood holidays up and down the Zambezi and Kafue rivers, out on the Great Lakes in Malawi, or off the coast at Maputo in Mozambique, game fishing in the Indian Ocean – but I knew nothing about trawling for pilchards. The captains looked at my soft hands and laughed in my face. Everyone declined our services, some not so politely. 'Go home to Mummy, little boy,' was perhaps the gentlest.

Someone finally took pity on us. The *Kingfisher* – a little trawler owned, like several of these pilchard boats, by a pair of affluent Cape Town brothers – was at jetty and about to cast off when we approached. Her skipper, a giant of a man named 'Boots' Botha, took us on for five weeks, on a commission-only basis. If we didn't catch we didn't get paid. At thirty-five years old, Boots was ancient to us – a hardened man of the sea – but he must have had a soft spot, or else he could see the desperation in our eyes.

The work would be hard, he said, we would be the dogs of the boat, doing all the tasks his experienced crew hated to do themselves – but in the evenings the beer would flow freely at the hotel where all the fishermen gathered and we would get a place to bed down in the boat's cabin.

That same day, we went to sea.

. . .

Like all new initiates, we were treated as pond life. True to his word, Boots gave us all the dangerous jobs which we jumped at because we knew no better. If there was a practical joke to be played, it was at our expense. My own initiation came early. Sent by the ship's engineer to bring up cotton wastes from below deck, I plunged my arm into a container – only to discover it was the engineer's latrine, the cotton wastes used in lieu of bog paper. From that day on I was christened *Spook-gat* or 'ghost's arsehole' in Afrikaans.

Those first weeks aboard the *Kingfisher* were back-breaking. Never had I put my body through so many sustained trials. Though I was barely twenty years old, my joints ached and my muscles groaned – and only after days of hard work did I grow accustomed to the grind. There was much to learn but, before the first week had passed, I gained a special position on board that went some way to elevating my standing.

The casting of trawler nets was a complicated business. With one end of the line attached to the trawler, and the other to a little rowboat towed behind, we would head for what the skipper thought were the day's best waters. At the back of the trawler, Boots Botha would survey the water for the first sign of a shoal. Usually it would be the darting of a pilchard just below the surface, perhaps even one or two cresting out of the swell. Pilchards gather in vast shoals, so as soon as one was spotted, we knew there were thousands more lurking underneath. It was at this point that the trawler would begin its circuit, lapping round the shoal in ever decreasing circles, bunching it into a tighter and tighter space. Sometimes the shoals would be so big that we'd have to unleash the rowboat, working the shoal so that it separated into two or three smaller shoals, whatever size best fitted our nets. As soon as the shoal was constricted, the surface of the water would come alive, quivering and glittering with the agitation of so many fish.

At the skipper's command, the rowboat would be thrown loose, its ties unfastened so that it could stream off, trailing the net behind. Soon there would be two hundred feet of net out in the water. Only then would the skipper bring the trawler around the shoal to pick up the rowboat again and retie it, the shoal being surrounded by netting.

The fish were crowded together close to the surface while, underneath them, the net hung open. Now came the moment to close the net, trapping the fish within. Around the bottom of the net ran the lead line, laden with lead weights to hold it down. It was this line that had to be gathered up, taken back on board the trawler and put onto a winch to draw the bag closed. Yet, the net could not be fully closed until the heavy steel rings around the lead line were taken off.

The critical point came when the whole bunch of the net was up. The rings had a thick cable running through them but, to take them off and bring in the net, another line had to be fed through so that the thick cable could come out and the steel rings be taken off one by one. A man at the back of the boat would reach for a stick and try to feed this new line around. It was a painstaking job, but nothing else could happen until it was done. The rest of us had to wait.

After three days of watching the crew clumsily feeding the line through the rings, I jumped forward and put my arm through the rings and pulled the new line through. I was the only one on board whose hands could fit through the rings. The trawler men were amazed, even though it seemed to me like an obvious thing to do.

The following day, when the net came up from the water, I was summoned. '*Spook-gat!*' cried the boatman. 'Here, *Spook-gat*, put your hand through here . . .'

I slipped my arm through the rings and fed the line again. I was pleased with my work. Every day I was saving the crew a half hour of frustration and impatience and, after that, the crewmen never looked at me with quite the same disdain.

• • •

At the end of every day, back at the jetties, suction pipes drew up our catch from the deck of the boat, and Boots Botha was paid. Nights were spent in exhaustion, or in drink, and come the next dawn, we would be back on shore, warming ourselves with coffee and waiting for the sun to spill enough light over the water to make fishing possible again.

We started to earn money. At first, it was enough for beer on nights when the hotels in Walvis Bay rang with the raucous sounds of fishermen who had come in from the sea. Then, as our catches grew bigger, so too did our cash and by the end of our trip I had made about £450, which was a king's ransom in those days.

But it was blood money, sometimes literally. At sea, men risked their lives daily. Fingers were sliced off at the knuckles when the sea suddenly surged, tightening or wrenching at the nets. Hands were mangled or crushed against the sides of the boats. And, on one occasion I will never forget, I saw a man lose his life to the fickleness of the sea – an experience I would later use in my novel *The Burning Shore*.

We were some distance off coast, with our nets already winching up, when our sister boat, owned by the same Cape Town brothers as the *Kingfisher*, drew near. Across the waters, we watched as they cast their nets, the line streaming off the back of the trawler. I saw one of their crewmen stumble, his ankle caught in the running line. For a terrible second, he stood tall, then the sea was dragging the line away, his body snapped taut – and he was gone cartwheeling over the side. As he hit the water, still entangled in the netting, his crew rushed to snatch him from the depths but it was too late. The line was already thirty feet under water. By the time he surfaced, he would be dead.

An hour passed. Maybe more. When it came time to draw in the nets, filled with pilchards, plankton – and the occasional shark or barracuda, to be cut free and tossed back into the water – there lay the man's body, already beginning to bloat.

After four weeks working the *Kingfisher*, we had gained the grudging respect of Boots Botha and his crew. Both Hillary and I were hard-working boys, and one night we all went out on the town. The hotel in Walvis Bay was heaving with trawler men, and the crew of the *Kingfisher* were already deep into their cups. At the bar, Hillary and the chief engineer were rounding up more drinks while I propped up a table with Boots Botha and the rest. It had been a good day. One of our sister ships had been trapped at sea, their net filled with so many pilchards from such an unexpectedly vast shoal that they were laden down, unable to move. The *Kingfisher* came to the rescue and we spent the day ferrying parts of their catch back to port and, in doing so, had the most profitable day in the crew's memory. Most of it was being spent in the hotel that night.

Boots was smashed out of his skull and he pulled me over for a heartfelt chat: '*Spook-gat*,' he said, struggling to remember my real name. 'Wilbur isn't it? You're a good man, I like you, so let me tell you. Every time you stick your *bleddy* arm through those rings, I get such a fright . . .'

Boots' eyes were bloodshot with beer, and he seemed to be laughing at some joke only he knew the punchline to, his spittle flecking my ear.

'Why?' I asked.

'*Spook-gat*, if the line breaks when your arm's in the rings, all those rings are going to separate – and they're going to have a pressure of about three hundred tonnes on them and your arm will look like a sliced loaf of bread.'

Now I understood the looks of consternation whenever I put my arm through the rings. I gazed around the room, at Hillary drinking, at the other members of the crew who all knew this simple truth that I did not. I had been risking my arm, perhaps my life, and not one of them had breathed a word. It was the law of the jungle and I was the little baby antelope squinting in the sun wondering why all the other animals had run away when a predator emerged. I smiled at my naivety. At least I was still alive to tell the tale.

The next day, as we rode the waves beyond Walvis Bay, casting our nets and preparing to draw them in, the cry went out – '*Spook-gat!* Put your hand through these rings!' I took one look at the grinning crew and told them in trawler man's language that I was never going to put my hand in there again. 'Go get your stick,' I shouted. They'd been rumbled.

• • •

The time we spent aboard the *Kingfisher* had been as gruelling as I could remember. Hillary and I set off eastwards, along the railway that would take us back across the desert, to Windhoek and, from there, to South Africa and Rhodes University; our pockets were flush, our bodies were strong, and my mind was filled with a new understanding of the sea. It was unforgiving and cruel, it took life with impunity, but it was also magnificent, wild and beautiful and rewarded those who understood her with the riches of comradeship and stirring narratives of life on the waves. In the years to come, I would return to those stories, to men like Boots Botha and the crew of the *Kingfisher*. Looking back, the seeds of future novels like *The Diamond Hunters* and *The Eye of the Tiger*, and even the character Lothar de la Rey from *The Sound of Thunder*, were all being sown in those experiences at sea.

Those novels were still more than a decade away – and, before then, the sea would come calling again.

• • •

The next Christmas holiday, I thought that, having survived working on a pilchards' trawler, I was tough enough to do a season with the whaling fleets which left from Cape Town in November and sailed down almost to the South Atlantic. I had heard from a friend that a Japanese whaling fleet was looking for labour.

The docks in Cape Town were vast, heaving with freighters, liners and pleasure boats. Before I was born, whaling in this part of the world was centred a couple of hundred miles up the coast at Durban, where the blue whales ran into the warmer northern waters, but this Christmas it was colder waters to which I was bound. Once signed up by a representative of the Whaling Company, I boarded a resupply boat, along with dozens of others like me, and we began the long voyage. Our destination was as far south as I had ever been in my life, and as far south as I was ever likely to go. We were bound for Antarctica, the cold majesty of empty ocean and icebergs. Down in those waters, the humpback, sperm, and southern right whales were to be our prey.

The whaling company had been in Antarctic waters since November, when the whaling season began, and the boat I was travelling on was one of many resupply vessels that regularly plied this route, delivering new men, goods and specialist supplies to the fleet. For five nights and four days we ploughed south, a journey of stultifying boredom, across boundless oceans, where there was nothing to see but the curve of the horizon, growing more pronounced the further we went. The crew on board, a mixture of South Africans and Japanese, were hard, taciturn men – and before we were one night out of port, I knew that this was no *Kingfisher*.

At dusk on the fourth night, we saw the blue expanse of the ocean broken, for the first time, by jagged peaks of white. Icebergs pocked the horizon and, as we entered the ice field, I realised we were close.

On the fifth day, we reached the site where the whaling fleet was working. It was the stench that hit us first. I had not encountered the foul smells of whale blubber and meat before, nor do I want to again. The odour was thick and loathsome, and seemed to taint everything in the atmosphere. The closer we came, the more the oily fug wrapped around us, suffocating us with its miasma of putrefaction and death.

In an expanse of open water, shimmering with the run-off from the butchery on board, lay the factory ship of the fleet.

Antarctic whaling was built around processing stations on the ice shelf itself, but the need for more efficient butchery – and to avoid regulation by any government in the world – had led to the first factory ships being built so that whaling could take place entirely at sea. When we boarded her, the factory ship seemed like a world in itself. I imagined the Antarctic as the place of beauty and grandeur I had conjured up by reading classic tales of exploration and heroism – of Robert Falcon Scott and his doomed mission to reach the South Pole, of Ernest Shackleton and the crew of the *Endurance*, abandoning their ship to the pack ice and yet somehow returning home without losing a single man – but there was little triumph or adventure in what the next month had in store. The factory ship was an open-air abattoir, her every surface slick with whale oil and blood. For the rest of the season, she was to be my home.

· · ·

If my first days aboard the *Kingfisher* had shown me how unprepared I was compared to the trawler men who worked those waters every day, my first days aboard the factory ship revealed how naive I had been to think of the trawler as any kind of preparation for a life like this.

Days were spent in long shifts on the factory deck. There were eight harpooning boats in the fleet. At first light, they would set out to hunt their prey, returning at intervals with rivers of blood trailing behind them. The carcasses of the whales were towed in by the catchers, and winched up the slide in the stern of the mothership by great mechanical claws. Then our work would begin. Armed with flensing knives, the crewmen sliced open the layers of blubber, systematically taking the great animals apart. The team of which I was a junior member hooked on cables that peeled the blubber off. It was hard, unrelenting work on a slippery, rolling deck, in gale-force winds which whipped across us, carrying with them all the freezing bitterness of the Antarctic. We were surrounded by heavy, moving machinery, while the knives swung with mad abandon by the Japanese could decapitate or disembowel a man. By comparison the pilchard trawler was a luxury pleasure cruise.

Once flensed – stripped of every scrap of fat, flesh and bone that could be processed, used or sold – the carcasses of the whales were pushed back out to sea. Somewhere, further south, they would wash up on the shores of the Antarctic ice shelf where vast bone yards would collect – a veritable skeleton coast.

I spent my nights in quiet solitude, too exhausted to do anything but sleep. I had no companions here – and no chance of making them. The men of the *Kingfisher* had become friends, but these whaling men were a different breed. Even those who spoke English had a glazed, faraway glint in their eyes. There was no camaraderie between them, only work, blood, blubber and bone.

By the end of the fourth week I felt as if I had been here a lifetime. The place was less a factory ship than a mobile slaughterhouse. The visceral mess of death was all around. I spent another long day toiling on the cadaverous deck, and, when I retired that night, every inch of me glistening with whale oil, I knew what I was going to do.

The next day, I made my way across the slippery decks to find the ship's doctor. I told him I had a pain in my abdomen that wouldn't go away. He laid me down, felt my gut but found nothing. He told me to go back to work. 'Surely,' I said, 'you don't want somebody to die on this ship? That's how bad it feels.'

He picked up a pen and began to fill out a form. He'd heard this story before and knew it wasn't worth questioning. That day, when the resupply ship came down from the Cape, there was one extra passenger on its manifest for the return route north. Two months earlier than I'd thought, I was saying goodbye to that floating hell upon the water. It would take me days to feel civilised again, weeks until I could no longer feel the residue of whale oil between my fingers, or smell the noxious vapour of the factory ship in my hair. The return journey was long and unsettled, the seas squalling under tempestuous skies – and Cape Town couldn't come quickly enough.

One day, I would write a novel called *Hungry as the Sea* and draw on my experiences in the Antarctic. *Hungry as the Sea* would be my twelfth book and the first I had ever written partially set in the US. It was a story about Nicholas Berg, the golden prince of Christy Marine, who had got to the top of the shipping world through hard work and ability, only to lose his position to a glib London city boy, who stole his wife for good measure. Now, with only a tugboat to his name, Berg had to brave the chilly wastes of the Antarctic, rescue one of his former company's luxury cruise liners and then prevent his cuckolder from killing his estranged wife and son.

I had no knowledge whatsoever of the big ships and the arcane world of high sea salvage. Safmarine, South Africa's merchant navy, was particularly helpful, being one of the big world players in maritime freight and shipping, but the greatest lure for me was Safmarine's ownership of two of the biggest and most powerful sea tugs in the world, the *John Ross* and the *Wolraad Woltemade*, known as the greyhounds or the vultures of the Cape, depending on your viewpoint. They both regularly docked in Cape Town. I spent hours aboard with the captains and crews who, very generously, shared their knowledge and stories of high drama on the worst seas of the world.

As for whaling and the Antarctic, if I never saw those icy wastes again, it would be too soon.

9

THIS HIGH-FLYING LIFE

The summer of 1947 was long and dry, and the further north we went the more blistering the heat. I had already been on this train for nearly three days, grinding our way from Johannesburg to Bulawayo, changing trains there for the final leg, and now, as we neared Lusaka, I was ready to believe that the holidays had truly begun. This was always a golden moment, a time when I could forget the strictures of boarding school and live as I wanted, running free on the ranch. My father's driver was waiting to meet me at the station and the delirious excitement of the school holiday stretched before me.

There was always work to do at home. My father, as a staunch Victorian, had little tolerance for idleness, and I could not get away with weeks of untethered abandon. But there was still time for hunting and shooting, reading and exploring – all the things that made me remember the ranch so vividly and with such fondness. On the third day of the holiday, I woke early, took to my bike, and set out for the Kafue River.

I was born between two world wars and growing up in the aftermath of the Second World War, I couldn't escape the consequences of war. I grew up around veterans, many of whom had been invited to the Rhodesias to settle as farmers or work as artisans. Our ranch had been built up from several smaller farms allocated to ex-servicemen who had then decided Africa was too hostile and harsh a place and had returned to England to build their futures in that green and pleasant land. But, of all our neighbours, there was one who had resolved to stay, and who was stoically making this corner of Africa his own. He lived two farms away and, as I cycled along winding dirt tracks and familiar scrub, I wondered what kind of reception he would give me.

I had first set out to befriend this man when I'd over-heard my father talking about him with our labourers. Apparently, he was a recluse and rarely seen in the social circles of the ranching world. He was also a former Royal Air Force pilot, a hero of the Battle of Britain who had come here to recover from his injuries.

The Battle of Britain was fought between July and October 1940 when the RAF defended Great Britain from the onslaught of the German Luftwaffe. As a boy, weaned on stories of the pilot Biggles and his escapades in the air,

the idea of brave British pilots dog-fighting with the relentless Luftwaffe as London burned below was thrilling stuff.
It was a story of valour, romance, heroism and sacrifice
that fired my imagination. Even now, as I remember
attending air shows and hearing the gut-thumping roar of
a Supermarine Spitfire's Rolls-Royce Merlin engine as the
aircraft soared into the heavens, or the sky sounding like
it was being torn in two by giant hands as the plane
swooped in a never-ending dive, I have shivers down my
spine. I once saw fourteen Spitfires and Hurricanes from
the Second World War take off en masse, the ground
shuddering with the combined raucous horsepower, the
air riven with the staccato pulse beat of their engines, and
I shall never forget the grace with which they cleaved the
sky. Later I would read that classic of Second World War
literature, *The Last Enemy* by Richard Hillary, a Battle of
Britain pilot who suffered terrible burns when he was shot
down by a Messerschmitt Bf 109. As a teenager, war
gripped me in its glamorous fist – it was a chance to test
your mettle, answer the call of duty, to become a man.
The price of military conflict was never in my reckoning.
That is until I met our neighbour for the first time.

His face had been burned beyond the talents of any
surgeon to repair. His eyes seemed like black holes set in
a mask of contorted scar tissue, his nose pinched and out
of shape. It was as if his face had frozen into an expression
of shock, as if set permanently in the moment of agony
as the flames tried to consume him. He had fought over

the skies of London during the Battle of Britain and was shot down when pursuing a group of German Dornier 215 bombers above the coast of Kent. He was reluctant to talk about the details but with time he gradually opened up to me. He said that Geoffrey Page, a fellow RAF fighter pilot, had described his early experience of flying Spitfires as 'the sweet red wine of youth', and perhaps he saw some of that in me, in my callow enthusiasms, my endless curiosity. He had opened fire on one of the leading Dorniers when suddenly the air was criss-crossed with a hail of flashing white tracer cannon shells. The escorting Messerschmitt 109s had attacked his squadron in defence of their bombers. A thunder burst of an explosion deafened his eardrums and he knew he had been hit. An ugly wheal of a hole gaped open in his port wing and flames started belching from the bottom of his cockpit. His engine vibrated violently and he thought he'd better get out of there fast. The fuel tank on a Spitfire is between the instrument panel and the engine, so right in front of the pilot was 90 gallons of volatile fuel, and suddenly it went up like a bomb, flames shooting over his face and hands. Instinctively remembering his bailout procedure, he jettisoned his canopy, grabbed at his Sutton harness to loosen it while his skin shrivelled like roasting meat in the searing blast furnace of his cabin. Somehow, he managed to jam his control column forward, pitching him out of the cockpit as the aircraft dropped away. He tried in vain to pull the parachute rip cord with his red raw fingers, over and over he grabbed at it, his hands slippery with sloughing flesh, until finally he gained purchase and his parachute opened with a sickening jolt. It was only when, off the coast of Margate, he hit the sea hard, feet first, and surfaced, gasping for air, his parachute luckily collapsing to one side of him, that he realised how badly burnt he was as the salt water pressed against his wounds like sandpaper. Months of pain and many operations later he was invalided out of the RAF and given a desk job for which he was grateful, although he also felt disappointed and guilty. He was ashamed of being wounded, felt somewhere deep inside of him that, by surviving, he had failed some ultimate test, and I realised that perhaps it was not just his facial disfigurement that made him shun company.

Just as the visible scars of that defining episode in his life never disappeared, the inner wounds never seemed to heal either, and I think he found my presence some sort of comfort. He was not much older than me – a man in his mid-twenties, perhaps, though it was hard to tell; he had the demeanour of a man much older.

I would visit his ranch whenever school term was finished. His was a cattle ranch and, coming from London, he had much to learn about farming. As I was the son of a cattle rancher I fancied myself an expert. I set about helping my friend the best I could about the nuances of caring for cattle, about the importance of dipping, of the various ticks and fleas cattle had to be protected against, the perennial problem of lions roaming across our ranch.

His hands had not been too badly injured and he could use them quite well, but he appreciated a second pair as I heaved and pulled and shoved and pushed, helping him work the land.

I got to thinking about how long a man could live a solitary life like this. Did he have family? Did he have other friends? What did a man do on his own at night, locked away in a prison he had made for himself? Did he want, one day, to have all the things other people dreamed about? Did he want to meet a woman and marry? He was in his twenties, with his entire life stretching before him. Had he given up on the rest of life already? And could a woman ever look at that scar tissue, those pinched eyes, and fall in love? These were questions I never asked.

Then, as mysteriously as he had come into our lives, my pilot friend was gone. One holiday, when I turned up at the ranch, he was no longer there. Soon, a new owner would take up habitation and work his own cattle along the banks of the Kafue. My friend had left no forwarding address, no letter explaining why he had left. For a while, his disappearance was a mystery to be picked over by my family and our neighbours, but soon he was just one more ex-serviceman who couldn't fall in love with Africa. I always wondered about that RAF man; perhaps Africa was too vast a space, constantly reminding him of the infinity of the sea and sky that nearly took his life, and perhaps he walked away from it all, seeking the oblivion he so nearly encountered during the war. Maybe he took his own life somewhere out in the bush, his body consumed by wild animals, leaving no trace but drops of blood in the dust, his spirit a wisp of smoke in the air.

I was sad to see him go. I would never meet my friend again but his presence would linger in my memory, ghost-like, for many years.

. . .

In 1973, almost thirty years later, the questions still preyed on my mind. I began to write the novel that would become *Eagle in the Sky*, my first novel set in the air, and the first that would make significant inroads into the all-important US market, climbing the *New York Times* bestseller list, something that wasn't repeated for any of my books until Nelson Mandela was released in 1990. As Charles Pick used to say, anything that came out of apartheid South Africa was tainted by association. Also Americans, bless them, never really understood the map of Africa, and as a result were at a disadvantage when it came to under-standing the setting of some of my books. *Eagle in the Sky* bucked that trend.

Eagle in the Sky would be the story of David Morgan, a young man who has the world promised to him but wants something more, something he has made. Though his family expect him to live his life in the boardroom of their financial empire, he finds himself instead drawn to the skies and, forsaking his predictable, mapped-out future, he leaves

Africa for Europe. As I began the novel, I knew Morgan would share the fate of my childhood friend. Badly injured in a fighter jet, he would spend the second part of the novel coming to terms with his injuries and finding redemption in the wild heartland of Africa. Being a Wilbur Smith novel, it was the love of a beautiful woman that would help David recover. I never knew what happened to my friend but, in the pages of my novel, I could give him the ending I hoped he had found. This love story – combining my enthusiasm for flight and my admiration for fighter pilots in general – would have its roots in personal experience. I had been in love with planes ever since I was a boy. I can still vividly remember the feeling of the wind in my hair, the ranch house dwindling beneath us, as my father took me up into the skies for the first time.

. . .

My father had bought his Tiger Moth bi-plane soon after we'd moved to the ranch, and it was in that tiny plane that I'd had my first taste of travel in the air. Strapped into the open cockpit with my father, dressed in hat and goggles as if I was flying in the Battle of Britain, we had risen above the ranch, banked sharply over the bush, and come around in a great arc, following the Kafue River as it flowed into the greater Zambezi. My father had been fascinated by aviation ever since the first successful flights had been launched when he was a boy. Sometimes, if I caught my father in the right mood, I was allowed to take hold of the joystick myself, and feel, for a fleeting moment, the giddy thrill of being in charge of this plane, thousands of feet above ground. For a seven-year-old boy, the rush was incredible. I knew that one day I too would learn to fly.

My father flew all over the ranch, but it wasn't until much later that I eventually got my Private Pilot's Licence (PPL). I wanted to pilot myself to the best hunting grounds in Africa, and not be beholden to anyone else's schedule when I planned to enter the bush. Some of the most challenging hunting grounds in inland Africa were accessible only by plane.

I learned to fly in Cape Town, in the mid-to-late 1960s, starting out in small bush planes. The Cessna 180 was a small American aircraft, seating four, and used all over the Africas by ranchers, hunters and small charter companies. It had handling characteristics similar to my father's old Tiger Moth in the way it took off, in the throbbing of the engine, the alarming rocking sensation every time the wind caught, and I graduated quickly to long solo flights, crossing South Africa from one coast to another. I could steer the Cessna onto landing strips deep in the bush where the uneven runways tested my skills to the limit. But there is a world of difference between piloting a light aircraft like a Cessna 180 over the rolling African bush, and the supersonic jet fighters I wanted to write about in *Eagle in the Sky*. There was little chance that I could be allowed to fly a Mirage fighter jet – the French plane flown by air forces across Europe and beyond – so I would have to settle for the next best thing.

A journalist friend, Andrew Drysdale – who would ultimately become editor-in-chief of the *Cape Argus* – introduced me to Dick Lord, a senior officer in the South African Air Force, who had started his career in Britain's Fleet Air Arm before going on to help found the US Navy's 'dog fight school' made famous by the movie *Top Gun*. Dick got me some time on an air force flight simulator in Pretoria. I wanted to find out what it would be like to be in a dog fight flying a Mirage fighter jet against a Soviet MiG.

Strapped into the simulator, the mock cockpit laid bare before me, I duly got airborne. Soon I was at two thousand feet, then five thousand, then ten. Intermittently, the intercom crackled in my headphones as the laconic major in charge of the simulation came over the air, reading out his orders.

I was soaring high, seemingly at ease in my jet fighter, when the intercom burst into static once more, and the major said:

'Mr Smith, you are flying Mach 2 in a vertical dive and you are five hundred feet from the ground. What are you going to do?'

I scanned the gauges. The last precious seconds I had were hurtling by. There had to be something here that could avert this catastrophe. I flicked a few switches, the sweat beading on my brow.

I concentrated hard, let my instincts take over. I knew exactly what I had to do.

Quick as a flash, I unstrapped myself, flung open the door of the simulator and looked him in the eye.

'You take over, Major!' I exclaimed as, behind me, the simulated jet carved a crater into the ground.

• • •

I had decided where my hero David Morgan would meet his fate. I was going to send him into the heart of the troubled Holy Lands, the wars being waged over control of the world's newest and most controversial state: Israel. South Africans had played a major role in the formation of the Israeli Air Force, with Cecil Margo – later a South African Supreme Court judge – having drawn up the force's blueprints at the behest of David Ben Gurion, Israel's primary founder and first Prime Minister. Later, Margo was to turn down command of the fledgling force to return to Johannesburg and work as an advocate – but the connection opened a door in my imagination, and through it David Morgan stepped.

The question remained: how to see this world first-hand, how to learn all the vital details of life as an air force pilot in one of the world's most incendiary places? Being a bestselling author had opened parts of Africa to me before, but in Israel my fame did not precede me.

Aaron Sacks was a plastic surgeon I knew from Cape

Town's Jewish community. Fifty years old, educated and suave, he had made his fortune by being one of the most talented and highly regarded in his field. Though he lived and worked in South Africa, much of Aaron's work had been carried out in Israel, where he treated pilots and other aircraft crew injured in accidents. Since its inception in 1948, Israel had been embroiled in a succession of wars with its neighbouring nations. There had been the war of independence in 1948, the war of 1956, and the incredible Six Day War of 1967 – all of them, sadly, providing work for a man of Aaron's capabilities. With his connections to the Israeli military, I had an opportunity to see first-hand the environment into which I was sending my hero, and soon I was boarding a plane for Tel Aviv. I made many trips between 1972 and '73.

Tel Aviv was a new city, barely sixty years old, but already it had outgrown and overtaken the ancient port of Jaffa on whose borders it had been founded – an experiment in peaceful cohabitation between Jewish settlers and Jaffa's mostly Palestinian population. That experiment had been tested time and again, but now it was one of the primary centres of the new Israeli state. This was a place, like the burgeoning cities of Africa, where the ancient and modern worlds met, a melting pot of peoples and cultures.

At first, the military brass had been very tight-lipped. They lived their lives on a constant knife's edge, waiting for the next call to arms – but, with introductions and favours, I gained permission to go into the air bases themselves. Shrouded in secrecy, I was escorted into a military transport and, after having spent long days with friends of Aaron Sacks, soaking up the nightlife and cafe culture of this complex city, I was driving through the desert scrub outside Tel Aviv, entering the restricted area where the Israeli air force prepared its defence of the nation.

As we passed through layers of camouflage, flanked by armed guards, I was instructed that what I was about to see was shown only to a select few outsiders, and even then, only those whose histories had been vetted and declared safe. Here, security was so tight that even the parents of the air crews on base did not know what their sons did. Wives had no idea what their husbands were doing, brothers did not speak about their work to brothers and on no account was I to write directly about what I would see.

It was a rare privilege. The air bases were new, precision-built buildings where combat pilots and ground crews spent their days in regimented silence, waiting for their orders. It wasn't long before I understood the deadly earnestness under which they performed their jobs. War was no game or adventure as I might have thought as a boy. This was a tinderbox of a region, and the political consequences of making the wrong decision in a split second were inconceivable.

Most of the crew and pilots who welcomed me were

young men in their late teens or early twenties. For them, this was a duty they believed in with the passionate commitment of youth. Although they were warm and accepted me into their mess, sharing their life stories, allowing me to see the insides of a Mirage fighter jet, or experience their training missions through the flight simulators on base, there was always a distance between us – there were things I could and could not see. In a world where secrets are currency, I realised, a novelist is a spy. This was not like the gold mines of the Witwatersrand, where through casual gossip and workman's banter I could build up the texture of the place, and I left knowing that, though I had gleaned enough to bring my novel to life, there was a world of detail an outsider could never fully understand.

One week after I returned from Tel Aviv, in October 1973, I was preparing to write my first chapter of *Eagle in the Sky* when war was, once again, declared in Israel. It was Yom Kippur, the Day of Atonement, the holiest day in the Jewish calendar and, seizing the opportunity, Egypt and Syria launched a surprise attack, crossing the Suez Canal to occupy the Golan Heights and the Sinai Peninsula, territories Israel had occupied since the Six Day War six years before. Very quickly, the situation spiralled out of control. The Americans rushed to support Israel, while the Soviet Union aligned itself with the Arab states, and once again the world was on the brink of catastrophe.

The hand-to-hand fighting was intense, but it was the battle in the air, where pilots were still getting into dogfights, that caught my attention. Those young men I had met, whose world I had shared in the air bases of Tel Aviv, were now in battle for real. Some of them would not come back. Others would end up like my friend from my father's ranch, or the character I was beginning to write about – trapped in a burning cockpit, disfigured or maimed by war, marked forever by one terrible moment in the sky.

With the knowledge that the story was repeating itself somewhere out there, I picked up my pen and started to write.

. . .

Eagle in the Sky was released in 1974 and became a tremendous success in the UK and particularly in the US. Perhaps there was something universal in David's fall from grace and the redemption found in his falling in love that drew American readers to the novel.

In the novel, David Morgan – handsome and gifted heir to a South African business empire – is blessed with a natural flying ability. Turning his back on the path his family mapped out for him, he joins the South African Air Force – but quickly tires of the routine and instead sets off for Europe to discover his true calling. In Spain, he falls in love with a beautiful Israeli academic, Debra

Mordechai, and is drawn to Jerusalem to be with her. There he meets her father, a senior staff officer in the Israeli Defence Force, who – stunned at David's skills in the skies – offers him a commission. Soon, though, disaster strikes.

• • •

I too was about to quit flying. In 1974, I was somewhere above Milnerton, north of the heart of Cape Town, when it happened. Milnerton lagoon was spread out beneath me, strings of palm trees adorning its banks. Somewhere, up the coast, the stark outline of Table Mountain hung, black against the blue of the sky beyond, with strata of white clouds scudding over its peak.

It had been a month since I last flew and, though I had been tentative at first, my hands were remembering and everything was falling into place. I had been in the air for several hours and now it was time to land, so I brought the plane around, setting my sights on the Ysterplaat aerodrome, just south of Milnerton beach.

I began to descend. I had done it a hundred times before and until now all my descents had been safe. Below, the aerodrome was becoming bigger and bigger. I checked my panels: I was steady at ninety miles an hour, a perfect speed for coming over the fence to land.

Suddenly there was a sensation like being thrust backward

and forward at once, a twist in gravity, as if the plane had been plucked out of the air by some unseen hand. It took my rusty mind too long to put together a response, but I knew what had happened. I'd hit a wind shear – from out of nowhere, a headwind as strong as 40 miles an hour had rolled over the plane. In an instant, my airspeed had been slashed to 50 miles an hour, almost half what it had been. The plane wasn't flying anymore. It was falling out of the sky.

Instincts took over. They told me to pull back, somehow wrestle the plane up into the air – but that was the wrong thing to do. The only way out of this was to go full throttle, to put the nose down, to keep her airborne long enough that she didn't land short.

In moments like this, seconds last hours. But that is not how it felt as I grappled with the steering column and I fought to correct the plane's path. Whether I had enough altitude left to recover was out of my hands. There was no way of controlling that now. I would find out soon enough.

The ground reared up, too suddenly and too soon. The Cessna's fixed landing gear touched the runway once, rose, touched again, and again. The uneven descent dragged the plane around. I reined the joystick back to right us. Then we were scudding down the runway, the landing gear touching down properly at last, the speed diminishing as I allowed myself the luxury of breathing deeply.

Somehow, by luck or hand of God, I'd managed to land safely.

After some time, the plane came to a halt. When I stepped out onto the runway, to feel the air now unnaturally still, I looked back at the Cessna, sitting there with its propeller still turning, as if nothing had happened. I stared up into a sky that did not look as tempestuous as it had done minutes ago. And I decided, there and then, that my flying days were over. I did not want to go the same way as my friend from the ranch when I was a boy, or like David Morgan, or the countless pilots whose calls for help have turned to empty static as they crash somewhere out in the African bush. Flying was not like driving a motorcar, something that can be picked up and put down at will. I was flying once a month – but, unless you were flying two or three times a week, your responses started to dull. Your hands and fingers need to react instinctively. You must be aware of the world around you in three-hundred-and-sixty degrees. When things go wrong in the air, they go wrong very quickly. There are no second chances.

I had ridden my luck long enough. From now on, if I wanted to fly, I would charter a plane, hire a professional pilot whose senses were being honed by flying a plane every day. If I wanted adventure in the skies, I would experience it in the pages of my books. For there was more to come, and ideas were forming for a Courtney novel set in the skies above war torn France

– to feature a grieving French beauty, Centaine de Thiry, who loses her lover in another cockpit fire and finds herself stranded on Africa's inhospitable Skeleton Coast.

But that was a story for another day. Right now, I had never been more glad to be alive.

10

THIS HOLLYWOOD LIFE

Hollywood had come calling early in my career. No sooner had print rights to *When the Lion Feeds* been sold to Charles Pick at Heinemann, than the screen rights had been optioned. Stanley Baker – best known today for his role in the blockbuster *Zulu* – was going to play Sean Courtney, with Peter O'Toole as Dufford 'Duff' Charleywood, Sean's best friend and partner in the goldfields. Meanwhile, historian and screenwriter John Prebble had been brought in to work on the script, and I was pencilled in to act as a technical advisor. Filming was planned for the southern Transvaal and Natal – but no film ever materialised. The rights to all my other novels had been snapped up, too.

Two years earlier, in 1969, I had met producer Michael Klinger. Acclaimed today as the most successful independent producer in Britain in the 1970s, he was disparaged in some quarters – British critic Sheridan Morley called him 'nothing so much as a flamboyant character actor doing impressions of Louis B. Mayer' – but he was no fool, he knew movies, and he loved my work. The son of Jewish Polish immigrants to London, Klinger had entered the movie industry through the two Soho strip clubs he owned. Effectively, he'd started as a producer of soft-core pornography, but he'd struck it rich by producing the cult classic *Get Carter*, one of the greatest British gangster movies of all time, starring Michael Caine and written and directed by the brilliant Mike Hodges. He purchased the rights to *Shout at the Devil*, buying *Gold Mine* before it was even published and securing the options for *Eagle in the Sky*, *The Eye of the Tiger* and even *The Sunbird*. Only the first two ever got filmed, ironically *Gold Mine* before *Shout at the Devil*.

It was not until I was handing in my third novel, *The Sound of Thunder*, to Heinemann, that I received my first original commission in the world of film, when a producer approached me to write the screenplay of Sir Percy Fitzpatrick's much-loved *Jock of the Bushveld*. First published in 1907, it was the true story of the author's travels with Jock, his Staffordshire Bull Terrier cross, in the 1880s as he worked his way across the Bushveld region of the Transvaal (then the South African Republic). It had been a childhood favourite of mine, the memoir recalling my grandfather's stories of his time as a transport rider, and I leapt at the chance. I spent the next months working on the script with Sir Percy's daughter, Cecily Niven, while Pretoria-based film impresario Emil Nofal set about auditioning dogs to play Jock. After much hard work, nothing ever came of the project. It was my first taste of the fickle nature of film.

In 1968 an adaptation of one of my novels hit the silver screen. In the summer of that year, *The Dark of the Sun* was released as *The Mercenaries*, only retaining its original title in its American release. The book was still banned in South Africa, but the film, directed by Jack Cardiff, made waves immediately for its graphic scenes of violence and torture. Rod Taylor, the gritty Australian actor, played Bruce Curry; the gorgeous Yvette Mimieux was brilliant as Madame Shermaine Cartier, renamed Claire for the film, while NFL legend Jim Brown, fresh from his role in *The Dirty Dozen*, was an incredibly believable Sergeant Major Ruffo. Though it was set in the Congo, the movie had been filmed in Jamaica, with interiors shot at Borehamwood Studios in London.

It wasn't just the title that had been changed in the transition from page to screen. The psychopathic Cockney barrow boy Wally Hendry – who kills Ruffo before Curry kills him in the final moment – became a Nazi war criminal named Heinlein, loosely based on the real-life Congo mercenary Siegfried Müller, who was notorious for wearing his Iron Cross, won during the Second World War, on his uniform. In the German-dubbed version of the movie, Curry became a German himself. Rechristened Willy Kruger, he was transformed in the translation into a Wehrmacht officer who had clashed with Heinlein over his fanatical Nazism. The German version also cut the scene where Heinlein murders two Congolese children, on the grounds of decency, which was a surprise given that the character was supposed to be a Nazi.

The film was one of the most violent of its time, but no more violent than the book had been – and neither was any more violent than what had actually gone on in the Congo, probably Africa's most violent conflict at the time and certainly one of the bloodiest. Even the director would later admit that the violence happening in the Congo was much worse than could ever have been depicted on film. In their research, they had encountered atrocities so appalling that it left them nauseated.

The Mercenaries might have been notorious for its graphic scenes, but it inspired a later generation of film-makers. Martin Scorsese described the movie as one of his 'guilty pleasures', while Quentin Tarantino used several tracks from the score in his film *Inglourious Basterds*, and even cast Rod Taylor in a cameo role as Winston Churchill.

As *The Mercenaries* hit the cinemas, I was putting the finishing touches to my fourth novel, the stand-alone thriller *Shout at the Devil*. It was loosely based on the sinking of the German Imperial Navy's *SMS Konigsberg* in the Rufiji River – an area of present day Tanzania where I had often gone to hunt and where, memorably, I hunted my first elephant. *Shout at the Devil* was made into a movie released in 1976. Its heroes, the drunkard American elephant hunter, Flynn Patrick O'Flynn, and the languid English remittance man, Sebastian Oldsmith, were played by Hollywood legends Lee Marvin and Roger Moore. What they were after – or at least what Flynn was after – was the ivory of the elephants in the Rufiji Delta. In the story, only one thing stands between Flynn and his prize: the psychotic German commissioner who rules the area with incredible brutality as if it was his own personal fiefdom. Their vendetta must take a back seat as the crippled German warship, *Blücher*, is moored in the same delta awaiting repair, and Flynn and Sebastian are forced by the British authorities to mount a daring raid to destroy the ship before it gives Germany an unbeatable advantage in the war for East Africa.

Before that, though, came my fifth novel, *Gold Mine*, and the movie that it spawned – *Gold*, released in 1974. *Gold Mine* had conquered the bestseller lists, selling over 100,000 copies in hardback, and Michael Klinger was hard at work raising the capital to produce the movie. MGM bought the rights for more than £30,000 and I was enlisted to write the film script for a further £10,000, plus I was in for a share of the film profits – which all sounded great to me. By the time the novel was published, Klinger had raised much of the £1,000,000 capital he needed from backers in South Africa – but, not for the first time, apartheid raised its ugly head. Roger Moore had agreed to star as Rod Slater – but, before shooting could begin, the head of the Association of Cinematograph, Television and Allied Technicians' Union (ACTT), Alan Sapper, announced that his union would not allow us to film in South Africa, his principled stand against the evils of apartheid. Roger was a member of that union and, if he went ahead, the union would blacklist all his future films.

Actors union Equity supported Roger, incensed that any other union would threaten the livelihood of one of its members. A standoff ensued, dominating the British newspaper headlines. Michael Klinger looked for a solution, and asked Sapper to suggest an alternative location. 'How about Wales?' said Sapper. Michael pointed out that Welsh coalmines were very different to African goldmines, and besides, the landscapes of wet and windy Wales were entirely inappropriate. It looked likely that the film's financiers would very quickly dump the project.

There was much discussion and further bad press before Sapper finally relented, instructing his union's members to make the decision themselves on whether to shoot in South Africa. At last, production could begin. A wonderful crew came together, each one of them determined to defy the racist rulings and work in harmony with South Africans, whether black or white. The movie employed many local South Africans, and there was never an apartheid problem on set. *Gold Mine* was a story without an overt political message, set in an industry that – as my personal research showed – was not divided along racial lines. However, there was a stark reminder of South Africa's political system that disturbed the cast: at ten o'clock every night, a siren wailed, indicating the beginning of the curfew. No black worker was allowed outside after this time – a situation many in the cast and crew found intolerable, and a reminder that South Africa's deeply entrenched racism touched every corner of life.

Gold Mine the novel had evaded the South African censors, but *Gold* the movie did not have so easy a passage. In the film, Roger was to share a romantic scene with Susannah York, who played the character Terry Steyner, in the bathtub. The scene had been part of the original book, with the heroine and hero chatting and having some fun and games in the bath, but it had initially been written out of the film script. The director, Peter Hunt, read the book again and liked the scene so much he worked it back in. What had passed the censors in print incited their anger on screen. They insisted it was removed from the South African version of the movie.

Roger was brilliant as Rod Slater and, like me, he took his research seriously, going deep underground in the mines of Buffelsfontein and Randfontein where the movie was filmed. He was a committed leading man, barely wincing when he contracted arsenic poisoning from the water in the mines – an affliction that turned his nipples green, prompting a rapid visit to a doctor. Roger even worked for free for the final three weeks of the shoot, when poor mine conditions meant shooting would have to relocate to a sound-stage in London.

When *Gold* was finally released, the critics were divided. The *Johannesburg Star* thought it was a triumph, predicting the great things it would do for the city on the global stage. The *Los Angeles Times* said the film 'is everything people have in mind when they talk about a movie movie. Its hero is heroic, its heroine is beautiful and kittenishly sexy, its villains are outrageously villainous, its characters crustily colorful. It has scope, scale, surprise. It has more punch than a 15-round fight and more corn than Kansas. It is a travelogue of South Africa and a fascinating audio-visual essay on gold mining.'

Others were not so enthused. *New York Times* critic Vincent Canby suggested the opening scene had been shot through a brandy glass because director Peter Hunt was 'embarrassed by the content of the film and was trying to hide it', while the *Wall Street Journal* was marginally less damning: according to their critic Joy Gold Boyun, the film had failed because 'it lingers too long on sentiment, sex and South African scenery and so loses the swift pace so crucial to this type of film.' When it came to be released in the USA, expectations had sunk so low the movie had to become part of a double feature.

I visited the set and enjoyed spending time with Roger Moore and Susannah York. I thought Susannah York was as cute as they came. When she died tragically from bone-marrow cancer in 2011, the London *Telegraph* remembered her as 'the blue-eyed English rose with the China white skin and cupid lips who epitomised the sensuality of the swinging sixties.' We had all got to know one another on set and one night we were out on the town together at a nightclub in Johannesburg and I asked Susannah to dance. We danced for a while, getting progressively closer and closer, and I thought this was going to be my lucky night . . . And then Roger appeared at her shoulder at about half past midnight and said: 'Okay, Sue, my girl. Bed time I think, we've got to film tomorrow. Come on.' And he took her by the arm and led her away. It was one of the great disappointments of my life. It was as close as I ever came to hating Roger Moore – if it was possible to hate such a sweet guy.

• • •

The relative failure of *Gold* didn't deter Michael Klinger, and it didn't put off Roger Moore either. He was to be back, two years later, when the movie version of *Shout at the Devil* hit the silver screen.

In the meantime, there was the launch of the only original film script I ever wrote that eventually made it to the screen. *The Last Lion* would later find a second life when I cannibalised its story for my 1989 novel *A Time to Die*. The movie starred Jack Hawkins, Karen Spies and David van der Walt, and was directed by Elmo Witt, with the story focusing on a terminally ill American millionaire who goes to Africa on a final expedition to fulfil his life's goal of hunting down a lion.

When the time came for shooting *Shout at the Devil*, Peter Hunt was back in the director's chair, and this time, Roger was joined by Hollywood legend Lee Marvin. As a former marine, part of an elite group who were dropped behind Japanese lines in World War Two, Lee was the perfect choice to portray hell raiser Flynn Patrick O'Flynn.

Although I had set the novel in East Africa, the movie would be shot along South Africa's Transkeian coast. Once again, before production had started, the British film industry was up in arms over what they saw as us condoning South Africa's apartheid politics by working in the country. The ACTT union had ruled against Klinger and his company for filming *Gold*, effectively prohibiting their members from working in South Africa. If they wouldn't budge, he would have to go to Rome to hire technicians.

Eventually production got underway, with the whole crew decamping to Port St Johns at the mouth of the Umzimvubu River in the Transkei. The crew were bunked in little houses overlooking the sea but the idyllic surroundings did little to mitigate the hostile political situation. The local mayor made it known that, if the production threw a party and invited any 'blacks', then we would be thrown out of town.

I spent a lot of time on the set of *Shout at the Devil*. Roger had brought along his glamorous Italian wife, Luisa.

She was typically Italian: fiery, passionate, and noisy. She terrified me. But it was Lee Marvin with whom I would become fast friends. He was as impressive off screen as he was on, dominating the set with his portrayal of Flynn O'Flynn. His magnetism in front of the cameras was matched by his feral zeal in real life. He was an unpredictable, riotous character, a handful for everybody, his life as colourful as any of the characters he played on screen.

Legend had it that, when Lee had one drink too many, his eyes turned red. Roger almost fell prey to the consequences of Lee's red-eyed volatility during the centrepiece of the movie: a gloriously brutal and bloody fist fight between Roger's Sebastian and Lee's O'Flynn. The fight was intricately plotted, the routine blocked and rehearsed so that every move was nailed down, but as action was called for the first take, Roger saw Lee's eyes turning red. Whatever he'd been drinking in his dressing room, it had pushed him over the edge – now he was drunk, and clearly thought he was in a real fight. It became one of the most stupendous fight scenes committed to celluloid, Lee's fists whistling past Roger's nose as he tries desperately to get out of the way, as authentic a portrayal of one enraged man trying to floor the other as you'll ever see.

Lee's love of vodka during filming led to all sorts of unexpectedly entertaining incidents. On one occasion, Lee was carrying the baby playing Roger's daughter, and almost dropped her. In fact, the baby wasn't a girl – we couldn't find one in Port St Johns, so we had to make do with a little boy instead. In the scene, O'Flynn was supposed to gently pick up the baby for the first time, cooing over it, but Lee forgot to support his head and he nearly ended up in the mud. And then the boy, who had been squalling like a force-ten gale, suddenly went limp and silent as if he'd fallen asleep. At first, everybody was amazed that Lee had this magical, calming effect on the child, but the reason was simple: Lee had breathed vodka fumes all over the boy, stupefying him instantly.

At other times, spurred on by the alcohol flooding his system, Lee's courage bordered on the dangerous. In a scene shot in Kruger National Park, where we went to film O'Flynn as an ivory poacher, an elephant had been shot by a tranquilliser dart so that, on waking, we could film Lee and Roger pretending to shoot at him. As the elephant woke, disoriented and filled with rage as they sometimes are, Roger and the rest of the cast – including Ian Holm, who was playing O'Flynn's mute servant and gun-bearer, Mohammed – turned tail and ran straight for the car before they could be trampled by this indignant and very large elephant. Wild with drink, Lee stood his ground. Oblivious to the fact that his gun was loaded with blanks for the movie, he fancied himself as the Great White Hunter, and wanted to face the elephant down single-handed. The elephant eventually walked away as they do when they see a rifle.

On another occasion, again having enjoyed a drink, Lee

My grandfather,
Courtney James Smith
(right & below centre);
teller of tales and the
inspiration for the
Courtney Series

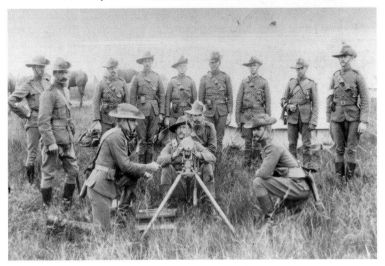

My mother, Elfreda, was my guardian angel. Her love of reading introduced me to the magic of the written word

My father, Herbert (centre). He meant everything to me. He was my God

My mother and father
on a jaunt

My childhood home in what was then Northern Rhodesia

Young Wilbur

My father with his Tiger Moth biplane before one of his trips
to reconnoitre the best hunting grounds for our annual safari

With my father after he bravely took on three lions single-handed – a
photo I still keep on my writing desk

At school at Michaelhouse – reading was my only refuge

Back home from school for the holidays

Success! Signing the contract for *When the Lion Feeds*

With my first publisher, friend and,
later, agent, Charles Pick

Receiving a Golden Pan from Charles Pick for sales
in excess of one million copies of a single book.
I'm lucky enough to have lots of these now!

Touring Europe with
When the Lion Feeds

Surrounded by mountains
of my books

I always enjoy meeting my fans at signing sessions

One of my early interviews

My own private island

Enjoying the spoils of success

With Lee Marvin and Roger Moore during the
filming of *Shout at the Devil*

At a party with Roger Moore and Susannah York — they starred in
the film adaptation of *Gold Mine*

I've been lucky to have many adventures in my life.
Childhood holidays in Durban sparked a lifelong
love for fishing that continues to this day

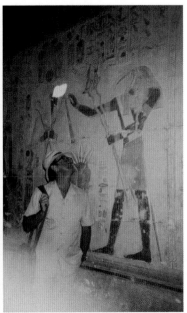

Researching the Egyptian Series

I've been lucky enough to have huge success in Italy over the years, and I was thrilled to be given the key to Milan. It's an honour I cherish every day

My helpmate, playmate, soulmate, wife and
best friend, Mokhiniso Rakhimova Smith

Enjoying the sunset

deprived a hard-working stuntman of his daily fee by performing a risky stunt himself. According to locals, the Umzimvubu River was infested with sharks and the script called for Lee's character to swim across the river to the wreck of the *Blücher* on the opposite riverbank. The plan was for Larry Taylor, an accomplished stuntman, to double for Lee, and the only shots we would need of Lee in the water were of him jumping in and starting to swim. Larry would then take over and continue the rest of the scene. Yet, no sooner was Lee in the water than his old marine training kicked in. Ignoring the cries of the director and crew, he surged unstoppably onwards, powering his way through the river until he had made it to the wreck on the farthest side. Incensed, Larry Taylor put his shirt back on and stormed off. He was perhaps the only man in history who lost out on a day's wages to the drink-fuelled bravado of the legend that was Lee Marvin.

With shooting complete, the cast and crew went their separate ways. There was one last hurrah for Lee when, changing planes at Rome's Fiumincino airport on the way home, he was beset by fanatical Japanese tourists who wanted his autograph and, again with drink pumping through his veins, he somehow lapsed into a post-trau-matic-stress episode, brought on by memories of his wartime service in Japan, and ran like hell out of the air terminal, screaming like a banshee.

About eight years later, when the movie had been and gone, I was able to catch up with Lee in Australia. I had come fishing for giant marlin along the Great Barrier Reef, and chance had it that Lee was there too. It was an unforgettable experience. We would spot the enormous sickle-shaped fins of the marlin from half a mile away. Then we would move in. The bait we used was a five-pound *bonito*. I would watch in awe as the marlin saw the bait, then attacked it with a savage swing of its great bill. As soon as the fish felt the hook, it would go berserk, the rod arching over and the huge reel screeching. Braced on the boat, I would take the full force of the fish's rage on my legs, while the marlin erupted from the surface of the sea like a missile launched from a submarine, dancing and tail-walking across the swells.

Lee and I spent our days on the Reef, and then the evenings carousing in port when we returned. On the final day, I landed a black marlin weighing 1012 pounds and measuring fourteen feet long. They hung it up at the harbour and I was bursting with pride. I'd just won membership of the legendary 'International Game Fishing Association Thousand Pounder Club' because of it. Lee returned to shore about an hour later. He had heard about my catch, and he sauntered over to the jetty to have a look.

'Not bad for a novice,' he drawled. 'Now, come and see a real fish . . .' We went to where his boat was tied up and there was an absolute monster specimen of a marlin lying on the deck – weighing 1200 lbs.

'Never mind, sonny,' said Lee. 'Let me buy you a drink and you can cry into your glass.'

That evening I learned not to try to drink level with Lee Marvin. It was another game that I was a real novice at too.

Shout at the Devil was far better received by the critics than *Gold*. Lee Marvin received rave reviews for his performance as the drunkard O'Flynn while Roger was praised for displaying the same debonair tongue-in-cheek wit as he did in the James Bond films. Yet *Shout at the Devil* was to be the last big film to be made of one of my books. I had been involved in scripting from the start of my career and, even as *Shout at the Devil* was released, I was being paid to write the screenplay for *Eagle in the Sky*. But I was growing increasingly uncomfortable in the world of film. On one occasion I was summoned to a script conference, a new experience for me, who had always thought of writing as a solitary, single-minded endeavour. Here I was in a room of a dozen people all casting their opinions, struggling to make their voices heard, each one of them trying to pull the story in a different direction. At the head of the room, the producer had called for silence when he opened the meeting.

'Gentlemen,' he began, addressing the script editors, 'we've got our work cut out to make sense of this codswallop . . .'

I was sat in the corner of the room and I looked up, considering him carefully. In that moment, I had learnt a very important lesson. In the world of film, the writer does not stand on the top of Olympus as he does in the world of novels, he's right at the bottom amongst the invertebrates, the very last in the food chain. It was the beginning of the end of my relationship with Hollywood.

The time had come to take stock. I was enjoying the riches and the attention that came with making a devil's pact with Hollywood, but I hadn't always enjoyed watching movies being made from my books. I liked some of the characters in the movies, but not one of them was who I'd imagined when I was writing. The characters in my novels felt like real people to me. I always lived with them for such long, intense periods of my life. I had developed them and their families, I knew what they looked like, how they spoke, how they would react in every possible circumstance. There is a straightforward, unobstructed relationship between a writer of novels and his readers, an honesty if you like. When a viewer watches a movie, they are seeing the product of many people's work, a collaboration between the actors and the director, count- less producers, cinematographers, make-up artists, set- designers, lighting guys and many more. But when a reader sits down with a book, it's just me telling a story and the reader recreating it in their imaginations. Something important, some sort of trust, will always be lost in the transition from page to screen.

It had been fun while it lasted, but this was not the world for me.

After *Shout at the Devil*, it was fifteen years before any of my works returned to the screen. In the intervening years, my novels would be optioned and re-optioned, but it wasn't until 1991 that *The Burning Shore*, one of my later Courtney novels, came to the screen as the television film *Mountain of Diamonds*. Later still, *Wild Justice*, *The Seventh Scroll* and *The Diamond Hunters* would all find new life as TV mini-series, but I had long ago stopped having any active involvement in the productions. To this day, I still don't. I never have a problem selling the rights to my books to other people – I've sold some of the rights several times over – but, from a writer's perspective, the best option is to sell the rights, take the money, and hope and pray no film gets made that might ruin your work.

. . .

One of the lessons my publisher Charles Pick had taught me was that I should write from the heart, only ever writing what I truly wanted to write. In the past years, it seemed I had stepped away from that ideal. The temptations of Hollywood, of seeing my characters up on the silver screen played by the idols of the age – Roger Moore, Lee Marvin, Michael Caine and others – had been corrupting me. Proud as I was of *Gold Mine*, *Shout at the Devil*, and *The Diamond Hunters*, I was aware they were the product of a young writer too deeply in love with the screen. Unconsciously, I had been chasing the dream of Hollywood adulation, and I felt that I was starting to write film-scripts rather than novels. It was the thin end of the wedge because then I would become a writer for hire, someone who was told by a director and producer what to write. Hollywood is a turbo-powered machine that only occasionally functions. It could be exciting when all the components came together, but often your work got torn apart, your credit taken away, the project stalled in development hell – and you were left with a bucketful of regret and a bruised ego. On top of that, I had been around enough film sets to discover the truth about the so-called 'romance' of movie making – they're usually deadly boring. There's not much going on and unless you are one of the main movers and shakers, there is nothing to do except a lot of sitting around and talking nonsense.

It had been a good ride, but I thought I was worth more than that. I was a novelist, not a screenwriter. I'd loved the cinema as a child – there had been a cinema up on the Copperbelt, and a Saturday Night Cinema club when I boarded at Michaelhouse – but they had never eclipsed books in my life. Novels were my craft. I belonged to extended narrative, pace, character, atmosphere, twists, drama, location, description, denouement. These were the components that made me the happiest. I was beginning to feel trapped, constricted in a way I had never been before. Since *When the Lion Feeds* had been accepted for publication, the work load was relentless. My publishers expected me to write a book a year, and quite rightly because it was the only way to build a strong reputation, by feeding your audience with regular, quality work. I wanted to approach writing as a professional, forging a relationship of trust between me and my readers. But I had been seduced by the lure of Hollywood, its glittering Faustian pact, and I was perilously close to being trapped in a writing treadmill. I was at the point where writing – which had been a passion of mine for so long, my first and only real love – was in danger of becoming a chore.

However, I had an idea for a new novel that would change all that, and which would be my passage out of the Hollywood factory. Writing it would mean going back to one of the most haunting memories of my childhood.

• • •

In the gathering dusk, the car came to a stuttering halt and, in the front seat, my father turned around. 'We're here,' he said. 'Wilbur, up and out.' It was 1941, and I was eight years old.

Outside, the oncoming night was silent and still. I helped my five-year-old sister out of the car and looked up at the succession of stone monoliths standing like giant sentries.

The overgrown ruins looked monstrous and menacing as the twilight shadows groped towards us, wearing the visages of men. The wind tumbling over the tallest towers seemed to be the whispering of ghosts from centuries past. I wondered what secrets lay hidden in the darkness. My sister crouched behind me, as if she would rather not see.

We had come to the ruins of Great Zimbabwe, once a city in the south-eastern hills of Zimbabwe near Lake Mutirikwe and the town of Masvingo. It was the capital of the Kingdom of Zimbabwe during the country's late Iron Age, the largest of many hundreds of smaller ruins now known as 'zimbabwes' spread across what was then Rhodesia's Highveld. We had arrived as the sun was setting because my mother was fascinated by the ancient world.

Today Great Zimbabwe draws tourists from all over the globe, but in 1941 the place was just another corner of overlooked Africa, left to be reclaimed by the wild. Europeans discovered this lost world in the late 1800s, but in my youth, there was no official acknowledgement that there had once been a thriving city here. The Rhodesian government, keen to protect Rhodesia as a European enclave at all costs, was putting pressure on academics and archaeologists to deny the great city had been built by African natives. But any schoolboy could see that this had been the heart of a kingdom with warlords and counsellors, merchants and soldiers, and possibly slavers and slaves. Dig into the history of Africa, my mother had taught me, and what you will find will be more fantastic than any fiction.

My father led the way. The ruins stretched for miles, the hills crowned by what had once been small towers – but here, in the heart of the ancient city, there was only one great edifice, a fortress built from stones of magnificent size. We passed along overgrown passages between tumbledown walls, through a great enclosure where the air was curiously still.

I sensed a communion with the past, with history's intangible myths. Every rustling in the night became the footsteps of some malevolent spirit, every shadow cast by the light of the scudding moon became the approach of a phantom who meant us harm. Soon, my sister started to cry. I tried to console her but the longer it went on, the more my reserves of strength began to crumble. I was not afraid of any material thing. Perhaps my mind was too full of H. Rider Haggard and his doomed sorceress, She Who Must Not Be Named, but it was the unearthly, the unreal, that petrified me tonight.

Archaeologists and anthropologists would spend their careers debating what kind of civilisation had been centred on these ruins. They would argue whether it was the seat of the Gokomere people, the ancestors of Zimbabwe's Shona, or whether it belonged to the tribes who would one day call themselves the Lemba or Venda. Some reckoned the city was between five hundred and a thousand years old, and that war, famine, pestilence or natural disaster had befallen its people and laid the city to waste. Nothing was certain.

• • •

Thirty years later, it was 1971 and I was sitting in my caravan in the Bvumba, the Mountains of Mist (Bvumba is the Shona word for 'mist'), which are situated on the border between Rhodesia on the west and Mozambique to the east. It's a beautiful place, often shrouded in early morning mist that clears during the day to reveal blue-green mountains with spectacular views, the abundant forests resonating with birdsong. Mist wreathed the headlands and thick miombo woodland flourished on the escarpments, half-masking the scent of the small coffee plantations in the valleys below. I had come here for the solitude I needed to write. I had also come to take back my independence, to recover my soul. The past decade had been immensely busy, so full of obligations, demands and my own ambitions that I was close to losing my way. The manuscript in front of me was half-complete, but already much bigger than the thrillers that had consumed each of my last few years. *Shout at the Devil*, *Gold Mine*, and *The Diamond Hunters* had all been blistering reads, highly charged, with adrenaline-driven plots like the best adventure stories, and they had been written with the expenditure of enormous emotional energy. I loved writing them, I was swept away by the drama and tension of their worlds – but I was determined that this new novel, *The Sunbird*, was to be something different. The challenge was daunting, but there was no room in my life for artistic ennui, indulgences like writer's block or appealing to the elusive Muse of Inspiration. My muse was my father's voice in my ear saying, 'Get on with it Wilbur, you lazy son of a bitch, there's work to be done.'

The Sunbird was going to be my most ambitious, richly imagined – and unfilmable – work to date. The germ of the idea had come from my experience as a boy during that night in Great Zimbabwe, and what the ghosts were telling me as they drifted through the ruin. I was developing my own theories about the history of the place and imagining my own lost city of Ophet, founded by castaway Carthaginians who had travelled south after suffering the depredations of the Romans in North Africa. They would come through Gibraltar, down an ancient river system now dried up, until they reached the mighty Nile, the birthplace of civilisation. I imagined they had crossed the Namib, as I would one day, and in Botswana found a fantastic civilisation, all of it to be undone by a villainous king, and rediscovered millennia later. The novel would be a two-part story set millennia apart and it would be much more ambitious and richer than anything I had written before.

• • •

Handing *The Sunbird* to my publishers, I had felt considerable trepidation. It was unlike anything I'd ever written, an epic in scope and length. I'd forced my imagination into territory I'd never visited before. My previous novels were slender in comparison – *The Sunbird* was almost longer than the previous two novels combined. However, it exceeded all my expectations. Even before the publication date pre-orders were four times higher than for any other of my books. I was so grateful and relieved at the respect my publishers had shown for the book. When my editors first read it, they were overjoyed.

The Sunbird is the story of Dr Benjamin Kazin, a hunchback academic, and it chronicles Ben and his assistant Sally's search for proof of a lost civilisation in the heart of untamed Botswana. Ridiculed by others in his profession, Ben is convinced that there was once a Phoenician settlement in Botswana and, spurred on by aerial photographs that he believes confirm his theory, he sets out to discover this lost city and eventually stumbles upon the archaeological discovery of a lifetime. Along the way, as he battles with unfriendly natives and murderous terrorists, spectacular cave paintings point toward the existence of a civilisation that was destroyed in a violent cataclysm many centuries ago. Only then does the novel reveal its true heart – no sooner is the reader swept up in Ben's quest, than the story spirals backwards in time to an imagined land of two thousand years before.

Since I was a boy, the phenomenon of civilisations rising and falling had been an obsession of mine: the Egyptians, the Romans, the Greeks, even the triumph and decline of the colonial powers in Africa. *The Sunbird* was an attempt to capture the sheer drama of these tumultuous events. The brutality and mysticism of the story were straight out of my memories of H. Rider Haggard; the doomed city of Ophet was a recreation of those terrified moments I had spent in the gathering dark of Great

Zimbabwe, my sister and I cowering in the midst of the enveloping night. I had taken the name of *The Sunbird* itself from my love of nature and the wild. I have always adored wild birds. The sunbird is my favourite of them all. There are 132 different species inhabiting the Africas, across Asia and even extending into northern Australasia. Like hummingbirds, they are tiny, brightly-coloured creatures. My garden in Cape Town is full of them, with a treasured nest of double-collared sunbirds next to the veranda. Spiritually minded people believe that they are the harbingers of harmony, that they can open hearts, bringing out the best in everybody. They believe the sunbird hates ugliness and discord and will always fly off to areas where there is happiness and beauty. There is a magic in those little birds, and they have been my good luck charms across the years.

The Sunbird gave me the confidence to create vast new worlds on the page. The irony was that, as with many of my other works, the screen rights were indeed snapped up by Michael Klinger. He would never be able to film it, though.

In the years to come, I would look back on *The Sunbird* as a watershed in my career. It even led to a little tradition. From that point on, every hardback first edition of my books would have an embossed sunbird on the front cover, in the lower right hand corner. I called my home in Cape Town, on the foothills of Table Mountain, Sunbird Hill.

That is the strange thing about a novel – you spend long months willing it into existence, but then it develops a life of its own. What starts as imaginary can sometimes become very real.

11

THIS HERO'S LIFE

I killed my first lions when I was thirteen years old. I did it to protect the family farm I had been charged to look after, and I was alone.

Every year my parents took time away from the cattle ranch to go on holiday together, down in South Africa or even further afield. Usually my father would leave his foreman, Peter, in charge, but this was the first year the responsibility had been given to me. Every day I saddled my pony and rode circuits around my father's fields, along the banks of the Kafue River and up into the forested hills at the height of the ranch. Down by the river, where the puku and lechwe grazed, the world could seem vast and unknowable while, in the dense trees of the north, I would see occasional impala, always spooking at my appearance and vanishing into the shadows. Sometimes lions passed through the ranch, on the hunt for wild game, and it was for signs of these predators that I vigilantly made my circuits. Only rarely did I see them; more often I came across the spoor they left behind, or the signs of a kill.

I entered the fields where my father's prized Brown Swiss cattle grazed. These were the animals on which the ranch's livelihood depended, hardy yet docile animals first bred in the Swiss Alps and capable of surviving in harsh environments as different as the snowbound mountains and the withering heat of inland Africa. As I came among them, I already knew that something was wrong. Most of the herd had scattered, disappearing off to other grazing grounds.

Lying in the grass in front of me was a cow, her chest cavity open and glistening with gore, her neck ruptured where some monster's teeth had torn it apart. I looked around. In the grasses I could see two or three other carcasses, all of them similarly maimed.

Whispering to my pony to settle her, as the scent of blood was making her jittery, I dismounted and approached the first dead body. I touched it with my boot. It was a fresh kill; the blood had not yet congealed.

I heard a low growl.

I turned my head slowly. In the long grass to my right, a pair of large, golden eyes stared at me over the mangled flesh of an ox.

I had been close to lions before, and flashes of that

night, five years ago, came back to me. This time there were no tent flaps to hide behind. My father would not stride defiantly from the dark and face them down. Instinctively I reached for the rifle slung over my shoulder. It was my father's rifle, and the same one that had felled the man-eaters that night.

I was lifting it carefully, positioning my aim, when the lion charged. He was a demon, his mane matted with the blood from his kills. In the corner of my eye, I could see two others in the field, both lionesses, their attention drawn by the snarling alpha male.

Fear did not come into it. It was my father who had taught me to shoot, after all.

I took the shot.

No sooner was it dead than one of the lionesses leapt at me. I wheeled around, shot again, and she fell at my feet. I did not wait for the other lioness to charge. She was watching me and pawing, creeping forward ready to strike: so I shot her as well. Only afterwards, as I was looking at their bodies, did I breathe out, and the adrenaline started to make me shake. But I had no regrets. It was me or them.

Two weeks later, my parents returned from holiday, and I was sitting on the veranda when my father approached. I told him what I had done. He looked at me in disbelief. He insisted I tell him the whole story. Afterwards he nodded, as if he was trying to convince himself it was OK. I had been foolish, he said, to confront the lions.

What had I been thinking? What if something had gone wrong? He stared at me for a while as if I was from Mars, someone he didn't recognise.

Later that day, he came over to me with a package which he was carrying with both hands. 'It's a gift,' he said, 'you may be a fool at times and you're going to get yourself killed if you're not more careful, but you've earned some respect.' I took off the wrapping. There, in my arms, was a brand-new rifle, its metalwork gleaming, its woodwork shiny with fresh varnish. It was the first rifle I'd owned that was not an heirloom, that belonged entirely to me. I could have cried with joy, not only because I now had my own rifle but because my father's approval was a rare and precious thing.

It was one of the defining moments of my life, and one I'll never forget.

• • •

It was 1996 and I was writing the novel that would become *Birds of Prey*, my return to the world of the Courtneys. *Birds of Prey* reached further back in time than any Courtney novel before it, back to the middle of the seventeenth century when the English and the Dutch were at war for the rich provinces of Southern Africa.

The words I was staring at were Francis Courtney speaking to his son Hal. 'If I'm being cruel to you,' I had written, 'it's because I know there is a destiny ahead for you.' They were deeply personal because they were inspired by what my father might have said to me. My father, of course, had been more prosaic: 'You'll get your arse kicked,' he had said, 'if you don't pull yourself together.' He had been gone for eleven years, and *Birds of Prey* was to become my epitaph for him.

I had been chronicling the history of the extraordinary Courtney family since *When the Lion Feeds*, first with a trilogy focusing on Sean Courtney's life in the late nineteenth and early twentieth centuries, and then with a five-book sequence that began in 1985 with *The Burning Shore*, continuing through to *Golden Fox* in 1990. The second series had been about the modern African world, but by 1996 I was keen to go back to the past. Many of my novels had followed the history of southern Africa to the present day so it seemed natural to return to the time of the early settlers. Since my experiences in Walvis Bay and my foray into the Antarctic sea, I'd been fascinated by the high seas and sailing, and seafaring in the seventeenth century provided a particularly rich source of drama and stories. It was also a good place to explore the relationship between fathers and sons. In writing the novel, I would recall the times when my father had pushed and punished me, instilling in me his own unstinting work ethic, as well as principles like duty, honesty, loyalty and never being lazy or indulgent. Looking back, as poorly as I had responded to his attitudes sometimes, my father had been equipping me for life, and I felt that more keenly than ever now that he was gone. Though it had been more than a decade, I still regretted that we had not grown as close as I'm sure we would be if he was around now. The lawless world of the seventeenth century, where patriarchy reigned, men could be men, and where families prospered or failed on the strengths of the bonds between their fathers and sons, was the perfect place to remember him on the page.

Birds of Prey was my homage to him, and it didn't matter that, if he was around, he probably wouldn't have bothered to read it.

· · ·

By 1972, I had made £1 million as a writer, a huge amount of money for anyone, particularly a writer, and more than I could ever have imagined making as a tax assessor, or even working for my father. I was not fabulously wealthy – at that stage I suppose I could have been compared to a successful doctor or a top lawyer – but it wasn't about the money for the money's sake: it was more the freedom that I had been able to buy, the freedom to travel, research and write. I had adventured and travelled from Europe to Alaska, from Africa to Russia, explored China and the United States, hunted, dived, flown and sailed. More to the point, I had done it before I turned forty – a mythical milestone that I had always believed was a critical indicator of whether you were going to make anything of your life

– or be consigned to mediocrity and unfulfilled expectations. I had my dad to blame for that; he used to say, 'If you don't make it by 40, you're not going to make it.' He'd done both, made it by forty and then lost it.

My father built his first fortune on the Copperbelt, that strip of sun-blasted Africa that I grew up on – and it began with a prizefight. Dad was a boxer of some repute in the mine workshop where he worked, respected for the size of his forearms and the powerful right hook he'd developed over years of being in the ring. When an old boxing pro arrived on the Copperbelt, taking on all-comers in a winner-takes-all bout, my father's mates cajoled him into signing up. The man was rugged and gnarled, hard as nails, and called himself Battleship Walsh.

The entry fee for these kinds of fights was normally a pound and if you went two rounds with Battleship or whichever bruiser had arrived on the Copperbelt, you'd get £5. If you knocked him out the prize money would double to £10. That was a lot of money in those days.

The night of the bout arrived, and there, under the African sky, the most influential people of the mining community had gathered, mingling under the canvas tents set up around the ring. The mine manager, Mr Walpole, was in his dinner jacket and bow tie, surrounded by his friends smoking cigars and drinking whisky. On the other side of the ring, my father's supporters from the mine workshop were deep into their cups and baying encouragement. My father stepped into the ring and walked around, clasping both his hands together above his head like a prizefighter, playing up to the crowd. They were hollering: 'Give him one, Smithy, give him one!'

Dad was busy acknowledging all his fans when the bell went. He hardly knew what was happening. Old Battleship Walsh came charging forward and straightened him out with a right to the nose, boom. His face erupted in blood, his Roman nose recast forever and he went flying backwards, over the ropes. It was virtually a king hit. Dad looked up to discover he was in the front row sprawled on top of the mine management, his blood spraying over their dinner jackets.

The managers grabbed him and pushed him back through the ropes. Battleship thought it was all over, his guard was down and he was looking forward to his prize money. Quick as a flash Dad danced across the ring and nailed him flat out with one solid punch.

There had only been two blows in the contest. With his smashed nose still pumping blood, Dad went around the ring with his hands held high again, acknowledging the fans for real this time. The cheers were so raucous it was as if the doors to a madhouse had been flung opened. The only one who didn't join in was Battleship Walsh: he was still laid out cold on the floor of the ring.

It was a memorable Saturday night – the £10 prize was in my dad's pocket and he was standing everyone drinks – it wasn't every day that a prizefighter got knocked out by a challenger. Everyone was slapping him on the back, even hoisting him on their shoulders like some conquering hero from the old times.

On Monday morning, a messenger came from the mine's head office to the single quarters where the unmarried men bunked to tell Dad the general manager wanted to see him. Dad dressed, picked up his bike and pedalled to the offices.

Inside, Old Walpole said: 'Smithy, you had a very good fight on Saturday night. You know, I enjoyed that very much. I think I've got a proposition for you.'

The mine engineer was sitting in the office and Old Walpole let him explain how the mine needed someone to make ventilation piping in 22-gauge galvanised iron to take fresh air along the underground drives, into the stopes (the open spaces or 'rooms' made in the process of extraction) and onto the faces where the miners would drill. Without it, the mine could not expand.

My dad could not refuse the offer. He started working in what was effectively a big thatched hut, where he taught a team of black guys brought in from the bush to cut, rivet and solder, and he soon built up a thriving factory, churning out thousands of feet of piping to ventilate the growing warrens underground.

The work was long and hard but soon Dad was making serious money. In a deal that would one day inspire the story of Rodney Ironsides and his stock-exchange scam, my father devised a way of turning this opportunity into his fortune. Whenever the mine was expanded, teams of men called blasters would go in, drill shot holes all day, charge them up with dynamite and then detonate it. The next shift would go in about four hours later once the dust had settled, and clean everything out. The blasters were supposed to remove all the ventilation piping before they planted their charges but the workers often overlooked this part of their job. Thousands of feet of piping were destroyed with each blast, and it all had to be replaced.

My father earned so much money he could become his own boss, and buy the ranch that would be our future home.

My father held strong views, knew his own mind and wasn't afraid of hard work. He was an artisan, the toughest man I ever met, and he bent the world to his own design. He schooled me in the same way too, never ceding an inch to another man in his life. He would do to them what he did to the Battleship Walshes of this world, not with his fists, but by beginning one step ahead, catching them unawares and being smarter. I thought he was the sun and the moon and the stars. I'd done a lot of stupid things in my youth, but my father was always there with a stern word and his belt in his hand to make sure I stuck to the right path. Not once did I resent it; my father was a staunch Victorian with a strict code of discipline – but a sense of fairness and justice as well. On our ranch, there were all kinds of ways for a boy to get himself killed. His rules were the best way of ensuring I didn't fall prey to any of them.

On one occasion, in my early teens, I'd seen a local

farmer demolish termite mounds with dynamite. His son was my friend Barry, and we hatched a plan to steal a stick of dynamite and make our fortunes by blowing up fish in the Kafue river and selling them.

With the explosive tucked under my shirt, Barry and I hired a canoe and the services of two paddlers. We took to the water and when we reached mid-stream I produced my depth charge. I lit the fuse and threw it overboard, but the paddler in the stern was so terrified he dropped his paddle over the side. The man in the bow desperately tried to paddle us away but he only succeeded in rowing us round and round in a tight circle over the smoking dynamite.

The dynamite exploded and hurled the canoe and everybody in it twenty feet into the air. Up above, in a spray of river water and debris, I began to think we'd made a mistake, and then we plunged back into the river with about two tons of dead and dying fish flopping around us.

Somehow, we made it to the bank without further casualties. The two paddlers were already scrambling off, as far away as they could get from these insane white boys. Barry and I were both so dazed we forgot to collect any of the fish.

• • •

My halcyon days on the ranch came to an end one year when, with me away at boarding school, my father sold the ranch, landing a second fortune to go with the first he had made on the mines. Our ranching days were over, and so, my father thought, was his working life. Content with the retirement fund he had built up, he took my mother down to Kloof, outside Durban in South Africa. But he made some bad calls on the stock market and went back to the sheet-metal trade he knew so well. He set up a business with me as partner in 'HJ Smith and Son' but ten years later it failed. Rhodesia had imploded into a long drawn-out war of independence, and my parents took their chance and returned to South Africa to live out their days. By then I had other means by which to help them out. My early novels had been very successful and I was finally able to give my parents what they had once worked so hard to give me: a home.

I would look back and know that my relationship with my father influenced the way I thought about the characters in my novels. Families at war, loyalties and rivalries, jealousies and love, these are the things that have dramatised all my novels. Like everything else, they are drawn from experience. The elemental conflicts of life – brothers against brothers, fathers against sons – have defined human beings since the beginning of time, and classic texts like the Bible and the Greek myths, and authors like William Shakespeare, have shaped the way I've constructed my stories.

• • •

My father died on 12 April 1985. I stood at his grave, with tears rolling. A great man had gone and the yawning absence in my life would never go away. I loved him and admired him and the world was smaller now. Dad had stopped smoking twenty years before, but the damage had been done. In his last days, he had become frailer, slighter, though in my eyes his soul never diminished and he remained the giant of a man who, on one terrifying night fifty years before, gunned down three man-eating lions and, in doing so, saved his young son's life.

Though we were dissimilar in many ways, in our later years we had come to recognise the same qualities in each other – the desire to work for no man that had driven my father to build his business on the Copperbelt and become his own boss was the same one that had driven me to writing. We both wanted to dictate the paths of our own lives. My father had little interest in novels, not even mine, although my mother said he carried around a copy of *When the Lion Feeds* in the boot of his car to show his friends. I was grateful that he'd seen me succeed even though it was in a profession he'd scorned, and I think there was some pride hidden in there somewhere. He had always been reticent with praise, perhaps he thought it encouraged laziness. There is one moment though that will always stay with me. On my fiftieth birthday, he'd called me an idiot for the millionth time. I said, 'Dad, you can't call me that anymore. I've proved you wrong. An idiot doesn't write bestsellers.' He grinned, looked at me keenly, and said, 'I guess you have!' And then he gave me a bear hug. Dad didn't hug much. It meant a lot to me.

And now he was gone. For some time now, I'd been picking him up regularly on Saturday afternoons, taking him for a drive in my Rolls Royce, or heading out fishing together. When he passed away, my world changed forever, leaving me with the regret that we had never been able to become true friends. Time, as it always does, had slipped through our fingers.

I often wonder what my father would have made of the twenty-first century. He would have been a man out of time. When my first child was born, my father took me aside. He had some important information to impart, the sort of advice you didn't get from Matron.

'My boy,' he told me. 'They're going to bring that baby back from the hospital any day now. When they do, wait for it to soil its nappy. Then confidently announce to your wife: "Stand back! This is my child as well!"'

'Then, undo the baby's nappy and stick the safety pin into the baby's bottom. The baby will squeal and your wife will never let you near a dirty nappy again!'

He was being totally serious.

In the end, I didn't take Dad's advice, but I had some sympathy with his view of a man's role in society. My father never bathed me, he never fed me, and he never changed my nappy.

• • •

I think one of the worst inventions of our century is political correctness. It has forced a generation of men to keep their masculinity under wraps, made them too timid to admit their true views about the world. Today, even the concept of 'hero' is not politically correct. In my father's time, our heroes were served up to us directly from the battlefield, commanding victorious armies, like Admiral Nelson, Wellington and Churchill. Or they were performing amazing acts of derring-do, discovering hidden parts of the globe, like Livingstone, Stanley and Baker. Growing up in southern Africa, I was in awe of the Victorian explorer and conservationist Frederick Selous – and not just because my father had met him when he was a little boy, and spoke of him as if he was a family friend. But where are the titans in public life today? Where is Winston Churchill? Where is Franklin Roosevelt? Where is Nelson Mandela?

If you look hard enough, there are people to admire – but they are private heroes, quiet lionhearts: the young British soldier who puts himself in harm's way in Afghanistan; the South African paratrooper, fighting a desperate rear-guard action in the Central African Republic, when he and his comrades shouldn't have been there in the first place; the police officer answering an emergency call without knowing where it will take him or what lies in wait when he gets there; the midwife who drives through a winter blizzard at night to deliver a baby. In South Africa, we have the unsung public protector,

Advocate Thuli Madonsela, who, while raising her two children as a single parent, took on the ruling party and President Zuma over profligate spending on his private rural retreat.

Yet, on the whole, there are no giants today, no role models in the public realm. We make our heroes out of ordinary people who have achieved prominence simply because their job puts them on the television or cinema screen, or they have become famous for being famous through ghastly reality television. Today's heroes are celebrities. Yes, they're different from the rest of us – they earn more, they visit more nightclubs, they may play better football – but Wayne Rooney is hardly Lawrence of Arabia, is he?

Although there may be a shortage of real men on the covers of magazines today these rules don't apply in my books. Eight hundred years before the birth of Christ, there lived a blind poet named Homer, who wrote two epic poems: the *Iliad* and the *Odyssey*. To this day, he is revered as the founder of literature – but he was also the first writer whose name we know to understand the human need for heroes and heroines. The names of Achilles, Ulysses and Hector echo down the centuries.

Like the heroes of my novels, my father lived life the way he wanted, in an era when a fortune could be made by a single blow in the boxing ring, where a man could provide for his family with only his natural guile and the rifle over his shoulder. My goal has always been to live life with the same zest as that with which I imbue the characters in my novels, underpinned by Kipling's words: 'If you can meet with Triumph and Disaster and treat those two impostors just the same . . .'

12

THIS HUNTING LIFE

'There is much mythic nonsense written about hunting but it is something that is much older than religion. Some are hunters and some are not,' said my favourite author and fellow hunter Ernest Hemingway in *An African Journal*. Hunting has been a fundamental human activity for over two million years. If we believe we are part of nature's ecosystem rather than uniquely created in God's image, then hunting was an essential means of survival. As a species, we have become more organised, less nomadic, and farming and agriculture have lessened the need to track, pursue and kill. Nowadays everything is commodified, packaged and mostly available on your local supermarket shelves. Something has been lost from the ritualised hunting practices of our ancestors where reaping nature's wild bounty was part of the cycle of life. It would bind families and communities in common endeavour, and allow us to feel part of something bigger than ourselves, something that demanded respect, consideration and reverence to maintain a balance of life and death.

To the ancient Greeks hunting was a heroic act that signified a rite of passage, and its importance was represented by the goddess of the hunt, Artemis, or in Roman mythology by Diana. On ancient reliefs in Mesopotamia, kings are celebrated as hunters of big game, and in Assyria and Persia representations of the hunting expeditions of the rulers adorned the walls of their temples and palaces. By Roman times hunting was considered a sport and became a spectacle as big game imported from Africa was let loose in the Colosseum and other arenas across the empire to be pursued and killed by noble warriors. Over the millennia, codes of hunting were developed to formalise the rituals and give them meaning as well as to sustain the practise. As hunting with firearms developed – as early as the sixteenth century in Europe – the potential for widespread slaughter became a danger, and conservation as a means of protecting wildlife for future generations became an important concept.

Hunting and fishing were very much a family affair with Ernest Hemingway and so it was with our family. When I was young, I would sit enraptured as my Grandpa Courtney told me hair-raising stories of his exploits hunting the big five game animals: the African lion,

African elephant, Cape buffalo, African leopard and black rhinoceros. The skills and codes of hunting that he employed were passed to his son, my father Herbert, and from him to me. These were my first lessons in hunting, and I remember them even now. The hunter was not a man obsessed with killing. He was not a wanton predator, taking life for pleasure. The hunter was a vital part of the ecosystem of Africa, the same as any of the other big predators who stalked our land. And, when I was dreaming of hunting my first impala, first kudu, first lions and more, while I sat at my grandfather's knee, I wanted to test myself like the hunters of old.

Those elephant hunters, my grandfather said, came for the ivory on which their livelihoods could depend, but they never took a female, only the old bulls who would die slow deaths by starvation as their teeth rotted and their frail bodies struggled with the burden of massive tusks. The hunters also returned the bounty to the local people who came to rely on them for their own survival. As the hunters were tracking the elephants, the rumours of their passing would spread and the local population would follow. With a successful kill, as the vultures circled overhead, the villagers, every man, woman and child, would appear from the bush with basins balanced on their heads. It was a celebration with dancing and singing, a triumph for the hunter and meat for the villagers. There could be fifty, sixty, even a hundred people gathered there, and, with the ivory taken, the festival would begin. Chunks of meat were carved, and someone might disappear into the belly of the beast, emerging to throw the choice parts – the heart, the kidneys, the liver – to his children, who would begin stoking up a cookfire. It was a carnival for the villagers, a rare feast of plenty and, by the end of the day, all that was left of the elephant was a pile of bones and the rib cage, left open on the veldt to be picked at by the vultures.

Those annual safaris led by my father were not only about the pleasure of being out in the bush for weeks on end. My father's licences allowed him to hunt unlimited buffalo, ten sable, and three elephants every year – all meat vital for sustaining the local villages scattered around our land. I learnt from my grandfather that hunting was a noble tradition, a taking and a giving, that the true hunter is a true conservationist. I would carry these lessons with me throughout my life.

• • •

A Time to Die, published in 1989, was not the first time I had confronted the realities of hunting in a novel – hunting had been a predominant part of my characters' lives as far back as *When the Lion Feeds* – but, together with its companion volume, *Elephant Song*, published two years later, this would be the first time I approached the complex interplay between hunting and conservation in my fiction. My father had often lamented the modern world – there were no real men left, he would say; modern Africa belonged to a generation who had never had to hunt to survive, and for them the hunter was an abominable figure, a destroyer of nature. This public perception of hunting was so far from the truth that I felt compelled to contest it wherever I could, and there was no better showcase than in my fiction, which could, by now, reach millions of readers worldwide.

A Time to Die, closely based on a screenplay I had written in 1972, *The Last Lion*, is the story of Sean Courtney Jr, a veteran of the Rhodesian Bush War whose brutal origins I had myself witnessed as a police reservist. Accepting a mission to help his dying friend, Colonel Riccardo Monterro, hunt down Tukutela, a legendary bull elephant whose tusks outweighed any other, Sean finds himself building a crack team of hunters and trackers from men he fought alongside in the Rhodesian Special Forces, before following Tukutela over the Inyanga and into the chaos of the civil war then erupting in Mozambique. It was a contemporary novel, only nominally a part of the Courtney sequence, and allowed me to fully express my lifelong understanding of hunting. This was not a novel about indiscriminate killing. It attempted to capture the incredible highs and lows of the hunt, the excitements, the danger at every turn, and the ineffable sadness of finally shooting your quarry – the ending of the hunt, of the animal's life, that always leaves a deep melancholy in the heart of the hunter but which makes him appreciate life more deeply. By setting the novel against the barbarism of civil war in Mozambique, I wanted to show hunting for what it is – an honourable activity compared to conflict and war, the bloodiest, most wasteful of human behaviour.

Elephant Song, my novel of 1991, went a step further, exploring the dark side of the hunting industry. While *A Time to Die* had been, in many ways, my homage to Ernest Hemingway's hunting memoir, *Green Hills of Africa*, *Elephant Song* was that novel's converse – an exploration of the underbelly of legitimate hunting: poaching and the viciousness, waste, cruelty and, indeed, the pointlessness of it all. I did not want the novel to be about the subsistence poaching many local Africans must do to survive, but about the link between big-money foreign demand and local supply. In ranging from the African bush to the world of high finance in London, it dissected the world's insatiable appetite for ivory and what it meant for the people of inland Africa.

I began hunting as boys of my age often do, with a pellet gun and tin cans lined up on a wall. Soon I had moved on to hunting birds and small rodents and, once my father had gifted me Grandpa Courtney's fabled Remington, I was able to go after bigger prey. On the annual safaris we made into the bush, my father would let me follow the hunters if I kept quiet, didn't trip over anything and under no circumstances opened my mouth to speak above a whisper. Of course, when you are eight, nine, or even ten years old, you are like a grasshopper and you keep up well enough, and silently.

I was so excited to be joining the men with their heavy rifles, expert knowledge and serious demeanour. I could take the wisecracks they made at my expense if it meant I was one of them. I would watch and learn their bush-craft, how they picked out spoor, knew the behaviour of all the animals, navigated the vast wildness, were sure-footed on the most precarious of ascents or descents of ravines and valleys, and understood when to safely rest, take food and water and smoke a pipe. They would hunt hard, pacing for miles as they walked down the elephants. They knew that the most effective and humane way to kill an elephant is with a brain shot. It results in instan-taneous death and no thrashing movement or alarm will unsettle other animals in the area. An elephant that drops from standing to its knees or lying on its side doesn't spook his companions who show the merest of curiosity. A heart shot however can send the elephant crashing through the bush for fifty to a hundred yards before it stops, scattering everything before it, and in thick bush it can be extremely difficult to find the fallen animal. My father and his hunters and trackers would know this from hard won experience. They were my all-conquering heroes.

My grandfather told me tales of one of his heroes, Karamojo Bell, a legend amongst elephant hunters for the amount of ivory he harvested during the golden age of hunting in East Africa at the turn of the century. Bell shot 1,011 elephants during his career, all of them bulls except for twenty-eight cows. He made meticulous records of all his hunts, how many shots he fired and how much money he made on every trip. On a single day, he tracked down and hunted nine elephants, and earned £877 from the ivory. On one expedition, he came home with ivory worth over £23,000, an eye-watering sum in today's money, although a modest haul in comparison with modern-day poachers. Bell was a fearless hunter, sighting his elephant at eighty yards, but preferring a close range of thirty to forty yards. As he wrote in his book *The Wanderings of an Elephant Hunter*: 'He [the bull elephant] knows the game and will play hide-and-seek with you all day long and day after day. Not that this silent retreat is his only resource – by no means – he can in an instant become a roaring, headlong devil. The transformation from that silent, rakish, slinking stern to high-thrown head, gleaming tusks and whirling trunk, now advancing directly upon you, is a nerve test of the highest order.' Having shot the first elephant, Bell would climb on top of the animal to avoid being trampled by the rest of the herd and to get clear shots of the other elephants. He was an exceptional marksman and could shoot cormorants out of the air with a rifle and was once seen shooting fish that were leaping from a lake. His success as an elephant hunter was not just about a good shooting eye, but also because of his careful cultivation of and diplomacy with the local people. At that time, huge parts of Africa were uncharted, and for some of the natives he would be the first white man they had set eyes on. Bell would bring gifts for the kings and tribal chiefs and would pay them for the right to hunt on their land. The respect he showed was amply rewarded as they would guide him to the location of elephant herds and the bulls with the biggest tusks. It was a relationship of trust rather than exploitation.

When we returned to our camp at night, my mother – who had spent the day making sketches of the landscape and wildlife around her – would have the fire going and the stock-pot boiling. After drinks we'd sit under the stars, listening to the hyenas and lions roaring in the distance, eating the fresh meat of the day's hunt and preparing the rest to be hung out and dried as *biltong* to feed the camp and take back for our farm workers.

The best hunters of the world are also the greatest conservationists. It is why there is no contradiction in me being a trustee of the World Wildlife Foundation. The reality is that there is a competition between man and game for land and water, and it must not be ignored – for, in Africa, if the animal pays, it stays. If the idea abhors you, if you believe no animal should ever be touched by man, then you are condemning the animal to potential extinction. If an elephant is not hunted, if it dies naturally, only the vultures and hyenas have food. Yet, if the animal is shot as part of a sustainable animal management programme, then the entire community benefits. When a hunter pays $250,000 to hunt an old elephant, the local people realise that there is real value in the animals who they see as taking land away from them, destroying their crops and threatening their safety. Rather than destroying animals, hunters are contributing to their continued existence – without the money hunters are willing to pay to go into the bush, the animals would be left to the mercy of poachers, discontented locals, and the ravages of industry and urbanisation as man spreads himself ever more widely across the world.

When it comes down to it, man and beast must find a way to live together and share this planet we all call home.

13

THIS AFRICAN LIFE

I was checking out of the hotel when I heard a commotion further along the reception area. Outside, it was a blistering day beneath the bare Australian sun, and I had been staying in Sydney for a book signing for my latest novel, *Rage*. As I stood at the desk, I could hear someone imploring the receptionist: 'But I have to see him, I have to see him.' I didn't take much notice, but then I heard my name. The hotel receptionist was saying to a young man who was about seventeen or eighteen: 'I'm terribly sorry, but Mr Wilbur Smith has already checked out of the hotel.'

I went over to them and said: 'Excuse me, I'm Wilbur Smith. Do you want to talk? Did you want to speak to me?'

At first the boy was speechless. He looked like he'd

seen the ghost of his mother. Then, stumbling over his words, he said: 'Oh thank goodness I have found you. Thank goodness I've been able to meet you because I've travelled five hours by train to see you and I have to tell you my story.'

I looked down and noticed his right leg was missing and he had a prosthesis attached. There was something heartbreakingly earnest about him. 'Okay, fine,' I said, 'I've got ten or fifteen minutes. Let's have a cup of tea together and talk.'

We found a table in the hotel bar and he told me how, as a youngster of thirteen or fourteen, he'd been going to school on the train with his friends and they were horsing around, as kids do. They climbed up onto the roof of the train and, as it ploughed through the Australian desert, they were pushing each other and racing up and down, daring themselves to perform ever more dangerous stunts like they were action heroes in a movie, and the young boy fell – in a second he was gone, tumbling from the roof and under the wheels of the train. His leg was severed, and its mangled remains were left miles up the track.

He looked at me with pain in his eyes. 'Mr Smith, I tell you, my life ended right at that moment. I was no longer interested in anything. I was done for with this disability, useless; there was nothing for me, no future, life wasn't worth living.' He reached into his bag at his side. 'Then I picked up your book.' He laid down a copy of *The Leopard Hunts in Darkness*. I had written the novel three years ago, and it was the fourth story in the Ballantyne series. In those pages, the hero, Craig Mellow, had lost a leg in a mine field during the Rhodesian Bush War, but he doesn't let it stop him succeeding in life. He triumphs over his disability and comes out almost a better man for it.

The boy was smiling. 'It changed me, this book,' he said. 'Today I'm Head of School. I'm the chairman of the debating society and the chess society and I'm an A student straight through. I owe this all to you.'

I almost burst into tears hearing that this young man had found hope, was given new heart because of a story I'd invented and a character I'd plucked from my imagination. These were the kind of readers who made me happy, who made me think of myself as a boy who loved books and reminded me of what was important, the transformative power of all stories.

. . .

The Leopard Hunts in Darkness inspired a great change in my life as well. Hollywood action star Sylvester Stallone, at the time famous for *Rocky* and *Rambo*, purchased the film rights, and for a fleeting moment the spotlight of the movie world was back on me. He rang me up in person, named a price. I said that sounds good, and the next day the cheque arrived in the post! He was keen to film it in South Africa and he wanted to play the character of hero Craig Mellow, but, like so many film projects, there was a lot of talk and, despite Stallone's reputation, very little action and the film never got made. In the novel, Craig Mellow – wounded veteran and bestselling author – returns to a newly independent Zimbabwe to discover that the ranch that used to belong to his family is in a state of ruin. Determined to revive his family's heritage, he sets about restoring the ranch to its former glory, bettering the world around him in the process. Four years on from that novel, Craig's dream of owning his own corner of Africa had become mine. It had been many years since the golden age of my youth living wild on my father's ranch, but the idea of one day carving out my own wild corner of the continent had become a dream that would not let go. Craig Mellow's story had been, to some extent, an act of wish fulfilment. I decided to make it real.

I stood on an escarpment, staring into the fading evening light. It was 1988, and I was deep in the bush of the Karoo, some 250km or two and a half hours by car due east from Cape Town. From one horizon to the next, the land belonged to me. It had once been a succession of farms that, one by one, I bought up to create a sprawling many-hectare ranch. I planned to reintroduce species of antelope and other buck, in particular eland that hadn't been seen in the area for almost three hundred years. Behind me sat a complex of ramshackle buildings that I intended to demolish and turn into a traditional Rhodesian-style homestead, just as Craig Mellow had done in *The Leopard Hunts in Darkness*, and my father had done with his own ranch, almost fifty years before.

I had spent decades roaming the world, writing novels and living life to the full. For the first time, I was going to settle somewhere. I would call the land around me *Leopard Rock*.

. . .

I had started writing the Ballantyne saga in the late 1970s, eager to return to the world of African history after a decade of contemporary thrillers. The Courtney series was, by then, only three novels, and they were published over a thirteen-year period. With the Ballantynes, I would work differently – writing all four novels in succession and chronicling the birth and growing pains of the country most dear to my heart: Rhodesia.

I had always known I would write about Rhodesia. I hadn't lived in the country for more than fifteen years and, while I was away, Rhodesia had gone through incredible upheavals. As I sat down to write the first Ballantyne novel, *A Falcon Flies* – the story of Zouga Ballantyne and his sister Robyn, who arrive aboard a slave ship to explore the wilderness beyond Moffatt's Mission in Kuruman, to evangelise, hunt, colonise and ultimately get rich – I had no way of knowing that the series would end with the death throes of Rhodesia and the birth of the country it was to become. History was unfolding all around me as I crafted my stories, real life blazing the trail along which fiction would follow.

While the Courtneys had been born from the stories of my father and grandfather, the Ballantynes had their roots even closer to home. The series was a labour of love and would be a celebration of the history and legends of a part of the world I was intimately familiar with. I planned to share the history that had fascinated me as a young boy, and the work of the Moffat Mission in Kuruman, South Africa. Robert Moffat was a Scottish pioneer missionary who travelled to South Africa in 1816 and settled in Kuruman, in the Northern Cape province, where he established the Moffat Mission. His daughter married David Livingstone, and Moffat's son, John, aided Cecil Rhodes's first steps in his colonial adventures.

The first Ballantyne novel, *A Falcon Flies*, had Zouga and Robyn Ballantyne arriving in South Africa and trekking north to the border of what would today be Botswana and Zimbabwe – while the second novel, *Men of Men*, saw Zouga meeting Cecil Rhodes among the diamond mines of Kimberley, and then helping that freebooter annex Matabeleland and Mashonaland for Queen Victoria and his own back pocket. It was a joy to write about the extraordinary enterprise of someone like Rhodes, who wasn't a military man, but a die-hard empire builder and pioneer.

These were novels built on the long hours I spent immersed in that history, with moments also inspired by my favourite authors – H. Rider Haggard had given Allan Quatermain the nickname 'Watcher-By-Night' after his own hero, the American military scout Frederick Russell Burnham, 'He-who-sees-in-the-dark', and I, in turn, gave Zouga the nickname *Bakela*, or 'He-who-strikes-with-the-fist'. The third novel, *The Angels Weep*, opened in the midst of the Matabele rebellions of the late nineteenth century, and then pitched the story into a conflict I knew only too well: the Bush War which had recently torn Rhodesia apart. Meanwhile, the fourth novel, *The Leopard Hunts in Darkness*, would move the story into what was then the present day – with independence from Britain, the formation of the new nation of Zimbabwe and its first faltering steps as the defeated colonists became common citizens, and former terrorists found themselves masters in the corridors of power.

• • •

In November 1965, I had isolated myself in the Inyanga mountains to write. The success of *When the Lion Feeds* had encouraged me to pen *The Dark of the Sun* and then *The Sound of Thunder*. I was writing about war – in this case, the Anglo-Boer War. It was a time of violent conflict, with Sean Courtney rising to become the leader of a commando unit running guerrilla raids in the veldt, but it wasn't only in fiction that the horns of war sounded. In the real world, the mountains where I had settled had become a frontier in a terror war of our own. Across the border in Mozambique, dissident Rhodesian *terrs* had made a base of operations, coming over the mountains in the dead of night to wreak chaos on our unsuspecting land.

Later that month, Ian Smith, the Rhodesian Prime Minister, made his unilateral declaration of independence, declaring Rhodesia a sovereign state independent from the British Crown. It was an act that intensified the disharmony already growing between the government and the black nationalist groups in the country, including the Zimbabwe African National Union – led by future tyrant Robert Mugabe – who stepped up their actions, indiscriminately killing citizens and inciting riots in townships across the country. This was the onset of the true Rhodesian Bush War, a barbaric conflict that would last fifteen tormented years and tear a once beautiful country apart. Every man of fighting age in the nation was called up in the defence of the country – and so, one morning, instead of receiving news of translation sales and movie deals, I opened my morning post to receive papers summoning me to duty.

The Unilateral Declaration of Independence had been imminent for some time. We had all known it was coming; the only question was when the storm would finally break. Now it had erupted all around us. I returned to Salisbury where I managed to write during the day but my nights consisted of long, tense patrols around the townships that circled the city as a member of the reserve in the British South Africa Police.

As evening paled to dusk, men all over Salisbury were preparing to discard their daytime roles, pretend that they weren't accountants, bank clerks, or salesmen, and report for another patrol. That night, I left my house and climbed into the waiting Land Rover. Inside were the three other men of my patrol. None of us had known each other before the start of the war, and we were unlikely to meet again after our service was over. It was tough work but we were stoic about it. We were not here as friends. Most of the men were like me, unmarried, in their early thirties, used to desk jobs by day. We had full-time police as overseers, but there had been no training. We were not drilled, and nor were we equipped as soldiers, not least because the international arms embargo placed on Rhodesia left us woefully short of gear. In standard-issue uniforms, with batons at our sides, we ran our patrols four or five times a week and, with whispers of all-out war on the horizon, hoped that a bullet wouldn't find us first.

The patrols were stressful, endless circuits around the townships, where strangers looked at us suspiciously but never said a word. Sometimes there were rumours of riots, crowds incited by the men we called *terrs*, the black nationalists threatening open war, but often they were ill-thought-out gatherings, disorganised and quick to disperse. We would be called out as a show of force to stop the riots in the townships from starting. Once, as we patrolled on foot through the early-evening dusk, a glass bottle arced overhead, shattering on the ground at our feet. When we looked back, a group of men had gathered in the dust road between the shanties, anticipating confrontation. These were only the first signs of what was to come. As the weeks and months went by, the nationalists found more ways to inspire terror: random brutality, atrocious attacks that provoked disunity and fear, barbarism for which the country had not been prepared. We were being called up more and more.

One weekend, we attended the site of a terror attack on a farm, a typically soft target. The fighting of the Bush War was mostly rural and, while citizens living in Salisbury and other towns and cities were largely safe from attack, there were no such guarantees in the countryside. Farmers faced the threat of violence every day and night. In their remote homesteads, there was little they could do to protect themselves from armed guerrillas determined to murder and spread fear. Too often, farmers had been cornered, smoked out, or butchered in their homes. Tonight, the terrorists had struck again. They had killed the kids, disembowelled them and thrown them into the pit latrines. Two black kids and one white kid. The terrorists didn't discriminate. They had also killed the mother, the farmer's wife, but the farmer had survived because he was away at the time of the attack. There are some sights you can never un-see, that are burnt into your brain, that will distort your entire view of humanity. Sometimes the images will reappear at night, mocking your hard-won sense of the rightness of things.

With the homestead locked down and soldiers swarming the land, we were dispatched to secure the dirt tracks leading in and out of the property. The hope of tracking the men responsible was small, and growing more distant every minute. That was how the *terrs* worked: one minute they were here, and the next they were gone, leaving ruin in their wake. The farmer would return to his homestead to discover he'd lost his entire family in the most awful way.

The incident crystallised my feelings that the whole Rhodesian situation was going to go one way. I didn't share Ian Smith's Battle of Britain defiance he was using to whip up white Rhodesian support. Having declared UDI, he committed his country to years of relentless bloodshed and horror.

I decided that, even though this country meant so much to me, I would have to leave. Also, I'd fallen in love again. This time it was with Jewell Slabbert, who I'd met at a party in Salisbury. In short order, we'd got married and she was pregnant, and I moved us down to Onrus River, just outside Hermanus in South Africa. I bought my parents a home in Somerset West. My dad was grateful but when I told him about my plans to get married, he just shook his head. 'If you're going to go through life marrying every woman who drops her knickers for you, you're going to be a very busy boy.' As always, he was spot on.

It was to be another fifteen years before the events I had absorbed would coalesce into the story of the Ballantynes. As they lingered in my mind, waiting to find an outlet, the Bush War exploded, found itself in a bitter stalemate, and then exploded again.

In 1984, as *The Leopard Hunts in Darkness* was being published, the insurgents who had waged war on Rhodesia were now in power in Harare – the city that Salisbury had become – but the same tribal rivalries of old continued, this time cloaked by a veneer of civility. Robert Mugabe, once a freedom fighter and now the nation's leader, had already brutally suppressed the Matabele people. And as my novel became a bestseller across the world, Zimbabwe banned it from sale.

• • •

We moved back to South Africa to evade the spreading tide of war, but there had been trouble brewing in that country too for a long time. I had been living in Port Elizabeth, writing my aborted first novel, when the Sharpeville Massacre occurred. In March 1960, the South Africa Police shot at crowds protesting the racist pass laws which were designed to segregate and restrict the black population. Black residents in urban districts were required

to carry passbooks when outside their homelands or desig-
nated areas, and they could be arrested if the passbook
didn't contain valid authorisation. A crowd of 5,000 to
7,000 demonstrators offered themselves up for arrest for
not carrying their passbooks outside the police station in
the township of Sharpeville in Transvaal (now part of
Gauteng). Police reports suggested that young and inex-
perienced officers panicked and opened fire, killing
sixty-nine people, including women and children, with
180 injured. Tear gas had been used, Saracen armoured
personnel carriers had ferried in platoons of police
carrying Sten submachine guns, while Sabre jets had flown
over the protestors at terrifyingly low altitudes. Since that
moment, the militant resistance against apartheid had
grown stronger and more organised than ever, and the
government had become fiercer in its opposition to the
ANC and the PAC. Only a year later, a Xhosa man named
Nelson Mandela would be convicted of sabotage and
treachery and begin his first year of imprisonment on the
infamous Robben Island.

In 1984, terror returned to Sharpeville, as another
protest march against apartheid turned violent and the
deputy mayor of Sharpeville was murdered. A group of
protesters known as the Sharpeville Six were sentenced
to death. In the *The Leopard Hunts in Darkness*, I had
chronicled the devastating fallout of the civil war in
Rhodesia; now, it was time to tackle apartheid, that most
contentious and complex of African subjects, in my next

series – a return to the world of the Courtneys. *Rage* was to be the beating heart of the second Courtney sequence. The first in the series, *The Burning Shore*, introduced a new branch of the Courtney dynasty when South African pilot Michael Courtney falls in love with beautiful French woman Centaine de Thiry, and when Michael is killed in action, Centaine enrols as a nurse on a hospital ship only to be marooned in the desert of the Skeleton Coast when the ship is torpedoed by a German U-boat.

The second, *The Power of the Sword*, was a Cain and Abel showdown between Centaine's two bastard sons: Shasa Courtney (who Michael had sired before dying in a plane crash) and Manfred De La Rey, whose father Lothar had an affair with Centaine after rescuing her in the Namib. The story charted the two men's rise through the 1920s, '30s, and '40s. It allowed me to weave fiction into fact, as Manfred ended up following a very similar route to the South African Olympic hope Robey Leibrandt, who stayed in Berlin after the 1936 Olympics and became a Nazi secret agent, re-infiltrating back to South Africa; while Shasa, having been wounded as a Hurricane fighter pilot in the SAAF in North Africa, returned as a special counter-intelligence officer, to hunt him down. It was another big book, broad in its scope, letting me tell a story against the wide canvas of South Africa's recent history, but it was precisely this that would land me in so much hot water in the third volume of the saga, *Rage*.

In *Rage*, the long and deadly enmity between Manfred

De La Rey and Shasa Courtney would come to a head, just as South Africa herself was engulfed in the fires of racial conflict. The novel would propel the bitter family rivalries I had always written about straight into a nation tearing itself apart.

Rage was a chronicle of South Africa itself, following Shasa Courtney and Manfred De La Rey as they get caught up in the politics of the fledgling nation and end up in parliament together. Shasa's wife has an affair with an African Nationalist leader and she is forced into exile as South Africa buckles under the defiance campaign of the 1950s and the struggle against apartheid takes root. The novel opens in 1952 and charts a period of almost twenty years, as the country lurches from the Freedom Charter in Kliptown, through the Rivonia Treason Trial, Nelson Mandela's incarceration on Robben Island, the horrors of the Sharpeville massacre and Prime Minister Hendrik Verwoerd's assassination in 1966.

When I started my writing career, I looked for inspiration in the adventurers of days gone by. Now, with *Rage*, I was acknowledging the very real dangers that South Africans were bravely living through daily. I had already witnessed the horrors that could engulf a country like Rhodesia, and around me there was concern that South Africa could head the same way. *Rage* was written in the mid-1980s, at a time when the nation was at a tipping point. Glasnost, the end of the Cold War, was blowing its winds of change across the world, and as the Soviet Union and Communism fell, the shockwaves were felt across sub-Saharan Africa with huge consequences for South Africa. Internationally, apartheid had been universally condemned and, as the 1980s progressed, trade unions, church groups, student societies and the Black Consciousness Movement, wounded but defiant after the death of their leader Steve Biko in 1977, continued to demand change. Nelson Mandela himself would be released in February 1990 by President F. W. de Klerk and, three years later, would become president himself. The death throes of the apartheid regime were a heady time.

I thought highly of de Klerk's predecessor, P. W. Botha, the Prime Minister throughout the 1980s. He was a tough and gnarly old politician more famed for his finger-wagging rhetoric and 'total onslaught' campaign against terrorists and communists. It was Botha who had started talking to Nelson Mandela while he was still in prison and, though he refused to dismantle it, Botha had begun tinkering with the apartheid edifice, removing the most hateful of the petty apartheid laws such as separate amenities for blacks and whites, and the criminalisation of sex between them. To many, Botha was the only reformist leader South Africa had had in 300 years. I told journalists on a publicity trip to the UK ahead of the launch of *Rage* in March 1987 that, though I saw South Africa becoming the third world country it actually was, I had hopes that, in the long run, a peaceful and just society could be built. My optimism was premised on the moderates triumphing in the space between the 'comrades' in the townships and the 'jackbooted followers of [right-wing extremist] Eugene Terre 'Blanche'. For that to happen the outlawed African National Congress would have to be brought into the political process and a formula found that could guarantee equality for South Africa's black population, while protecting the rights of the white minority. I said I would like to see Nelson Mandela released and included in a government of national unity. I still had deep reservations about the structure of the ANC and, if it was not controlled, feared it would go the way of African liberation movements before it and become a classic African one-party state, complete with a president-for-life. Whatever happened in the next few years was going to be vital for the longevity of this firebrand of a nation.

By the time *Golden Fox*, the sequel to *Rage*, was published in 1990, it would only be another year before Nelson Mandela was released and the first steps were being taken toward reconciliation, and healing the nation's wounds. Nelson Mandela showed his true worth and justified his international acclaim when, in an unprecedented act of African statesmanship, he stepped down from the Presidency after only a single term.

Rage reflected the real-life dramas being played out in modern Africa, and the sequel *Golden Fox* continued the trend. Shorter than the others, it was more of a spy thriller, with one of the minor characters from *Rage*, Shasa's daughter Bella, as the heroine. I was fond of Bella in *Rage*, but had no idea what she was going to get up to. Then in *Golden Fox* she came into her own as a spy who infiltrates the government. It often happened: I would create someone with no apparent future then suddenly, later, I realised what they could do. I didn't have conversations with my characters as I had heard some authors do. My characters just lived in my mind and my writing for me to watch and record. I would often be asked if a character was me. Was I the devil-may-care big game hunter, adventurer and ladies' man, Sean (in either *Rage* or *When the Lion Feeds*), or his brother Garrick, the runt of the litter in *Rage* and the cripple in *When the Lion Feeds*? I suppose, in truth, I identified more with Garrick. Like me, he was a loner fuelled by a determination to succeed, often surprising those around him.

It wasn't Bella, however, who stood out and grabbed all the attention, but a minor character, Vicky Gama, the wife of the novel's jailed leader Moses Gama. Vicky had been introduced in *Rage*, but now in *Golden Fox*, with her husband still incarcerated on Robben Island, I had written a scene in which I depicted Vicky, the 'black Evita' and 'mother of the nation', as a topless gin-swilling sjambok-wielding sadist, beating up a young member of her athletic club, who she suspects of being a police informer. It all took place in a mansion in Soweto, which Vicky had built from overseas donations to the struggle against apartheid.

My books are pure fiction, there are no hidden messages, no matter what people want to think. My characters are totally fictitious – I'm a storyteller – but some people drew parallels between Vicky and Winnie Madikizela – or Madikizela-Mandela, as she is known today. In the week *Golden Fox* was released, Madikizela-Mandela was being named in court during the trial of her bodyguard, Jerry Richardson, who was accused of murdering a young activist by the name of Stompie Seipei. Stompie, a fourteen-year-old member of the ANC Youth League, had been kidnapped with three others on December 1988 by Madikizela-Mandela's bodyguards, who called themselves the Mandela United Football Club. Stompie was killed on New Year's Day 1989 and his body dumped near Madikizela-Mandela's house. He was found five days later in the veld. His throat had been cut. Richardson, the Mandela United 'coach', was convicted of the murder even though he claimed in court he had only been doing Madikizela-Mandela's bidding; and, a year later, Madikizela-Mandela was convicted of Stompie's kidnapping and being an accessory to his assault. Madikizela-Mandela was sentenced to six years in jail, reduced to a fine and a two-year suspended sentence on appeal. Richardson got life.

The reality was that *Golden Fox* was written some time before Madikizela-Mandela was named in court, but, whatever I wrote, I couldn't please everyone all of the time. Some people would be delighted by passages that might offend others. In the novel, the scene in which

Vicky Gama attacks the suspected informant did not refer to any particular person. I was writing stories, not political allegories. It depicted a type of person who could have existed in the period in which the novel was set.

It was not the only moment the novel came close to the realities of modern South African life. *Golden Fox* had the daughter of a fictitious South African ambassador to London wheedle her way into the Cabinet to get her hands on top secret information – including a poison gas being manufactured in South Africa by an Armscor-like entity – to give to the Russians and Cubans. As much as it was the work of my imagination, recent newspaper headlines had claimed that the assassinated white Swapo leader Anton Lubowski had been a spy for South African military intelligence – and it had been proved that Commodore Dieter Gerhard, the commander of the all-important Simonstown naval base outside Cape Town, had been a spy for the Soviets all along. Like *Rage*, *Golden Fox* showed just how the realms of fiction and fact intertwined. *Golden Fox*, though, would be the last time I sailed that close to contemporary political history. The reason was simple: I was a professional storyteller, not a political pundit.

As it was, the books were almost writing themselves. Anyone outside the country wouldn't believe what we were living through daily, and as always in Africa, tragedy lurked around the corner. We had a bad experience in July 1989 when a hit-and-run driver knocked down and killed our domestic servant Gladys Siqele. She was outside our Bishopscourt home in Cape Town walking with a friend back to her house when a car mounted the pavement and mowed her down. I was out of the country on a book tour at the time. My wife thought she might have been targeted because of my books, by another 'Wit Wolf'. The original 'Wit Wolf' (white wolf), a disaffected and disgraced twenty-three-year-old South African Police constable named Barend Strydom, was sitting on death row in Pretoria for a shooting spree he conducted in full uniform with his service sidearm that claimed seven African lives and wounded fifteen more on 15 November, the previous year. He claimed to be the leader of the White Wolves, but that turned out to be a figment of his imagination. He was sentenced to death but escaped the noose as the National Party Government under F. W. de Klerk had suspended all executions. He was released in 1992 as one of 150 political prisoners and granted amnesty by the Truth and Reconciliation Commission after the democratic elections in 1994.

We posted a R10,000 reward for information about Gladys' death. The police asked us if we or Gladys had any enemies. We didn't, at least none that we knew of, but we told the police of an incident a couple of weeks before when a car swerved towards a black pedestrian and then drove away at high speed.

The tyre tracks swerving towards Gladys, who had been on the opposite side of the road, were as clear as daylight.

The car had to have been travelling at high speed because Gladys was killed instantly.

Gladys had been with us for twenty-one years and was the mother of four children. We went to her funeral and it was one of the most moving experiences of my life. Under the hot sun, in the gentle red dust, the deep, pungent home-smell of Africa all around us, there were 300 to 400 mourners singing of their love for Gladys and for mankind as if it was the total spirit of Africa given voice. That day, as the tears ran freely down my face, I celebrated that I too was an African, that only here amid tragedy, could I feel such a powerful, unbreakable bond.

Four days later a 32-year-old police sergeant approached his station commander and confessed he had been driving the car. Almost a year later Jacobus Michael Charles Andrews appeared in the Wynberg Court on a charge of culpable homicide, alternatively reckless driving. In October, he was convicted of culpable homicide and fined R1,000 or twelve months' jail. Nothing would bring Gladys back; we did what we could for her children who were all adults, but his sentence was only a slap on the wrist.

We were very sad and very angry.

• • •

After the euphoria of the general elections on 27 April 1994 that swept the African National Congress into power, it was as if the genie had been let out of the bottle. There were rampant expectations, an economy in decline and freebooters on the side turning a profit at every corner through state tenders and the abuse of state resources. The most frightening thing though was the criminal violence – fed by the flames of disillusion, especially among African youth. At one stage, there was a real fear that South Africa could become like Lebanon and those who were able to would simply leave the country and settle elsewhere. It was made worse, paradoxically, by the new adherence to the doctrine of human rights. The police were virtually powerless, and the courts had been rendered impotent to hand down sentences of any meaningful deterrence. I have always believed that to survive we must have laws and morality. I'm not a great practising Christian, but religion has a very strong place in the formation of our society because it teaches people ethics. We are spoiling whole generations of people now. You don't have to work, you can claim benefits; if you want to write obscenities on the walls and go on the football pitch and swear your head off, you're a hero. Human rights, while in principle absolutely essential and admirable – and I'm an unwavering supporter – can be abused and criminals can go free if you have a good lawyer, enough money and know the right people.

The situation though wasn't bad enough for us to leave South Africa forever; that would only happen if the country became ungovernable, ruled by a mad racist in an environment where I felt physically threatened – in other words in a situation like that in countries to the north of us, in particular Zimbabwe under the despot Robert Mugabe. I have witnessed inhumanity which changed my attitude when in Rhodesia during UDI, specifically that those systems which had been fine in Victorian times were now long past their sell-by date.

I knew that apartheid was such an iniquitous doctrine and that it couldn't persist, but I wasn't able to stand up and say so in public. I already had the Bureau of State Security (BOSS) watching me constantly. I had a tap on my phone for years. I was walking down Muizenberg beach in Cape Town after apartheid ended and a chap came up to me and said, in an Afrikaans accent: 'I know you.' I replied, 'Have we met?' and he said, 'Ach, no, we haven't met, but I worked for BOSS and for a year I had to sit and listen to you on the telephone. Old Wilbur, you boring!'

I said to him, 'Well whatever you do, please don't tell my readers!'

Whenever I returned to South Africa from my long researches, it was always with excitement mixed with trepidation because of the violence and the crime. After the ANC came to power, we had forty-eight years to catch up with in six months and a lot of people had been left behind. It was OK to be free, but freedom meant respecting others and their property. I had a man who walked around my Cape Town house with a dog, and I had security fencing, but I was most concerned for the lives of the people who worked for me. They were the ones at risk. I could protect myself but they were vulnerable.

There were two very positive changes for me when apartheid ended, and they both involved Nelson Mandela. South Africa's acceptance into the global community thanks to the international reputation of Madiba meant that my books were now selling well in the US, for the first time ever exceeding the sales in the UK, which had always been the benchmark. In fact, US tourists visiting in huge numbers to Cape Town would often ask where I lived and the tour guide would drive them up to Bishopscourt. One day, I was in my oldest clothes with a hat over my eyes when a luxury coach pulled up.

'Do you know where Wilbur Smith lives?' one of the coach party asked.

I said, 'No, but Dr Chris Barnard, the world-famous heart transplant surgeon, lives just down the road,' and off they went. I valued my own privacy a lot more than I valued Chris's.

The second was the holding of the rugby world cup in South Africa in 1995. The South African Rugby Board had won the rights to host what would only be the third ever world cup, although it was the first for our national team, the Springboks, because they had been excluded from the first two because of apartheid. It was Mandela who won the game – and the country – for us, in one of the most incredible acts of reconciliation ever witnessed. It was so great that a book was written about him and the rugby world cup by journalist John Carlin, called *Playing the Enemy*. Clint Eastwood subsequently made a film *Invictus*, with Matt Damon as Bok captain Francois Pienaar and Morgan Freeman as Mandela.

Nelson Mandela remains my hero to this day. I had the privilege of shaking his hand and, having grown up and lived my entire life in Africa, understand the true greatness of his achievement. I am one of those South Africans who worried what the shape and face of my own country and indeed the continent would become when he died. Sometimes, I thought, self-styled philanthropists like former British Prime Minister Tony Blair and pop stars Bono and Bob Geldof were doing more harm than good by wanting to treat the symptoms and not the causes of the problems in the continent. One of these was their insistence on writing off international loans, which to my mind was like rewarding bad governance and unaccountability. It wasn't about them not understanding the African mind, but rather that they ignored the reality of the African concept of government. The whole structure was predicated on tyranny, controlled by one person, from Shaka in KwaZulu Natal to Mzilikazi in what became Zimbabwe. They committed terrible atrocities to consolidate and stay in power – a pattern that had continued with terrible consequences in modern Africa, such as when Mugabe put down the Matabele dissent using his North

Korean-trained Fifth Brigade. Even Kenneth Kaunda of Zambia had resorted to force when his people were starving. And then there were the kleptocracies of the Central African Republic and Mobutu Sese Seko's Zaire (today the Democratic Republic of Congo) where money that was supposed to help the people was shamelessly looted and deposited off shore, gratefully received by unscrupulous Swiss bankers.

The dictators don't accept the idea of using money to generate more wealth for the country. They either spend it, or steal it – and then when the country can't repay the billions they have been loaned, the West will be asked to write off the debt and advance another tranche.

The dictators then think, 'Oh boy, we're on a good wicket here! We'll never have to pay anything back. When is our next gift coming?' This isn't about black or white. It's human nature.

South Africa's own problems were similar yet nuanced: the apartheid government had impoverished all black South Africans, and so they had nothing to lose. It didn't take long, much like post-perestroika Russia, for some of the better-known erstwhile Marxist freedom fighters to metamorphose almost overnight into big time capitalists and tycoons. We even had a phrase for it in South Africa, the 'gravy train', or the propensity of activists to lose their principles for the allure of directorships, a practice only exceeded by another phenomenon – not exclusive to South Africa either – of *tenderpreneurs*: people who have become obscenely wealthy by using their political connections to wangle state jobs and contracts.

Which is just another reason why Nelson Mandela was so special. We had all watched with trepidation and more than a little sadness as he began his slow, inexorable decline. The attention to his series of health scares was nothing less than ghoulish, but that was what happens when you see a great man going. When he died on 5 December 2013, I wrote: 'An African giant has fallen, but the legend that was Madiba will echo down the centuries.' I don't believe I will be proved wrong on that. The entire country went into mourning, with scenes that hadn't been witnessed since the country first went to the polls as one on 27 April 1994. I don't believe we will ever see that kind of national kinship again, especially not in my lifetime. It's a pity, but an incredible gift to have lived through a period which traversed Nelson Mandela standing in the dock under a possible death sentence on terrorism charges, being banished for the better part of his adult life to a rocky island in the middle of Table Bay, and then emerging twenty-seven years later to pull a fractured country together – and then stand down as he had promised after only a single term in office.

It was unprecedented in the ways of Africa, and nigh-on unheard of internationally. We were poorer for his passing, but far richer for having had the privilege of knowing him.

• • •

Perhaps because of its subject matter, and how closely it hewed to the world falling to pieces around me, *Rage* had been my most difficult novel to write. Yet, somehow, it had worked – and readers fell in love. The novel sold almost a million copies in 1988, and was an international bestseller. It also broke the world record for the longest ever South African novel, with the paperback weighing in at 626 pages, breaking the previous record holder – Madge Swindell's 1983 novel *Summer Harvest* – by 26 pages.

The stigma of South Africa's apartheid regime had dogged me my entire career. As Charles Pick used to say, it was one of the reasons my novels had not taken off in the United States as quickly as they had in the rest of the world. For Americans, everything that came out of South Africa was damaged by association with the political regime. It was a similar story in other parts of the world. On a publicity tour in New Zealand, I was accosted by fourteen scruffy men from HART – the 'Halt All Racist Tours' movement. They were the same mob who had successfully disrupted the South African Springbok rugby tour in 1981, flour bombing a rugby ground and almost inciting an all-out civil war between All Blacks rugby fans there to see a contest between the two greatest rugby playing countries in the world, and protestors who wanted to see the end of apartheid. They wanted to present me with their 'Racist of the Year' award, which I declined with thanks. Clearly, they hadn't read anything I had ever written. The fact that I was white and South African was enough for them to denounce me. Later, when I was questioned on New Zealand television's *News Hour*, I counterattacked by accusing HART itself of blatant racism – the labelling of me, just because I was white. It seemed they thrived on racial conflict – without it, they wouldn't exist. My books, I said, had always been anti-racist – in fact, my early books had been banned because of friendships and sexual relationships that crossed the colour bar. One thing is certain: I abhor racism, and I always will.

Stories moved me and inspired me – since my childhood – and the idea that they should aspire to do more than that had never really occurred to me, or, if it had, I never truly entertained it. *Rage* and *Golden Fox*, however, became the focus of the perennial debate between popular and literary writing in the most unexpected way.

In 1991, the South African novelist Nadine Gordimer won the Nobel Prize for Literature. I was involved in the periphery of the award after a fan, Andrew Kenny, wrote to a Johannesburg newspaper, the *Star*, asking why I hadn't been considered by the Swedish committee. I had never met Kenny before, but his opinion seemed to strike a chord with a great many readers, and soon letters to the editor flooded in, reflecting both sides of the debate. Kenny's argument was that, compared to the number of people who read Nobel laureates like Gordimer, my novels – and others like them – had an immense reach, one that could influence many more people and contribute to their understanding of the modern world. Far from being pure escapist fun, Kenny argued, books like mine were the only ones that could hope to affect the way we lived our lives. Like many critics before, Kenny didn't hold back on what he thought were my shortcomings – my books, he said, were unsubtle, my dialogue stilted, my people caricatures; my stories were filled with unbelievable sex and far-too-believable violence. Yet, if he had to choose one book to explain South African politics to a foreigner, he would unhesitatingly choose *Rage*.

Other letter writers added their voices to the chorus, with one even suggesting a special South African prize for popular fiction to recognise me and pacify Kenny. It was an unusual and unsolicited affirmation. I had never set out to write high literature – not since *The Gods First Make Mad* had I made that mistake – but I enjoyed the idea that my characters and stories could make a difference to people's lives. It was all much ado about nothing, and I found it amusing, and gratifying for showing me what incredible fans I have. I have always tried to ignore critics. In the early days, it had been terrible when they hated my novels – and the idea that they were the arbiters of good taste was always galling to me – but now it didn't matter. I was no longer a new writer. Whatever the critics thought, my readers were not going away. They are the people who buy my books, read them, and tell their friends all about them. They are the only ones I think of whenever I pick up my pen.

Sometimes fellow authors, especially the literary types, turn puce at the thought of my popularity. I have always thought that we should be standing together – the literary writers and all the other authors – but instead they deride us for being 'airport writers', and sneer at our commercial success.

Yet, William Shakespeare was a popular writer in his day. Perhaps he would be surprised to know about the lasting place he has in English literature. His audiences at the Globe were made up of the working masses; this was a place that Londoners could come to laugh at the ribald Falstaff, and not necessarily gape in awe at the beauty and imagery of the language. Shakespeare's crowds wanted to see the story at the beating heart of the play. Centuries later, the same was true of Charles Dickens, one of the greatest storytellers in the English language. As Andrew Kenny had said, it is the popular author who has the chance to really touch hearts and minds.

I had a fan in the highest office of the land: former president F. W. de Klerk, the man who eventually freed Nelson Mandela, unbanned the ANC and set South Africa on the path to democracy. I first met him in 1995, after he had stepped down as deputy president in the new government of national unity, and we chatted for some time. He took me to task for *Rage* and my portrayal of Manfred De La Rey, who he recognised as being inspired by B. J. Vorster, the prime minister interned during the Second World War for his membership of the Ossewa

Brandwag, the right wing pro-Nazi militia. Many years later, when I met F. W. again at Alfred Mosimann's private dining club in London, I greeted him heartily. 'Hello, F. W.!' I exclaimed, and he looked up and said, 'Hello, old Wilbur, it's good to see you again.' I was flattered that he'd remembered me.

On one occasion, I went up to the north of England to visit an independent bookshop which, although small, had been selling a lot of my books. Halfway through the afternoon, the owner, a lady, came up to me and said, 'There's a retired colonel who lives in the village and he relies on me to pick him four books a month to send to him. I think it would be a lovely touch if you could inscribe a copy for him and I'll send him one of yours. His name's Colonel Bailey . . .'

'Sure,' I said.

I duly inscribed the flyleaf, 'To Colonel Bailey, with best wishes, Wilbur Smith.' And that was the end of the story – or so I thought. A year later, I popped into the same shop for a cup of tea and a chat with the owner. 'You'll never believe what happened with that book you signed for Colonel Bailey,' she said.

'Oh yes, what was that?'

'It came back the next day, with a note from him, saying, "Dear Mrs Smith, I've been dealing with you for fifteen years and this is the first time you have ever sent me a spoilt copy. Please take this book back and send me a clean copy."'

I collapsed in laughter. So much for the allure of my signature.

Sometime later, I had the opposite experience while on a flight from New York to London, after a fishing trip in Alaska. I had a proof copy of my latest book and was going through it, correcting typos, when the chap sitting next to me leaned over.

'I see you're reading Wilbur Smith,' he said.

I nodded.

'Tell me honestly, what do you think of him as a writer?'

I feigned deep thought for a moment and then said, 'Well, I think he's a fine writer. I'd place him alongside Hemingway and John Steinbeck.'

My neighbour warmed visibly and leaned in closer. 'I know him,' he beamed. 'I know Wilbur Smith . . . he's a close friend of mine.'

'No, really!' I said, never having met this gentleman before.

'Yes,' he went on. 'And I'll tell you something else. You know the character of Sean Courtney, the hero of *When the Lion Feeds*?'

I played along. 'Do I know him? Of course, he's one of my favourites.'

'Well,' said my newfound friend. 'Wilbur based him on my life!'

'No!' I said, with just the right amount of incredulity.

'Yes,' said the man. 'I'll tell you what, if you give me

your card, I'll go to Wilbur and get him to send you a signed photograph of himself. We're so close, there's nothing he wouldn't do for me.'

So I gave him my business card, which he pocketed without a glance. I haven't heard from him since.

• • •

Leopard Rock: even now, these two words return me to the perfection of a night obliterated by stars.

In our old Rhodesian-style farmhouse, reminiscent of my childhood home, I lay awake, listening to the animal sounds. Intermittently, I slept, only to be woken by the bark of a kudu, or roused, in the morning, by the beauty of birdsong around the ranch house windows. At Leopard Rock, I was in practice a game farmer – doing game counts, checking populations and, if necessary, arranging for the extra numbers to be sold at auction for transfer to other farms. But the recompense was huge. In the morning, the blare of city life long forgotten in the stillness of the wild, I would go out into the veld. Sometimes I would spot the occasional leopard, or sit quietly and watch the herds interact. I particularly enjoyed observing them after the ewes had lambed, and the cows calved, to see how the little ones adapted to their new environment. There is no better feeling in the world than seeing a young animal take its first steps and knowing that the land around them, the only world they will ever know, is safe and free because you have made it that way.

The sole purpose of Leopard Rock was to preserve the game I had been systematically introducing: the springbok, kudu, eland and impala, all of them imported from game farmers and released to live wild and give rise to greater herds. Our staff lived on the farm, maintained the land, and, wherever possible, protected the game from poachers, as well as from the leopards who sometimes wandered through. When we first founded the farm, some of the locals were living in very poor conditions, almost in cattle stalls, and our immediate order of business was to build proper houses, install hot and cold running water, electricity and television. We made sure everyone had access to medical check-ups each year, enlisted the staff in pension schemes and helped their children enrol in school. Every Christmas, the staff and their families would gather at the farm house to share gifts and party together, long into the night.

I'd discovered that Leopard Rock was not only a place where I would conserve animals, it was a way of helping the local African people as well. It gave me great pleasure to be the laird of the estate – or, as they would say in central and East Africa, *'Bwana'* – but being laird came with responsibilities. Once, I was in the middle of an interview when the phone rang. The farm manager was frantic on the other end of the line. One of our labourers had driven his tractor through the electric cables and severed power to the whole of Leopard Rock. Calamities like these would often pluck me out of the isolated world of writing, but what Leopard Rock took from me, it gave back in abundance.

14

THIS DESERT LIFE

We had set out from Luxor into the glare of the sun in October 1989. Now, just before our first nightfall, I saw stars blossom across the sky, and felt the first chill of the desert. Gone were the monuments and temples of the West Bank Necropolis, the splendour of the Valley of the Kings, the thousands of tourists who flocked to Luxor, so many more than when I had first travelled to Egypt in the early 1970s. Ahead of us were the rolling dunes and undulating sands of the dry *wadi* that we were following. I was travelling with my companions, the Bedouin we had taken as guides, and the three snorting camels laden with our packs. This was a trail the Bedouin knew well, passed down from their forefathers: a caravan route for the merchants of ancient Egypt to ferry their wares; a route along which African slaves had been driven by their Arab masters many centuries before. Every step I took I shared with those people plucked out of history. I could feel their ghosts and forgotten stories swirling around me as keenly as I felt the lacerations of the desert sand in the wind.

In two weeks, we would arrive at the turquoise waters of the Red Sea, to dive into the magnificent coral reefs and swim with the thousands of species of fish unique to that part of the world. Between now and then, however, there were two hundred miles of desert, and already the sand was caked to my face, riming my nostrils, scouring the back of my throat. Soon, I fancied, I would look like Lawrence of Arabia – only not as good looking as Peter O'Toole in the film. In many ways, I had lived with the desert all my life. It is a part of Africa as vital to me as the bush in which I loved to lose myself and hunt. For the past decade, I had been inspired by it as a source of stories, the deserts of northern Africa as important to my novels as the bush of the south had been when I started my writing career. In this trek, I was going to reaffirm my love for this most inhospitable landscape. I had, I suppose, been building up to this pilgrimage my entire life.

· · ·

My father inspired my love of the hunt: he stood in my eyes for all the heroes of southern Africa; but it was my mother who made me consider the past and understand that Africa was a place of ancient civilisations, customs lost to the mists of time, and wild unknowable gods. She told me tales of the Pharaohs who once ruled northern Africa, of the cursed tombs they had left behind, and of the treasure hunters who still toiled in the desert to uncover the secrets of that blasted land.

My mother's fascination with Great Zimbabwe had led me to create Benjamin Kazin and *The Sunbird*, and it was her enchantment with Ancient Egypt that would open another door through which a eunuch slave named Taita would introduce himself to the world. Nothing had captured my mother's imagination more fiercely than the discovery of Tutankhamen's tomb. The nineteen-year-old Pharaoh had been discovered eleven years before I was born, when my mother herself was a young girl filled with dreams, and the memories of the discovery had stayed with her ever since. Lying in bed at night, she told me about Howard Carter and George Herbert, the fifth Earl of Carnarvon, descending into the darkness of the tomb, how the flickering lights of their flaming brands revealed by degrees the mummified remains of the boy king. 'It was waiting in the deep caves, Wilbur. Not a stone had been moved. Not a figure out of place. Lying on his back with his golden death mask hiding his face, was King Tut himself . . .'

On 26 November 1922, Howard Carter had chiselled a small hole in the corner of the doorway of the tomb, and by the light of a candle could see that the many gold and ebony treasures were undisturbed. Lord Carnarvon asked, 'Can you see anything?' and Carter replied with the now famous words: 'Yes, wonderful things!'

It is difficult to imagine today, but the discovery of Tutankhamen's tomb was a huge event. The tomb had been found almost intact, a scene untouched for millennia, and then the men who entered the tomb died in quick succession, giving rise to the belief that the tomb had been cursed. It was the perfect set-up for a media frenzy. Lord Carnarvon died six weeks after the tomb was opened; George Jay Gould, an American financier, developed a strange fever and died in France six months after entering the tomb; Prince Ali Kamel Fahmy Bey of Egypt was shot dead by his French wife of six months in London's Savoy Hotel shortly after he was photographed visiting the tomb; Sir Archibald Douglas-Reid, a radiologist who X-rayed Tutankhamen's mummy, died from a mysterious disease just over a year later; and Carnarvon's two half brothers both passed away – one from blood poisoning, and the other from malarial pneumonia. Later, Carter's personal secretary was found smothered in his bed; his father committed suicide by throwing himself from his seventh storey apartment – and the most inexplicable story of all came when Carter's messenger discovered a cobra, the symbol of the Egyptian monarchy, sitting in the bird cage in Carter's house, having already devoured Carter's canary. It was an entertaining confection, a grisly but addictive spectacle, just like the best stories. Arthur Conan Doyle, the author of *Sherlock Holmes*, blamed 'elementals' created by the boy king's priests, while one newspaper printed a legend that would solidify the curse in the public consciousness for generations to come. *Death shall come on swift wings to him who disturbs the peace of the king!* it declared – leaving aside the fact that these words never appeared on the hieroglyphs found in the tomb. Like all good fabulists, the newspapers didn't let the facts get in the way of a good story. Tutankhamen's curse had the nation gripped.

To a boy who had experienced the desert infrequently – the arid expanse of the Kalahari stretching into an infinite horizon when we went out on our annual safaris – the idea of desert kingdoms, of supernatural curses, and a boy king not much older than myself, contained the elements of thrilling fantasy. In stories like these, the desert became a place of magic and mysticism. I did not write a desert story of my own for many years, but the tales my mother recounted excited and inspired in me new narratives of wonder.

. . .

It was not until I crossed the Namib as a student that I truly understood how merciless the desert can be. The Kalahari supports more life than most deserts, its plains green and fertile when the rains come, but the Namib is featureless to all except those who know it best, a place of scorched earth beneath an inferno of a sky.

In those early years, I had a child's view of Egypt as a place of pharaohs and queens. It was only after *When the Lion Feeds* was accepted for publication, and I was en route to London to meet my publishers, that I was able to visit the country for the first time, when BOAC stopped off in Egypt.

Cairo in those days was a very different city to that which greets visitors today. There were few tourists wandering the streets or hordes laying siege to its monuments. The feluccas plying the waters of the Nile were sailed by local travellers and fishermen, not holidaymakers eager to touch the water of this ancient river. I stood on the river bank all those years ago, looking upstream, and imagined the intrepid travellers who had followed the watercourse in ages past, seeking its fabled source – not just the Victorian explorers whose stories I had loved, but also the Roman legionaries and Greek soldiers. This was the birthplace of civilisation and, over the decades to come, it would keep calling me back.

Alone, I wandered through the City of the Dead. It was a corner of Cairo where hundreds of tombs were occupied as dwellings for the poorest people of the city, a place where the living and the dead mingled, where the modern and the ancient worlds met. Later, I spent long hours in the Egyptian Museum with its unrivalled collection of pharaonic exhibits. These days it is a grand museum, home to one of the greatest treasure hoards in the world, but back then it was more of a repository, an echoing warehouse through which I was permitted to wander and let my imagination roam. Nothing was labelled, priceless items were piled haphazardly in obscure rooms, even Tutankhamen's famous death mask was housed in a ramshackle glass cupboard of the kind you might find in a rundown jeweller's store. In a corner, a guard had propped his rifle against the wall and was casually smoking a cigarette, seemingly unconcerned by the magnificent history all around him. As I made my way along the halls, I imagined myself as a pioneer – unearthing little-known and overlooked gems, walking a few paces behind Howard Carter and the Earl of Carnarvon as they revealed to the world what had remained hidden for nearly four thousand years.

My first visit to Egypt was fleeting, but my return trips became longer and longer. I went back in 1974, while I was researching *Eagle in the Sky*, and thereafter, whenever the deserts called, I would jump on a plane and land in this extraordinary country. Part of my excitement was caused by the Nile itself, a mythical feature of Africa, a river which had bewitched many before me. The Nile had given sustenance to settlers since the dawn of time. Gradually, various tribes of hunter-gatherers came face to face with each other, forced to the verdant riverbanks by the encroaching desert, and there they peacefully commingled, building structured societies in order to survive.

I explored the ruins and ancient places, the kind you

can only visit now under the watchful eyes of sentries and guards. On those early visits, I was allowed to clamber wherever I wanted. At Giza, where the Pyramids rose vertiginously into the sky, my guide helped me to the zenith of one of those fabulous constructions. At the pinnacle, heaving and out of breath, I gazed from horizon to horizon, absorbing a space so vast and empty, yet crowded with the intense bustle of the past. I ventured off the beaten track to see the old Coptic Christian monasteries deep in the desert – where all that was needed to see a glimpse of life inside was to open your wallet – and the magical Faiyum Oasis beyond Cairo, where for a brief moment the desert is green and alive, and the ducks are plentiful and waiting to be picked off.

On another trip I went north, to where the Nile meets the Mediterranean Sea. There, sixty miles west of Alexandria, lie the cemeteries of El Alamein, the last resting place of those soldiers who died in 1942 in one of the most decisive battles of the Second World War – when Montgomery's Eighth Army defeated Nazi Germany's Rommel. It was a personal pilgrimage to remember the Rhodesians and South Africans who, it is often forgotten, played their part in that victory. Afterwards, I flew south to Aswan, site of the massive modern dam across the Nile. I picked up a cruiser for a ten-day trip downriver. It was one of my life's great experiences, sailing backward through time as the river wended its way north, bound for Luxor and Karnak, with all their temples and museums.

It was on a subsequent trip that I sailed over the Valley of the Kings in a hot air balloon and saw the ancient world reaching out to meet the modern above. As I hung there, floating serenely, I could see al-Qurn high in the Theban hills, and the place where Tutankhamen himself was discovered, as well as the burial mounds of the Theban Necropolis stretching out all around. Perhaps my love for this landscape was something I had inherited from my mother, but I could see many and varied stories of Egypt spread out on the landscape beneath me.

One day in 1988 came a moment so perfect, so thrilling, that it would echo forever after in all my fiction, and bring to life a new character who would never let me go: Taita.

. . .

Egypt, the Pyramids and Great Sphinx, the mighty Nile whose waters fed half the continent: this was an Africa unlike anything I had ever written about, and now I was holding a piece of it in my hands. In 1988, I stood in the heat of the desert on the West Bank of the River Nile. Guide lines and ropes had been stretched out by the archaeologists working the dig to which I had been invited. For weeks, they had been peeling back history just as a writer peels back the layers of his story – and now, where once had been arid scrub and sand, the evidence of a former civilisation rose out of the sun-blasted crust in eerie outcrops of stone. Below, in the cavernous black hole of her tomb, lay the remains of a queen unrecorded by history. The academics believed she had died and been mummified as early as 1780 BC, at a time when the Hyskos people led an invasion from the Near East and settled the eastern river delta, but it felt like she was here with me now, whispering into my ear.

The queen had been buried with all the treasures of her lifetime. I had been writing about treasures like these from the time I wrote *The Eye of the Tiger*, but no fiction could compare with the truth of what was unearthed in these ancient tombs. Death masks of gold, circlets inlaid with precious gems, figurines captured in intricate detail depicting the age-old gods of the river. There was no precious artefact, however, that would affect me more than the one I held in my hands today. This was no gold, no sceptre with sapphires pressed into its hilt, no death mask capturing the perfect likeness of the body it kept hidden underneath. These were papyri, pieces of pith of the papyrus plant, woven together to make ancient parchment – and, across them, were inscribed hieroglyphs beyond my understanding.

My hands trembled as I touched the scrolls for the first time. These fragile pieces of papyrus contained a message from almost four millennia ago. I traced the arcane symbols with my finger. Here was a connection between me and the past. I thought about the queen, lying undisturbed in her tomb while nations rose and fell in the world above her, wars were waged, men made inconceivable machines, conquered the planet, set sail for the moon. I considered the man who might have rhapsodised about her in these scrolls and in that moment, I knew that they had been waiting for me for four thousand years.

Later, once the scrolls had been translated by experts at the University of Cairo, I was able to read what this ancient figure had committed to paper. The scrolls were written as a personal tribute to the woman the author had loved, the great queen whose body had been brought back to the light. The scrolls revealed a lot about the writer as well – it was his opportunity to extol his own genius and power, to brag about what an extraordinary person he had been. The script was not conducive to conveying subtle emotions, but there was something here, something that would tug at me for years to come. The author, whoever he had been, was an endearing braggart, and he had other qualities. He was faithful, he was loving, he was full of compassion for animals and people. There were gaps in his narrative where an author might let his imagination run free; here was a character whose skin I eagerly wanted to inhabit.

It was in that moment that Taita was born.

River God was my twenty-fourth novel, written in the pure isolation of the Seychelles, gazing out over the azure waters of the Indian Ocean. It was the first novel I had written using a word processor after handwriting all my books before that, but it had been forming in my mind for decades before I committed a word to the page. It was a novel that brought together so many of my fascinations, influences and obsessions.

River God was published in 1993. It is an epic novel, one that whisked its readers nearly four thousand years into a past I had researched exhaustively over the preceding years. This was an act of writing that owed much to *The Sunbird* before it – but there was one vital difference: where, in *The Sunbird*, I had built the city of Ophet from my imagination, in *River God*, Egypt had to be cultivated from hard research.

The novel shocked my readers. For a decade, I had been writing high-octane novels set in present day Africa – the final parts of the Ballantyne sequence, and the second part of the Courtney saga – but *River God* was a change of pace, a step beyond the boundaries my readers had come to expect. Not all the responses were positive. One woman wrote to me and said: 'I read the first few pages of *River God* and it wasn't you and I put the book down because I couldn't read it and I hope you're going to write a decent book.' I wrote back and apologised for disappointing her and about three months later, she wrote to me and said, 'I did it. I read it and it's the best book you've written by far.' I think that, when people got over the initial shock, they accepted it.

I wanted to take my readers into brave new lands, but some of them were finding it difficult to equate Egypt with Africa. 'Oh yes, but it's different,' they'd say. 'It's

Arabic.' That may be true for Europeans and Americans, but it is never so for Africans. To us, Egypt is as African as the Cape of Good Hope. I have always seen Africa as one single horse-headed continent. All of it shares a mystique, and it is bound together by great rivers, by wild animals – historically the habitat of the African lion, for example, extended from north to south – and by a savage spirit that is all pervasive. Africa has a wildness that the cultivated lands of the northern hemisphere will never understand, and the Nile embodies that mystery, that magic. It is the most extraordinary example of living history in the world. The evidence is around you if you ever take a boat upriver. It becomes a time machine. The farmers tilling the land and working the water wheels have been doing so since the surrounding monuments were built by the pharaohs. It is here that a man can be intimately connected to the past, perceive that time is greater than any individual. Here, you truly understand how fleeting a man's life is, how small he is compared to the great turning world all around us.

If *River God* didn't appeal to some readers, there were many more who enjoyed it. I couldn't have predicted it, but it brought me four times as many readers as any of the Ballantyne and Courtney novels before it. They came for the living, breathing world I had conjured up from painstaking research and a writer's best weapon – *willpower* – but they stayed for the novel's hero. Taita is a man unlike any I had written before. I had sown the seeds for him in Benjamin Kazin, but Taita was the antithesis of all the Courtney and Ballantyne alpha males, all swash and buckle, around whom my writing had always been focused. Taita was emasculated, gelded by his master, Lord Intef, after being discovered sleeping with a young slave girl. As a eunuch, he knows the power of love, but can never fulfil it, and he has devoted his life instead to acquiring great wisdom and wide knowledge. He was a Renaissance hero. Readers from all over the world seemed to empathise with his plight. The power of unrequited love, the agony and the ecstasy, drew millions to Taita and kept them enthralled.

Taita may have emerged from the scrolls but, along the way, I had given him parts of myself as well – not my history, as I had done with the Courtneys and Ballantynes, but aspects of my personality and character. I had developed something of a soft spot for Taita, a brotherly affection perhaps, and I was as eager as my readers to know where his story would take him.

I followed *River God* with *The Seventh Scroll*, a different kind of novel which, nevertheless, continued the story of Taita's life. Set in the modern day, *The Seventh Scroll* was indelibly linked to the history of *River God*. It was not what my readers had been expecting – but I was having too much fun. The lost worlds of Ancient Egypt had invigorated my writing as no other novel had done for decades. They renewed my confidence, allowed me to spread my wings once again.

In *The Seventh Scroll*, Taita, who had captivated me in *River God*, returned with all his tricks and ploys, to conceal and safeguard the burial of Pharaoh Mamose and his vast treasure. For the first time, I wrote myself into the novel for a giggle, and fictionalised the excitement I had felt when I held those unearthed forgotten scrolls, but in typical Smith fashion I concocted a love affair, a vainglorious collector, his Teutonic muse and PA, and a fight to the death in the gorges of the Nile. The current British Foreign Secretary, Boris Johnson, who reviewed it, said: 'It would be hard to give away the plot of the latest yarn of pharaonic pillage because there is so much of it. In the opening thirty pages the heroine and her husband are stabbed, burnt, bombed, burgled, flayed and, take it from me, it works its way up from there.'

If there were misgivings, it was that the story effectively condoned the thieving of African artworks by European collectors. That wasn't the intention, but nonetheless at least one book reviewer argued that, even if that had been the case, there was nothing wrong with it. As James Mitchell of the *Star* wrote: 'I have heard one complain that the behaviour of Wilbur's heroes in *The Seventh Scroll* is immoral in that they are looting the artworks which should belong to Ethiopia. Whether their aim is to get them for Sir Nicholas's private hoard or Royan's Egyptian museums, the fabulous treasures will be leaving their geographical hosts. The unspoken agenda was that even fiction should have a moral basis. With that I agree. Yet such criticism is naive. Ethiopia is in chaos at the present time when this novel is set. Any such artworks would in real life be sold off to the highest bidder . . . undoubtedly to be hidden away in some Texan vault. If this sounds rather like the usual justification for the British retention of the Parthenon Marbles removed by Lord Elgin and whose return is frequently demanded by Greek governments, then so be it.'

In the years that followed, my beloved Taita would not let me go. His stories kept crying out to be told. *Warlock*, my first novel of the new millennium, continued Taita's odyssey as I journeyed away from the true history of *River God* to the world of mysticism and magic that the Egyptian series would eventually become. It was H. Rider Haggard again, making himself known in my writing. In *Warlock*, following the death of his beloved Queen Lostris, Taita retreats to the desert to mourn, and in that inhospitable land, he transforms himself into a warlock, adept at harnessing the powers of the occult for good purposes. With his newfound talents, he returns to serve Pharaoh Tamose and to bring up his son Prince Nefer. Soon, Tamose is betrayed and murdered by his right-hand man, who then sets himself up as regent of Egypt. It is Taita who must protect not just Nefer, but the whole of Egypt as well.

When I completed the novel, I decided to change direction again. I launched into *The Quest* with great vigour. It was different, it danced to an unusual beat, and it was perhaps self-indulgent to give Taita his manhood back in the end, but I had become very, very fond of Taita. *The Quest* is an adventure further into the realms of witchcraft and magic. It was quite well received: *Publishers Weekly* said: 'Once again Smith deftly blends history, fantasy and mythology, but newcomers should be prepared for grisly deaths and mutilations.' Another critic mentioned that the novel had created a 'chronicle of otherworldliness which crosses the line from the true historical novel to a work of fantasy and, in so doing, harnesses and recaptures myths out of the mysterious dark continent with which he is so familiar.'

I have always prided myself on my research, and while writing *The Quest* I decided to experience fasting, to put myself in the shoes of Taita, who of course had done much the same in his journey to become an adept. Fasting is a well-documented practice, particularly among seers and sages. It is part and parcel of most of the world's great religions: with Islam making the month-long Ramadan fast one of the five pillars, while Judaism enjoins its believers to abstain for an entire day during Yom Kippur.

But, soon after *The Quest* was published, perhaps the greatest heroine I had ever known, my mother Elfreda, passed away.

My mother had been on her own for more than twenty years since my father died. In all that time, not a day went by when she didn't think about and miss him. I had always thought my mother was invincible. I thought she would reach her centenary and live beyond it but, when she turned ninety-five, she looked at me and said, 'Wilbur, I am very sick.'

'You're not, Mom,' I replied. 'You're very strong.'

'My darling,' she said, 'you don't understand. Your dad wants me – he *needs* me with him . . .'

'Mom,' I said, 'you know you're going to get there and his first words will be, "You silly woman, where the hell have you been for the last twenty years? Now go and make me a cup of tea."'

She smiled and said: 'I'll do anything to hear him say that again.'

Before she died she made me promise I would look after my sister, Adrienne. It was no hardship whatsoever; I have always loved my little sister.

My mother had been a staunch Anglican throughout her life. It was one of the only distinctions between her and my father. An agnostic through and through, Africa was my father's only god. After she passed away, I stood in the crematorium with my wife Niso and Adrienne, and committed her body to the flames. Later that day, I returned to my study in Cape Town with her ashes sealed in a special box.

I placed her on my desk, surrounded by all the novels of my lifetime. It had been my mother who first showed me how books could be the doorways into magical worlds. It had been my mother who weaned me on stories, who inspired my fascination with Egypt, who had encouraged me to follow this seemingly impossible dream. Without her, there would have been no Courtneys, no Ballantynes – no Taita. And so, every day, as I picked up my pen and continued to write, she sat alongside me again. The woman who had first stoked my love for reading had not gone, there were still many stories to tell.

A couple of years later though, I felt she wanted her remains joined with Dad's. He hadn't wanted to be cremated. He said, 'No cremation, thank you very much, that might hurt! I'm not taking any chances, just do me the old way.' He is buried at Somerset West, so we opened a small shaft in the grave and placed my mother's ashes next to his coffin and put a little sign on the gravestone. The first thing we do when we come back to South Africa each year is go out to say hello to them and put some proteas on their resting place. It's a very good feeling. Peaceful.

15

THIS AMERICAN LIFE

The motorboat roared along the river as I sat in its prow, the breeze reddening my face, making me feel as raw as the country we sped through. On either side, the riverbanks gave way to forested hillsides, black spruce and tamarack clinging to the slopes. In my lap rested the prize catch of the morning – seventeen pounds of gleaming river trout. It had been a good day's fishing.

This corner of the world, far removed from the sun-burnished scrub and bush of my childhood, had a special appeal to me. Alaska still had a frontier spirit about it, an elder world of rugged individualists where the wilderness prevailed and mankind was in the minority. It is the largest state in the United States by area and one of the least populated, a place where lonely souls can seek solitude, or eke out a living in the wilds far from the prying eyes of neighbours or everyday interference. I had been coming here every year. We would fly into Anchorage from London, a night flight taking us over the North Pole and the barren outreaches of the Arctic Circle, and from there make our way to the distant King Salmon, a place with a population of about 700 people. Staying at the remote King Salmon Inn, where travellers mingled with the men who worked the red salmon in the rivers and the bay, we would gather our supplies before heading out into the wild. By sea plane we would fly out to a location we were sworn to keep secret – no local fisherman wanted the prime sites of the salmon in these rivers to be revealed – and from there we would follow the rolling waters, our days filled with fishing and cookfires at night.

When we steered the motorboat to the riverbank and waded up to shore, the low sun was shining brightly above the tamaracks. We tramped across the rocks, toward the trees where our packs had been stored, and suddenly I glimpsed a dark looming shadow towering over the provisions we had left behind that morning. It was one of the biggest grizzly bears I had ever seen. I stopped in my tracks and stared. Perhaps he hadn't seen me yet, for he did not look up, nor seem to notice us at all. My first thought was, 'What a beautiful beast.' His fur was brown with darker colouring on his legs, blond-tipped on his flank and back, and he had a prominent shoulder hump typical of his species. Then I saw his claws like curved daggers, which had to be three or four inches long. His snout was down, and his front paws were engaged in ripping something to shreds. It looked like a man's torso, but I couldn't see the glisten of blood and I did not sense the death throes of some poor victim. I should have backed away but curiosity got the better of me and then I realised what had lured the bear into our camp. In King Salmon, I had provisioned for the trip by buying an expensive anorak to keep out the often ice-flecked wind of this part of the world. With the sun so strong this morning, I had left the anorak behind and had forgotten I'd stashed several bars of chocolate in the pockets. Bears have an excellent sense of smell, better than that of a dog, and he must have sniffed out this unexpected treat from a long way off. He looked pretty content tearing my anorak to pieces, with his nose and half his face covered in the sticky, melting chocolate. I hoped his appetite was sufficiently sated for him not to decide that his main course could be human flesh.

Grizzly bears tend to be more aggressive than black bears when defending themselves, but they usually try to avoid contact with people, and, despite their physical advantage – the male can rise to a standing height of seven feet and weigh up to eight hundred pounds – they rarely hunt humans. However, it can attack if surprised at close range or protecting a food source, textbook behavioural characteristics I was, right now, in grave danger of triggering.

As if sensing my presence, the bear paused in his

rummaging and lifted his head. Two black eyes considered me from a thick thatch of brown fur. They seemed to find me wanting.

From a distance, I stared at the grizzly. He was at least six hundred pounds of pure muscle and stood four feet wide at the shoulders, his fur shining with run-off from the river. It was naturalist George Ord in 1815, who, after careful study, formally classified the grizzly bear, not for its appearance but for its character, as *Ursus horribilis* ('terrifying bear').

This was not the first bear I had seen. Hardly a trip went by to this part of the world when one of these lumbering giants of the forest did not make themselves known. I'd lost count of the number of times the wardens had lectured us before we set out into the wild. 'This is bear country,' they said. 'Never forget – *you're* the inter-lopers in this part of the world.' They were eager to impress on us that, if a bear attacked, we should not scream – because, or so it seemed, loud noises would upset them. Sometimes we would see bears fishing from the banks of the rivers as we rode past. Once, a female grizzly had charged us – only to be repelled when our guide pulled his pistol and fired a warning shot over her head. They are magnificent creatures, true monsters of the wild, and this specimen eyeing me was one of the species' finest.

Some kind of madness must have possessed me, because I did not feel fear, only outrage that he had torn apart my gear. Rather than the bear's fight instinct being triggered, it was mine, and I charged straight at him.

I screamed, waving my arms indignantly like someone who had just been pick-pocketed. I was trying to drive him away, but I soon realised I was on my own, my fellow fishermen lingering behind, either because they were terrified or because they couldn't suppress their laughter. Before I knew it, I was almost upon the bear. Seemingly unperturbed, he stood his ground. I was near enough to smell his heavy carnivorous scent, to see the ripple of the wind across his pelt. Then he moved with lightning speed. One instant, he was on all fours, claws still tangled in the remains of my anorak, the next, he had risen on his hind legs to his full height. Seven feet above the earth, his front legs stretched out wide as if he wanted to hug me in one final embrace, he opened his jaws and, from the bottomless cavern of his belly, erupted a sonorous, outraged, furious roar, a sound like no other in nature.

I stopped dead. The bellow filled the forest, blotting out all other noise. I looked up into his salivating, chocolate-smeared jaws. I looked at the savaged remains of my chocolate bars and my mangled anorak, relieved I wasn't still inside it. What fire had been in me was extinguished in a second. If the bear desired my coat, if the bear fancied the chocolates, he was welcome to them.

I turned and ran.

I did not look back until I was near the river. When I finally stopped and turned, expecting the bear to be at my shoulder and ready to pounce, he was nowhere to be seen. He'd left as nonchalantly as he'd arrived, having pillaged what he came for, and he was probably far away settling down for a snooze. He was not the only one who had disappeared. My companions had vanished. Eventually I heard a rustling in the bushes and from behind trees and under dense cover my friends emerged, one or two of them appearing to be doubled up, trying to hold in their guffaws of laughter. One of them came up to me, slapped me on the back, and said, 'Wilbur, you're the king of the jungle.' I would remember that grizzly bear's roar for the rest of my days.

It was to be some time before the bush plane returned to take us further along the river.

• • •

As a boy brought up on the remote Copperbelt of Northern Rhodesia, the United States had always been another world. In the days before 24-hour television news, and the instant access of the internet, images of that fantastic place across the ocean came only through the films and books I devoured. In John Ford Westerns, America was a land every bit as rugged and uncivilised as the Africa about which my grandfather spun stories, while in the pages of a John Steinbeck novel it was a continent of people striving to make their own way and do their best for one another. I grew up believing in an America of long open roads and fast cars, of daring frontiersmen pushing their way West to civilise a continent, of the glamour and glitz of Hollywood and the West Coast.

I first visited America in 1965. New York, that melting pot of a city and latter-day capital of the world, was a dizzying revelation. The seething metropolis of sky-scrapers and tightly crammed streets was far removed from the open skies and rolling bush land of my child-hood. I returned to the skies and continued further west to a city I had seen garlanded in lights on the silver screen, of whose temples I had often dreamed. Las Vegas seemed to embody the excess and appetite of America. I lost a week there, in a whirlwind of shows, soaking up the atmosphere and absorbing the vast energy of that fabled city of the desert. Nevada was stark and beautiful, its desert as hot and unforgiving as the deserts I knew in Africa, but it was not the sun-burnished steppes and endless sagebrush that I had come to see. I was not a gambling man – I never have been, despite the exotic allure of cities like Las Vegas – and, apart from one feeble attempt at a game of baccarat, I did not lose myself at the tables of the great casinos. For me, it was enough to hear and feel America's raucous lust for life.

That week, in October 1965, was the beginning of my lifelong love affair with the United States.

When the Lion Feeds was launched in the United States in 1965. *The Dark of the Sun* followed soon after. Then came *The Sound of Thunder*, *Gold Mine* and more. It wasn't until *Eagle in the Sky* in 1974 that my work climbed into the bestseller lists in America, but it didn't mean my readership wasn't slowly growing, nor was my love affair with the United States any less enthusiastic. As the years passed, I was finding more and more reasons to travel to the States. However, I had always known I would never set a novel in America. My agent Charles Pick's advice to 'write what you know' meant my novels would always be rooted in the Africas that had made me who I was. So my trips to America were never about work. Instead, the United States represented a place of adventure and enjoyment, a place of release. Every year I'd visit Alaska to fish for salmon and river trout; I skied for decades in Utah, outside Salt Lake City, at Robert Redford's stunning Sun Valley ranch in Montana, and, most memorably of all, at Beaver Creek in Colorado, where the ancient White River National Forest is capped in snow in winter, and the churning Colorado river grows steep banks of ice. I had learnt to ski in Europe after *When the Lion Feeds* was published and, though I would ski all over the world – in Australia's Blue Mountains, between the volcanoes of Japan, on the picturesque slopes of Switzerland – I was never very good at it. It didn't stop me from hurtling down the mountainsides of Beaver Creek with the forest and jagged peaks flashing past, or riding high in the chair lifts and seeing the untamed backwoods stretching out in every direction.

I sought out the best fishing and bird-watching locations

where I could experience America's nature in all its glory.
I had fallen in love with the wild places of America. It is
a continent like no other, a country where desert gives
way to fertile plains, where one mountain range can
encompass both the barren red and greys of the Sangre
Di Christo in New Mexico, and the snowy evergreens of
the northern Rockies. In no other country do these landscapes meet and combine: the otherworldly redwood
forests, with trees vaster than any in the world, the arid
sagebrush and desert, the snow-capped mountains and
Great Lakes, the long empty stretches of highway pock-
marked with villages and towns where hard-working
Americans craft out their lives. There is more to see in
the United States than a single lifetime could ever take
in.

Nevertheless, I gave it a go.

. . .

In 1982, I was immersed in the saga of the Ballantynes.
The Angels Weep had just been published, and the series'
apex, *The Leopard Hunts in Darkness*, was beginning to
take shape in my imagination. But, for several years, the
workload had been intense – and never more so than with
the Ballantynes, whose long history poured out of me in
a fevered few years of work. I needed a break, something
to restore my energies. It often happened in the middle
of a novel, when I'd lose my way, feel the fear of the story

running away from me, and a sudden safari or skiing expedition gave me the clarity to return to the novel in a fresher frame of mind. 1982 was the first year I had taken out of writing since *When the Lion Feeds*. Something was needed to let my creative well fill up again, and there was no better way of escape than to voyage out into the far-flung places of the world.

We began in Barrow, the overnight flight from London bringing us across the unsettled wilderness of the Arctic Circle. Outside the city, the headland of Point Barrow marked the northernmost tip of the United States; north of here was empty tundra, a thousand miles of barren whiteness stretching to the very end of the earth. Barrow was an oil town, so remote from the rest of the United States that people still relied on hunting to survive, carefully managing and harvesting the seals, polar bear, caribou and walrus which lived beyond the borders of town. From Barrow we journeyed south, through the untamed national parks where bears and wolves held sway, and at last to the Katmai peninsula. This wild part of the world was easy for a fisherman to fall in love with. A lifetime could have been whiled away here, with only me and the fish in the rivers, the river trout happily taking my bait wherever it was cast.

After our sojourn in America's frozen north, it was time to make a pilgrimage to that other far-flung state, Hawaii, as far from mainland America as London is from Cairo. In the cobalt waters of the Pacific there was yet more fishing – only, here, our hunt would be for a fish that could fight back.

I have always loved fishing for marlin. There is an elemental thrill in the tug of war, something pure in the fight, which had appealed to me from a very early age. By now I had fished for marlin all over the world – in the Indian Ocean where my father and I would sail out together, on Australia's Great Barrier Reef, where Lee Marvin beat me to the prize – but the Pacific blue marlin is the largest of the billfish species and it had always been my ambition to land one. The waters of Hawaii have an almost mythic status for marlin hunters. Here, the largest marlin ever caught with rod and reel was brought in at an enormous 1,805 lbs – ten times the weight of a powerful man – by Captain Cornelius Choy from Oahu island in 1970.

The blue marlin is one of the most beautiful fishes of the ocean. They are deep blue on top and silvery white below with a large dorsal fin and a long, lethal, spear-shaped upper jaw. They are extremely fast swimmers and use their spears to thrash through schools of fish, circling back to consume their stunned and mutilated prey.

We set out with the dawn, bound for the deep waters where the marlin lay. The Pacific seemed unnaturally still that morning. From west to east, north to south, the ocean shimmered in the sun but was calm. The skipper cast out our lures and we began to ply a circuit of the waters, waiting for the lures to be taken. We were using live bait, small skipjack tuna to tempt the marlin, but for long hours, there was nothing; the marlin remaining elusive in the blackness below. On the boat, there was nothing we could do but wait. Most of the time, patience is the fisherman's best friend.

Almost two hours later, I was standing on the flying deck, ready to admit defeat, when the lure closest to the boat disappeared in a sudden cascade of water and the reel started screaming, the line peeling away at a terrifying rate. I looked at the skipper, the skipper looked at me and in that split second, the adrenaline coursed through our veins. I sprang for the fighting chair, snatched the rod and reel and clung on for dear life as the skipper buckled me in.

In only a few minutes I knew that this was a big fish. I could feel his power reverberating in the line, sense how wild and frenzied he was becoming at the knowledge he had been snared. Then, as if from nowhere, the angle of the line started coming up and a monstrous blue marlin burst out of the sea, leaping and grey hounding away from the boat.

The battle began. Soon, the marlin had drawn the line to its full extent; almost five hundred feet of line now lay between me and the beast. I began to reel him in, felt the bite as the reel fought back. It had been spinning so fiercely that the oil in its runner was boiling, bursting out of the seals in clouds of scalding vapour. I continued to hold up the rod, draw in the line on the reel. My whole world had closed in. There was nothing but me and the marlin: his raging defiance and my determination to bring him aboard.

One hour of combat turned into two as time slipped by in a haze of muscle strain and mental focus: two hours into three and then four. My right hand was scraped and cut up, my left arm in paroxysms of cramp, but I fixed myself to the reel and centred my mind and would not let go. Hemingway's words flashed through my brain from his own chronicle of marlin fishing, *The Old Man and the Sea*: 'Man,' he had written, 'is not made for defeat . . .' By now I could feel the fight in the marlin fading. I too was exhausted, but little by little I brought in the line, and every turn of the reel gave me the strength to rotate it once more. After four hours, the war was nearly over. The marlin rose from the water – first his sword, then his body, and finally the razor-sharp contours of his tail. He must have been the most spectacular fish I had ever seen, a true-blue gladiator of the deep.

At last, I staggered from the fighting chair on trembling legs, and with aching arms stood over the marlin as it came alongside the boat and the skipper hauled him on board. Here he was, lying on the deck beneath me: five metres long from tail to the tip of his sword, five hundred kilograms if he was an ounce, deep azure, slippery silvery white, a heft of compact muscular power. I had bested him, but now that he was caught, it was only right to return him to the oceans to live another day. Perhaps some other fisherman would take on the arm wrestle in another bout of sport or he would win his next challenge, but he deserved to be free and untamed. Sadly, the decision was taken from me. I was quite upset with the Hawaiian authorities, for, like every true hunter, I am as much a compulsive conservationist as I am a compulsive fisherman. I normally catch and release and I wanted to put him back into the waves but that year the marlin was the one fish the authorities were not allowing to be released. I looked down at him with great sadness. This was the end of his journey, and, despite the unfortunate circumstances, I would take his metre-long sword as a trophy and a tribute.

It stands in a place of honour in my study to this day.

• • •

There was a journey I had been dreaming about making for a long time, one that recalled the best of the American legends, and, as we stepped off the plane at LAX airport, into a bustling crowd of Californians from every walk of life, the anticipation stirred us onwards. The long ocean road from Los Angeles to San Francisco was a part of the Americas I felt I knew already, mainly through the novels of John Steinbeck I had read ravenously many years ago. Now it was time to see it for myself.

I had been drawn to the West Coast of America long before I had come to the United States. New York City would always be a dizzying, frenetic place, and I love its Broadway shows, Christmas lights, restaurants and museums, especially the galleries where you could see some of the most stirring pieces of art in the world, like the French Impressionists I had always admired. But the West Coast embodied an aspect of America with which it was impossible not to fall in love. California was the home of Hollywood, the playground of the rich and famous, and it would never lose its allure, even after my own disillusioning escapades in the world of movie-making. The West Coast is magical, California unique.

We had been staying in the Beverly Hills Hotel, idly fantasising about partying with the glitterati, when the temptation of wild places and vast, open skies became all consuming. I was a spontaneous traveller, but once a decision had been made, I always planned it in intricate detail. For a day we pored over maps and guidebooks, and the next morning we were on the road: up from LA towards the sprawling wilderness of Yosemite National Park.

The moment I first saw the park I knew I would come back time and again. A meticulously preserved piece of old America, Yosemite is one of the continent's true marvels. El Capitan, the granite cliff looming over the valley, put me in mind of the rock-climbing adventures of my youth, while the groves of giant sequoia trees were spectacular. Leaving our car behind, we ventured deeper into the park, and for long hours we roamed its scrubby sun-baked chaparral, marvelled at its stately groves of trees so vast a man could walk through tunnels carved into their trunks, its alpine meadows and turbulent water-falls. This was America as it was long before the Europeans arrived. All around us, the forest was ancient woodland as it was back then, never logged, never exploited. And the bird life that abounded in those shadowy groves was enough to make me want to spend another lifetime here. There were woodpeckers, crows and black finches, tiny flycatchers darted in the branches, while regal great grey owls made their roosts up high. There were grey wolves and bears as well, though we did not see them, but it was enough to imagine them carving out an existence in a corner of the country preserved entirely for them.

Back at the car park, I heard something shriek behind me. A terrier jumped out of its owner's car and ran around in circles, clearly afraid of something.

I looked up in a nearby tree and saw a bald eagle enthroned in the branches surveying the commotion below, as majestic and haughty as any of its kind. The eagle spread its immense wings and dropped out of the tree like a cannonball. It hurtled past my head and snatched up the yapping dog. Silent at last, the dog was up in the air, skewered by enormous talons, and whisked off into the trees and beyond.

There was a moment's silence in the car park. Then the dog's owner stared up to the trees. She rushed off to find the game warden. She returned to the car, racked by tears, her husband comforting her.

As he climbed into the driver's seat, he caught my eye. He winked, and could hardly suppress a grin. He pumped his fist and let out a 'whoop', then found his poker face again and slid into the car next to his devastated wife.

It seemed the eagle was not the only one who had had enough of that yapping little dog.

Beyond Yosemite, we continued our journey north, returning to the coast to follow the ocean road through the mountain country of Big Sur. Here, the Santa Lucia Mountains edge dramatically into the Pacific, with the Ponderosa pines and Douglas firs blanketing the foothills in rich dark green. Along the highway, coastal redwoods stood like sentinels, guardians from another age.

This country had once been the heart of a gold rush, similar to the stampedes for the Witwatersrand that I had written about in *When the Lion Feeds*, but the Santa Lucias had kept Big Sur so isolated that only the most hardy, intrepid travellers had ever made it here. Now, although more people had arrived with the highway, the land still felt wild and remote. The Los Padres Forest was alive with the sound of coyotes at night. Once, at the side of the road, we stopped to see the spoor of a mountain lion, come down from the peaks to hunt Bighorn sheep and California deer in the lowlands. As we trekked north, condors and falcons turned overhead, or considered us menacingly from their hiding places in the forest's uppermost branches.

North of Big Sur, we travelled for long days in Monterey

County, until we found ourselves in Salinas, with the striking Gabilan Mountains looming over us to the east and the wide, open expanses of the Pacific Ocean in the west. As we followed the coast, staying in the small towns and villages, I imagined we had entered the pages of a John Steinbeck novel. At the edge of the road, farmers sold produce straight from their trucks. The hospitality of the local, rural Americans was so far removed from the frenzy of the big cities that it seemed unreal. Along the way, classic American songs played on a loop inside my head, Kris Kristoffersen on permanent repeat.

I admired Hemingway for his passionate evocation of hunting in *Green Hills of Africa* and for the way he blazed new trails in his writing. However, I loved Steinbeck more. My favourite Hemingway had always been *For Whom the Bell Tolls*. I loved the sparseness of his writing, the way he saw people so clearly, the deft, delicate brushstrokes that defined character with such economy. I loved, too, that he was essentially a tragic figure, an unhappy man disguising his uncertainty behind a carefully constructed macho image. But Steinbeck held a different place in my heart. His humanity is a searing light shining into his characters' souls, exposing their truth and vulnerability. I had always loved *Cannery Row* for its humour, pathos and empathy with people who are struggling with poverty, their low-rent tragedies. It is a wonderful insight into Depression-era America – touching and moving and funny. *Tortilla Flat*, too, showed his towering love for downtrodden humanity

– and, if he was a little left wing in novels like *In Dubious Battle* and his unforgettable *The Grapes of Wrath*, well, I could forgive him that. In *East of Eden* he had created two warring brothers who I could only aspire to match with Sean and Garrick Courtney.

These abundant lands were bursting with stories. Steinbeck had called it 'the valley of the world', and inside One Main Street in Salinas we found the National Steinbeck Center, a museum dedicated to his life's work. We spent many hours absorbing every aspect of the exhibitions: Steinbeck's handwritten manuscripts and journals locked behind glass; the Model T Ford from the movie of *East of Eden* sitting out front, while images of James Dean as Cal Trask played on repeat; and, finally, the green camper that Steinbeck lived in as he wended his way along the highways of rural America, writing *Travels with Charley* along the way. One day was not enough to take in the scale of Steinbeck's achievement, so we came back the next, and the day after that.

John Steinbeck had lived his life as I aspired to do: always searching, always travelling, writing what he knew about most intimately of all. When, several days later, we reached San Francisco, and the end of our journey, I was thinking of him still, and eager to pick up my pen.

Our American voyage was over – but only for a short time. I knew this country would keep tempting me back.

. . .

Every year I received letters from American readers who convinced me that this truly was a special country. I had one reader who would write to me from Florida every time I released a new novel. The thought that someone, out there, was waiting for my stories was more sustaining than I had ever imagined. His daughter, Sandi Smith of Crossville in Tennessee, sent me a card when he died. 'Dear Mr Smith,' it read. 'My father was so impressed with your stories, I thought you should know that one of your books, *The Sunbird*, was buried with him. I have also read all your books and enjoyed them.'

There was a man called Jack, living in Houston, who was also an avid reader and who wrote to me whenever a novel was published. After several years, I received a letter from him saying, 'Dear Wilbur, I'm sorry to have to tell you, but our relationship has to come to an end because I'm 89 at my next birthday and my eyesight is going, and so I won't be able to read your books in future.' It just so happened that, a week before, I had been sent a large-print edition of my latest book from my publishers, produced for people with poor or failing eyesight. I put the book in a jiffy bag with a letter that said, 'Jack, it doesn't have to end. You've got to put up with my books for a while yet. Here is one that you can read.' I heard from his wife afterwards what had happened. Jack opened the book and was so overcome with excitement that he wrote two letters. One was to me thanking me for sending him the book, saying how much he enjoyed it, and how much my friendship meant to him; the other was a letter to his son in New York saying, 'Look what Wilbur Smith has sent me, isn't this fantastic!' When he took the letters to the post office, his eyesight was so bad that he got them mixed up and he sent me the letter meant for his son, and mine to his son. I remained friends with his wife for a long time, until I finally received a letter saying, 'I'm terribly sorry to tell you that, just before his 92nd birthday, my husband Jack passed away, but in his will, he stipulated that all your books had to be in the coffin with him to go on the next voyage.' She sent me a photograph, and there was Jack, in the coffin, looking very dapper in a nice dark suit, a white satin pillow under his head and my books all around him. 'Jack,' I thought, 'good voyage, mate. Thank you very much.' That was one of the sincerest compliments I have ever received.

In another lifetime, I am certain I would have made America my home, but we are only given one lifetime, and for me America will always remain that vast, rich place of people and stories, constantly changing, constantly growing, a place that brought so much pleasure in my life.

16

THIS DIVING LIFE

The golden rule of diving is: dive alone, die alone. Beneath the surface, with the waves crashing above, it was a rule I had broken too often.

Thirty feet below the sparkling waters of the Indian Ocean, I checked the gauge on my oxygen tank and watched it tick over, every breath an increment closer to empty. It was 1995 and I had been waiting here, trapped beneath a coral ledge, for too long, and time, as it always does, was running out. Somewhere up there, dimly perceivable as a rippling shadow, Judith – the manageress of my Seychelles estate – waited patiently on our yacht, with no way of knowing what was happening below. In recent months, she had skippered the boat for me on many occasions, keeping a watchful eye as I explored the depths of the sea with not another diver in sight. I loved diving, the weightlessness felt like the ultimate freedom, the graceful agility the medium allowed was a release from surly earthly bonds, and I'm convinced man evolved from the sea as we are drawn instinctively to open water; to me it's like coming home. The solo diving experience appealed to me even more profoundly; there's a purity about the isolation, the raw solitude of having nothing else to rely on but your own ingenuity and instinct. This was my domain, no other human for miles in every direction. But this time I was not alone. Between me and the safety of the boat hung three grey reef sharks, six feet long from their broad, menacing snouts to the tips of their tails. Black points ran along each of their dorsals, but most unnerving of all were the black holes of their eyes, like coals set in a mask of grey stone.

The grey reef shark is the first shark species discovered to display threat behaviour. It adopts a 'hunched' posture, dropping its pectoral fins and swimming from side-to-side in an exaggerated motion when it's threatened and is preparing to attack. It has been known to attack divers and it is astonishingly fast, launching itself like a harpoon by covering twenty feet in a third of a second.

So far, the sharks circling above me were luxuriating in the warm waters, placidly indifferent.

I had not noticed them arrive. I knew these stretches of coral as intimately as the gullies and scrubland of Leopard Rock, and came here often to watch the magical sea life: the angelfish and parrotfish, the peacock groupers and black and white snapper. One fish, the five-hundred-pound Napoleon wrasse, had become my first underwater fan when, upon dropping a bit of my picnic lunch one day, I discovered he was partial to hardboiled eggs. After that, he would find me whenever I dived and come begging for food like a faithful hound. The Napoleon wrasse, also known as the humphead wrasse, has almost comically thick lips, two black lines behind its eyes and a hump on its forehead. Added to its strange appearance, its colouring is like something out of Disneyworld, or an animation by Pixar. It varies from blue green to vibrant green and purplish blue, and is stunningly iridescent, a confection of colour.

I knew reef sharks patrolled these waters, but they had never bothered me before and I had never bothered them. This seemed like a good arrangement, and one I was keen to maintain. But now they were in danger of breaking our unspoken contract, nosing around with what looked to me like increasing curiosity and, when I checked my tank again, I had only a few minutes left.

I was no novice under the water but, as the sharks' grey hulks obscured the light from the surface, I began to feel like one. I'd broken the golden rule one too many times, and it crossed my mind that I was about to become a headline story: reckless novelist meets his grisly end in island paradise . . .

I learned to dive in Rhodesia, long before *When the Lion Feeds* had transformed my life. My first forays under the water were in the dazzlingly blue waters of the Chinhoyi Caves, north of what was then Salisbury. The caves are a vast, beautiful complex of interconnected caverns, and beneath the surface lies a network of submerged tunnels that challenge even the most adept divers. In those caves, divers can plunge up to one hundred metres into the water, exploring places the sunlight has never reached. Later, driven by my fascination for coral and underwater life, groups of friends and I would head for the Mozambique Channel to camp, dive, spear fish and host *braais* on the beach. Over the years, I'd gained more and more experience. Spurred on by my friendship with South Africa's champion diver David Cohen, I had dived the battleship wrecks that litter the ocean floor around the remote Pacific islands, and the ruins of even older ships on the bottom of the Mediterranean Sea. The underwater world is a rich and miraculous domain. It is the only place that can never be mapped by satellite; it's a geography as uncharted as in the days of my father and grandfather before him. Down here, you could still be a pioneer, but this world also has its dangers.

I crouched beneath the coral, trying to conserve my breath, and to appear as small as possible to hungry mouths and sharp teeth. Up above, the sharks dropped their pectoral fins. Seemingly hunched over, they began to dance from side to side, a motion that could only mean one thing.

The tank was near zero. The sharks were ready to

attack, to inflict the kind of damage on me I'd only read about in books and newspapers. But if I knew anything, then, I knew this: I was not going to die under the water, not without a fight. It was only thirty feet to the surface. If I was lucky, I could get up quickly without suffering the horrors of decompression sickness, but first, I had to get there in one piece.

There was only one route to the surface from here: I was going to rise straight through the middle of the sharks.

Drawing my last breath, I threw myself from beneath the coral, fixed my sights on the light above, and began to rise. Slowly at first, as I didn't want to unnecessarily startle the predators, and after about four metres I was level with the reef sharks and still rising. Refusing to be mesmerised by the pitch black of their eyes, I averted my gaze, but they had seen me. The kicking of my fins had drawn their attention, the frenzy of bubbles and churning water I left in my wake.

Ten metres from the surface, bright light began to play all around me. Somehow, I fought my way and broke the surface, and, tearing the mask from my face, gulped greedily at the fresh air. The boat was only metres away. I swam for it with every ounce of energy I could muster, saw Judith coming into focus above, and reached out my hand. Moments later, I heaved myself over the side. Lying spread-eagled on the deck, I noticed that Judith was staring into the depths from which I had come.

When I dragged myself to my feet, she pointed into

the water. Just under the surface hung the grey shapes of the reef sharks. They had swum behind me, she said, following me and cresting the waves just as I had scrambled into the boat.

'Judith,' I said, in as steady a voice as I could manage, 'it's time to go.'

It was the last time I dived alone.

• • •

Cap Colibri: my former exotic island home. It appeared out of the ocean, a stripe of golden sand, capped by deep, lush vegetation.

I had been going to the Seychelles for many years. I had known the cut diamond expanses of the Indian Ocean ever since I was a boy, fishing with my father in the same Mozambique Channel where I would one day set my maritime thriller *The Eye of the Tiger*, but the idea of owning my own island in the Indian Ocean had always been a hopeless dream. However, I kept coming back. First I did so to indulge my passion for game fishing, for the Indian Ocean has some of the most spectacular fishing grounds in the world, with black marlin, sailfish and queen mackerel in abundance. Later, it was to dive in its crystal-clear waters, and witness first-hand the phantasmagoria of coral lurking under the surface. As my writing career took off, the Seychelles became a getaway, somewhere I came to wrench myself out of whatever novel I was working on, to recuperate before I went back to battle with the story once again.

In 1989 I became the proud owner of a twenty-seven-acre plot at the southern end of Cerf Island in the Seychelles, part of the Sainte Anne Marine National Park, a string of islands surrounded by reefs due west of Mahe. I will never forget my first sight of Cap Colibri. The pristine beach was ringed by impenetrable jungle and, as I approached our new home, I felt like Robinson Crusoe, hacking my way through the bush with a *panga* in hand. This was a corner of the world that, like Leopard Rock, would be my retreat from the mayhem of everyday life. But more than that, it was an island steeped in mystery and had a thrilling story of its own.

When we arrived at Cap Colibri, the beach and land around our estate were pocked with holes, small craters dug in the earth. The more we explored the island the more cavities we'd find, some hidden by vegetation, others lying in plain sight. They were not the work of island rodents, but of shovels and spades. A fisherman from further up Cerf Island told us the island's secret. Cerf Island had once been a haunt for pirates. Rumours persisted that great treasures had been buried here and travellers would turn up determined to find it. What we had found was the evidence of the human hunger for buried gold.

Nobody had ever found the treasure of Cerf Island, but the previous owner of our estate had discovered the extent desperate men will go in their lust for riches. Word had gone around that he had found the treasure, hoarded it away and not told a soul. Local fishermen claimed he was sitting on a fortune and, across the islands, covetous eyes began to turn his way.

The rumour was unfounded, but one of the neighbouring islands housed a penal facility and, on a moonlit night, a plan was hatched. Stealing a boat, the convicts sailed to Cerf Island and forced their way into the house that was now ours. They tied up the owner, threatened and tortured him; but he could not tell them where the treasure was hidden because he did not know. The truth was, the treasure was a fable that had developed a life of its own. The convicts murdered him in his house and fled without a single gold coin.

It was not the only story of piracy and legendary treasure that haunted these waters, and it was another local myth that would inspire the third Courtney sequence, planting the seeds of the novel that would one day become *Birds of Prey*.

Legend has it that the Seychelles is home to untold buried treasure, if only someone knew where to look. Once upon a time, this had been pirate country, a group of islands far from the authority of the British or any other empire, where men could do as they pleased and the rule of a captain was the rule of law. The treasure of the Seychelles had grown out of the real-life exploits of Olivier Levasseur, a French pirate more commonly known as the Buzzard, or *La Buse*, in French. Levasseur was born to a French bourgeois family in 1688 and became a naval officer before obtaining a Letter of Marque from King Louis XIV during the War of the Spanish Succession. The letter was effectively royal permission to wage war on Spanish ships as a 'privateer' – a mercenary of the seas. When the war ended and he was ordered to return home with his ship and crew, Levasseur had other ideas. He had developed a taste for the life of a privateer and had no intention of changing his ways. The riches he had pillaged from Spanish ships were too tempting to ignore, so he crossed the line, becoming an outlaw and pirate. He sailed and plundered down the west coast of Africa, before moving east, into the Indian Ocean.

By now, Levasseur was blind in one eye and wore a patch. After establishing an alliance with two British pirates, Edward England and John Taylor, he embarked on a campaign of robbery unmatched in the annals of piracy. With the help of England and Taylor, he captured one of the Great Mughal's richly laden pilgrim ships to Mecca, attacked the Laccadive Islands deep in the Indian Ocean, and sold the loot to Dutch traders. As his fortunes grew, so did Levasseur's confidence as a pirate captain. Edward England was accused of being too humane by the barbaric Levasseur and Taylor so they marooned England on Mauritius and went on to carry out what was heralded as the greatest act of piracy in history: the capture of the Portuguese galleon *The Virgin of the Cape*. The galleon had been carrying the Bishop of Goa and the Viceroy of Portugal to Lisbon, and was laden with gold and silver bars, priceless works of art, pearls, diamonds, and silk, as well as the seven-foot-high 'Flaming Cross of Goa', a spectacular piece of gold work set with emeralds, diamonds and rubies, so heavy it needed three of Levasseur's crew to carry it. The *Virgin*'s men surrendered without a fight, their cannons already lost overboard in a storm, and the value of the treasure has been estimated at one billion pounds sterling in today's money. The haul was so huge that the pirates could afford an act of magnanimity: they left the passengers unharmed, and sailed off into the sunset, the richest pirates in all the Seven Seas.

The plunder of the *Virgin* sent shock waves around the nautical world. So feared had Levasseur become that the governor of Reunion Island, east of Madagascar, tried to broker an amnesty to all the pirates of the Indian Ocean. For Levasseur the price was too high – he skipped the parlay and settled down, in secret, right where I now stood, in the heart of the Seychelles. There he buried his treasure and tried to live a peaceful life, but the past caught up with him. Levasseur met his end, an unrepentant pirate, on 7 July 1730, but, as the noose was put around his neck, he made a declaration that would echo down the centuries, ensuring his legend continued. 'Find my treasure, the one who may understand it!' he exclaimed and cast a necklace containing a cryptogram of seventeen lines out into the crowd.

In that moment, Levasseur inspired generations of treasure hunters like the ones who had come to dig up the beaches of Cerf Island. He captured the imaginations of writers too, his story leaving a lasting impression on Robert Louis Stevenson, whose novel *Treasure Island* is a classic of the genre. Basil Rathbone played Lavasseur in the 1935 Errol Flynn film *Captain Blood*. He had inspired me to turn back to the Courtneys and imagine what the lives of their ancestors must have been like, sailing the same seas as Levasseur in piracy's Golden Age.

This beautiful, unspoilt island was a place to seclude myself. Its history was ravishing and ebullient and from sunlit cove to jungle headland, you could feel its vitality all around. A place like this had already given birth to legends. Now, it would give birth to fables of my own.

• • •

In typical Smith fashion, Cap Colibri started small, but grew as the years went by. We began with a main house built in the traditional Seychellois style, with deep, shadowy verandas wrapped around the entire building. It had a large open-plan living area, four bedrooms and three bathrooms, a kitchen and a scullery. Then we built a two-bedroom home for the night watchman and a three-bedroom home for the housekeeper and other staff. We kept the original trees, from redwoods and mango to monkey puzzles and banana, giving the setting an exotic character, and, in the grounds, we built a separate air-conditioned building that would house my study. Geckoes, tree frogs and chameleons were in abundance alongside the brilliant coloured birds, making our fantasy island paradise a reality.

Cap Colibri was a unique place to rest and read. It seemed to encourage contemplation. Facing out onto the sea, there were few distractions. When I sat at my desk to write *River God*, I could lose myself in the deserts of ancient Egypt; when I worked on *Birds of Prey*, I was smelling and breathing the same air as Hal and Francis Courtney. People could have built rows of high rise condominiums and I would never have seen them as my view was uninterrupted. The estate was kept in a state of constant readiness, and I could go there with only a brief case and a zip disc containing my work, whenever the need took me.

The fish off Cerf Island were plentiful. I would go out fishing for a medium-sized tuna, only to end up with a black marlin on my line. My part-time boatman, Jean-Claude, described himself as *un pêcheur dangereux*, a fisherman of danger, and every trip he would take me to a secret location where we would catch beautiful red snapper or grouper. I would go diving whenever I could. The reefs of the Seychelles are rich in life, vast edifices of coral, and I would also explore the numerous wrecks such as the *RFA Ennerdale*, a World War II tanker that ran aground off Port Victoria in July 1970 after delivering oil to Royal Navy ships patrolling the Suez Canal. The tanker sank in just the right depth of water so you could reach it quite easily, but usually I was the only one swimming through the wreckage, exploring my own private realm.

Cerf Island quickly became a place of unforgettable memories: Christmas at Cap Colibri, then my birthday in January, surrounded by family and friends; long days at sea, fishing and diving, or lazy days in the sun, followed by *braais* on the beach, or wine around a bonfire. I'll never forget sitting under my own palm tree, whisky in hand, watching a burnished gold Indian Ocean sunset over the lagoon. Those days were priceless and, sometimes, I pinch myself to believe that I lived them and they weren't all a dream.

• • •

Time and again, chance and good fortune have changed the direction of my life, but sometimes, when the stars align, a person you encounter can eclipse every story ever told. So it was for me, on the eve of the millennium, when Mokhiniso Rakhimova stepped, by accident, into my world.

London was grey on the day my life changed forever. It was that time of year when the seasons change, and I was soon to embark to Spain for several days for the annual partridge shoot which always drew me to that part of the world. For the time being, I was alone, and wandering.

It was 18 January 2000, and I found myself outside the WHSmith bookshop in Sloane Square (now a Hugo Boss Store). There, also peering through the window at the books on display, was perhaps the loveliest woman I had ever seen. I couldn't take my eyes off her.

Something compelled me to follow her when she entered the bookshop. As she browsed the shelves, I picked up a book from a table and tried to read it, but I kept looking her way. Who was she? I thought, where did she come from? What was her story? She had been drawn to the shelves of a rival author, was thumbing through the pages to decide which novel to buy and it was then that I seized my chance. I said hello and apologised for disturbing her. She looked at me coolly, weighing me up, and then she smiled. As I started talking, she said that she was a student and that her tutor had recommended she buy a long book to read aloud, something to help improve her English. 'I've just the thing,' I said, took her hand and led her to another part of the shop where the authors with names beginning with 'S' were displayed. 'Here,' I said, 'this is what you should read.' There, in front of us, stood a wall of my novels with my photograph staring back from a publicity poster. I don't think she recognised me, it was an early photo, for she seemed unimpressed. I selected a book – to this day I can't remember which one – bought her the copy, and insisted on signing it. As I scrawled my name and thought of a suitable inscription, words like 'you're the most beautiful woman I've ever met' and 'please can I see you again' tumbled through my mind. I didn't know what to write. And a voice was whispering to me: Smith, you can't let this moment go. For the first time in my life, words were failing me, and I had to resort to an age-old line: 'Aren't you hungry?' I asked.

Soon, we were settling down for lunch at Caviar Kaspia in Mayfair (now closed). I had known she wouldn't say no – she was, after all, a student – and she devoured a large portion of excellent caviar. I found out her name meant 'Moonfish' in Persian, and that she had been born in Tajikistan, a former state of the old Soviet Union. She had a law degree from Moscow University and had come to England on a working holiday, hoping to improve her command of the English language.

When I told her I was a full-time author she was sorry to hear that I was almost penniless, as in the former USSR, writers were broke. She had never heard of Wilbur Smith, and for that I was thankful. It was the beginning of a whirlwind romance. At a single stroke, she transformed my life. What experience had taught me is that love is all. There is simply nothing that can compare with the bonding of a man and a woman – as one, they have the strength of an army. It did not matter that she was much younger than me and, so it seemed, it did not matter to her. Love breaches all time, it unifies difference, it is the essence of our being, and when it draws two people together, all boundaries melt away. In Tajikistan's tradition of arranged marriages, there was no slur about being with an older man; in fact, they tended to choose an older man as a provider, a protector, a devoted and loyal companion. But none of that mattered.

The next morning, when I woke up, I realised that I had fallen in love.

> *Hear my soul speak:*
> *The very instant that I saw you, did*
> *My heart fly to your service*
> William Shakespeare, *The Tempest*

Five months later, in May 2000, we were married in Cape Town, at the magistrate's court with my lawyer as a witness.

I had taken a flyer, I had gambled on love, but it has paid off handsomely. I have not regretted it for a single moment. I have been rejuvenated in every possible way and in a manner I never thought possible. It's so exciting to see life through the eyes of a modern girl, an intelligent, sensitive, generous woman who is so deeply committed to me and to what the world has to offer. I was at a point in my life when I seriously considered giving up writing.

Niso put paid to that immediately: 'OK, my darling, who are you now?'

I said, 'A writer.'

She said, 'Who will you be when you retire?' and ever

since then, for the last eighteen years, the word 'retirement' has been banned from our vocabulary.

A new chapter in the story of my life was about to begin.

• • •

When you are a young man, you want to conquer the world. You want to own everything, to be the lord of all you survey. But, when you are older, and life has taught you its lessons, you want to get rid of inessentials, to shed as many material possessions as you can, for your life to become more compact and settled again.

So it was that, after Niso came into my life, we looked forward to our future together by shedding the past.

Since my run-in with the reef sharks, I'd lost my appetite for diving. It was like the feeling I'd had when flying into the Ysterplaat aerodrome in Cape Town all those years ago. If I didn't stop sometime, I knew I would die. I stopped diving in July 2003. Another reason was that Niso was allergic to coral. Every time we went diving, she came out in a rash, looking like a pink leopard. It was time to sail away from Cerf Island for the last time.

Leopard Rock was already a memory of the past. I sold the estate to a Cape Town businessman for a fraction of the money I had poured into it, but I secured lifelong visitation rights to a little cottage on the property and, besides, I was happy to see it go, knowing that all the species I had reintroduced to the reserve would flourish for generations to come. Life was changing for me – and new excitements were ahead of me with Niso.

• • •

Before I departed Cap Colibri, however, the Indian Ocean gave me one last gift. His name was Hector Cross.

The legend of Olivier Levasseur had provided the inspiration for *Birds of Prey*, but it was piracy of a very different sort that would bring Hector Cross to life.

It was the end of a long day's fishing, and the sun was setting over Port Victoria on Mahe's north-eastern shore. The port was alive with yachts and fishing boats returning from their day's trade but, as Jean-Claude – my dangerous fisherman – brought us closer, a small boat was going the other way, working against the tide to leave the port. It was an inflatable dinghy with a guttering outboard motor, and it was not until it drew near that I saw the men on board.

The boat was laden with jerry cans of fuel and other supplies were piled high and roped securely. Between the supplies stood a group of men with eyes as cold as ice. At first, it struck me as odd that these men should be setting out to sea as darkness was falling, but I raised my hand in the protocol of greeting all the same. None of the men moved a muscle. No one returned my greeting – a breach of sailing etiquette that caught me off-guard.

Then, slowly, the man at the rear of the boat returned my stare. He was impassive, his eyes lifeless, deadened and glassy like those of a long-landed fish. I had only seen eyes as cold and menacing once before when, as a boy, I had come face to face with the Black Mamba at the water tank outside my father's ranch house.

The inflatable passed, disappearing into the dusk over the sea. I looked over at Jean-Claude; he seemed to know what I was thinking.

'Somalis,' he said. 'Pirates, Wilbur. They were in port to resupply. Their ship's out at sea . . . somewhere.'

I turned back to the ocean from where we had come. Not once, as I cast my line out, had I thought about the other type of men plying these waters. But Jean-Claude was adamant. Had we been in a slightly different place, or run across them at another time, our day might have turned nasty. Pirates, he said, don't plunder ports like Victoria anymore. They earn their living by hostage and ransom, acts of terror played out for all the world to see.

I would never forget the way that man looked at me. His eyes boring into mine, assessing my worth, calculating what profit to him I might possess. It chilled me to the core. One night, some years later, I started thinking about the plot of my next novel. I began to envisage the heir to one of the world's most powerful oil corporations, falling into the hands of men like those. I imagined the intense interaction of ransom demands and hostage negotiation.

I thought of an ex-SAS operative, now turned private contractor, who finds himself given one last mission: to go against the pirates and take the law into his own hands. His name, I decided, would be Hector Cross, and he would be my newest hero.

I knew Somalia well. It remains a fascinating place, not because of its warlords running rampage in what is an epically failed state, nor the fact that their ragtag soldiers once downed a US attack helicopter in Mogadishu, a story famously captured in the movie *Black Hawk Down*, but because of its tantalising ancient history. Apart from having the longest coastline in Africa, Somalia was also the first place in Africa with an Islamic influence, established by some of Mohammed's original followers who fled from persecution in today's Saudi Arabia. Somalia was once an important conflux for commerce, and the location of the fabled Land of Punt, ancient Egypt's close ally in trade, and a place I had written about as far back as *The Sunbird*. During the Middle Ages, Somali kingdoms dominated the region, only to be pushed back by the British and Italians, who arrived to colonise along the coast. Muhammad Abdullah Hassan – forever remembered by the British as the 'Mad Mullah' – fought a two-decade guerrilla campaign against the British, forcing them to erect blockhouses and commit to the same kind of counter-insurgency warfare they had pioneered in South Africa during the Boer War. When the country became independent in the 1960s, it quickly transitioned into a military dictatorship and, from 1991, was engulfed in a civil war that raged for ten years. Today, it is a country in the throes of rebuilding, but still held back by unrepentant warlords who run their own fiefdoms, and constantly give succour to pirates like the ones whose path I had crossed.

Those in Peril was to be my attempt at understanding modern day piracy and getting under the skin of those dead-eyed men who had considered me from their inflatable that day. Modern piracy is an organised big business. In 2011, the year *Those in Peril* was published, almost $160,000,000 was paid in ransom to Somali pirates, including £13,500,000 for the release of the Greek tanker *Irene SL*. In all, 1,118 hostages were held, most for more than six months at a time. And though there is a massive international effort to patrol the Indian Ocean, western hostages are still being taken, including South African sailors. The seas are as they ever were: a nation to themselves, beyond the laws of civilisation.

The pirates patrolling these seas are developing new tactics, changing the rules of engagement. They're using sophisticated radar equipment and off-shore bank accounts – instead of desert islands – to hold their booty. A popular view is that the Golden Age of piracy is a romantic lost era, but in Somalia, a country where the young grow up with few economic opportunities, modern day pirates are held in high regard. They are seen as glamorous, heroic rebels bucking the system, by young boys who aspire to their lifestyle. In *Those in Peril* I wanted to undermine those ideas, to reveal the Somali pirates for what they are: ruthless criminals; men with no humanity. As I was to learn, poring through the records of encounters with these pirates as I brought the story of Hector Cross to life, these men are professionals. If you are kidnapped off the African Horn, it's simple: stay put. Either you will be released or you will be killed, and as a captive you don't have any control over it. Escape attempts are always met with quick, merciless executions.

In *Those in Peril*, Somali pirates kidnap the spoilt, beautiful daughter of a rich oil baroness, demanding a twenty-billion-dollar ransom for her return. With time running out, and her daughter's life held in the balance, Hazel Bannock must turn to the man at the head of her private security for help. Between them, they take the law into their own hands.

This was also a book about the relationship between a tough man and an equally formidable woman. I named Hector Cross after the great hero of the *Iliad*, and like many of my heroes, he is a professional soldier, now in charge of a global private security company. I built him, and the lesser characters in his employ, from the profiles of men I had known who carried out their deadly business in Afghanistan, in the Gulf, in South America and Central Africa. I had spoken to these men and heard their tales of the dark business of war, and, though I will never be able to publicly acknowledge their input, nor pass on the stories they have told me, they have found voice in the steely, capable character of Hector Cross.

I had been writing about strong men all my life, but in *Those in Peril* another character entered my imagination who would be a powerful counter-balance to Hector Cross. I decided there were enough tough guys out there, and I was beginning to think that nowadays, as Norman Mailer entitled his 1984 novel, *Tough Guys Don't Dance*. It was time to put together some new steps on the dance floor, get my guys jumping and singing a little louder to a different tune. I had always respected the power of women, and I relished the challenge of writing a strong, believable female character. Centaine Courtney had been the first of those, but in *Those in Peril* I needed something more, a heroine as clever and competent as the hero, as ruthless in her quest for victory, as adept at facing off against the villains.

I find strong women fascinating, I enjoy their independence, their self-containment and self-belief. My mother, Elfreda, was as resilient, in her own way, as my father, and, I think, much more unbreakable. The mother will hold the family together – and the same can go for countries, for nations themselves. From Queen Boadicea of ancient Britain, to Indira Gandhi, to Margaret Thatcher, Angela Merkel, Queen Elizabeth: these are the kinds of women from whom I would find the inspiration to build Hazel Bannock.

Margaret Thatcher, who everyone knows as the Iron

Lady, was determined to always be number one, to be the best at whatever she turned her hand to. I remember the time I went to a stock signing at my publisher Macmillan's Basingstoke warehouse to sign copies of my latest novel before they were sent out to the bookstores. I sat down at a table and signed three thousand books in their stockroom. Ten days later, Maggie Thatcher went to the same warehouse to sign her book, the first volume of her autobiography I believe it was. The staff said to her, 'Oh, Wilbur Smith was here last week.' Maggie frowned and asked, 'How many books did he sign?' and they said, 'Three thousand, which is a lot!' She looked at them and said, 'Give me four thousand!' That's the kind of spirit I loved and wanted to capture in my character Hazel Bannock, somebody who could stand their ground with Hector Cross. That indomitable resolve would be the heart of the novel.

The gambit paid off. *Those in Peril* was a *Sunday Times* hardback number one bestseller for several weeks, with yet another strong opening week's sale. Its success was taken as proof that hardback book sales could yet survive in an era of ebooks and the threat to traditional high street bookselling, and what was particularly heartening for someone like me, who had started his career fifty years before with pen and paper, in an age before computers and instant communication, was that it topped Apple's iBook chart.

Once, the Courtneys had changed my life, offering me

a career of which I could only have dreamt. Then, along came Ben Kazin and Taita, to show me that heroes did not always have to be Herculean men of action. Now, with *Those in Peril*, I had given voice to my lifelong faith in and admiration for women who took centre stage. That novel was evidence that my days of conjuring up new characters and new stories were not over yet. As one chapter of life closes, another always opens.

I might have left the Indian Ocean behind, but with Hector Cross it would follow me wherever I roamed.

• • •

For a while Niso and I spent some time in Switzerland. We both loved skiing after I introduced her to the sport, so we bought a flat in the Swiss village of Davos in 2001. I had skied in Davos every year for twenty-five years. Switzerland is beautiful, the winters are a fairyland of delights and the skiing is exhilarating. I stopped skiing in 2007, however, listening to the voice in my head: 'Wilbur,' it said, 'if you're over seventy-five and you're skiing then you're a fool, because you're going to break something and over seventy-five it doesn't mend so easily.' Niso is something else altogether. She's like a rubber ball – falls, bounces up and is off down the slope again.

Niso only knows one speed and that's flat out, straight down the slope, no turns, no slowing down. Only one thing is capable of distracting her: her love of children.

Once when I was still skiing and she had just started, I told her to follow me down the mountain, and we set off. I was about half way down when I looked back and there she was, far, far behind me. She'd been distracted by a whole bunch of kids, about twenty of them on a school outing. And while they're talking away, she's picking up speed. Eventually I call 'Niso, Niso', and she calls back, 'I'm coming, I'm coming.' And she did. Straight into me, knocking me off my feet and out of my bindings.

When we got up and dusted ourselves off, I said, 'Look, you'd better ski down on your own, my bindings are broken, I'll walk.' But she'd have none of it. 'No,' she said, 'If you walk, I'll walk too.' She's such a selfless person, and it's at moments like these you realise why you love someone unconditionally. And it's also when you find out why people ski down mountains. It's no fun trudging down-hill through knee deep snow, carrying your skis – you feel about as dignified as a prehistoric mammoth.

Switzerland is not far from Paris, which I have always loved. The chalet in Davos allowed us to pop across the border to eastern France to stock up on excellent wines, cheese and other local produce. I have always found the French, outside of the big cosmopolitan cities, to be extremely warm and friendly. Niso and I used to cycle a lot on the quiet roads in France and often when we stopped for a breather, Madame would come out of her home to offer us water or just to pass the time. Nothing, though, beats the culture in Paris, and both of us love visiting the

Musée d'Orsay, topped off with duck and raw seafood at La Coupole, where Hemingway used to eat. Alternatively, the mussel dishes and bouillabaisse at La Méditerranée, on the Left Bank, are delicious – all rounded off with excellent French wine and Cognac, of course.

· · ·

London is where we now make our base for a large part of the year, but during the summer of 2002, we lived in Ireland, in a village called Midleton, near Cork. The Irish are very positive towards writers and artists, but neither Niso nor I could handle the weather, and found Irish humour a bit puzzling. Niso was bored to tears one day, so I said, 'Go and see the Blarney Stone,' and she said, 'What's that?' I explained what it was and off she went, but she got a bit lost, so she turned into a side road and, seeing a sign above a building that said 'petrol pump and general store', she pulled up and went inside to ask for directions.

There was a woman behind the counter. Niso asked her: 'Do you know where Blarney Castle is?' The woman answered, 'Yes,' followed by a long silence. So Niso said, 'Well, can you tell me where it is?' The woman responded: 'Oh, I thought you were asking if I knew where it was.' There was another long silence, so Niso tried again: 'I want you, if you know where it is, to tell me. Can you tell me how to get there?'

The woman said: 'Where is your car?' Niso pointed to her car and said: 'There it is, outside your shop.' The woman said: 'Well you can't get there then.' 'Why not?' said Niso. 'Because it's facing in the wrong direction,' the woman replied. So Niso said: 'If I turn the car around can I get there?' And the woman said: 'Yes.'

All this of course was played out in music hall Irish brogue.

Then there was the time Niso went to buy Brussels sprouts. She went into a grocer's and asked, 'Do you have any Brussels sprouts?'

The man behind the counter replied: 'Is it Christmas?'

Niso said: 'No, not for another six months?'

'Well then,' said the man, 'you don't get Brussels sprouts. They only come at Christmas.'

It wasn't long before the allure of the emerald green countryside, usually obscured by rain, wore off entirely and we went looking to make our home in London.

17

THIS WRITING LIFE

'm often asked at readings or publicity events: 'Wilbur, I've written a novel, how do I get it published?' I think the answer is persistence, never give up, or as Samuel Beckett famously said: 'Fail again. Fail better.' There is of course luck, which is largely out of our hands, but I do believe we can create our own luck by willing it, by being so devoted to what you want to achieve that possibility becomes probability. And there is human chemistry, finding the right people who love what you do to enable you to do it.

You need to find the right agent who understands your work and can navigate the intricate pathways to the right editor and publishing house for your book. I sent my first novel *The Gods First Make Mad* to a number of literary agents and many of the copies of the manuscript were returned without even being read. I knew this because I'd put tiny dollops of glue in between some of the pages to see if they'd come unstuck – they were still stuck together. However one agent, Ursula Winant in London, saw promise in my work, agreed to take me on and took a punt. She sent my novel to twenty or thirty leading publishers and collected a similar number of rejection letters. It seemed my career as a best-selling author had crashed during take-off.

Rejection is one of life's harshest experiences. It's like being mugged on a dark night and being left battered and bruised, and you can't fight back. You're on your own, carrying the weight of utter defeat. My advice is to use it as a spur, pick yourself up and build some muscle, tone-up your defiance, your resolve, your ambition – fail better.

After a year, Ursula got in touch with me again and enquired about my new novel. I was amazed that she was so encouraging. I started writing again. This time I wrote about what I knew. When I had finished *When the Lion Feeds*, I sent it to Ursula. She was brilliant, she loved my novel and rang me to say so. She prepared to do battle on my behalf. She had known Charles Pick at publishing house William Heinemann for twenty years. As I have already mentioned, Charles was a special blend of innovation and experience, knowing every important detail about publishing. He had started as an office boy at the age of sixteen with publishers Victor Gollancz. His next job was in sales. Shortly afterwards, he tried to sell a 'marvellous new book' called *Burmese Days* by an author named George Orwell to a Hampstead bookshop. Standing behind the counter parrying Charles's pitch was a part-time assistant called Eric Blair, who admitted he knew Orwell very well . . . It was Orwell himself.

Charles's skill was his ability to work with a broad range of authors and develop them into household names. He published J. B. Priestley, Paul Gallico and Monica Dickens, Charles Dickens's great granddaughter, among many other authors.

Ursula was determined that Charles would be my publisher.

She rang him up and pitched, saying she had just read this wonderful manuscript that he was going to fall in love with. Charles demurred: he'd heard this sort of sales patter many times from agents; but he knew and trusted Ursula's taste. It was when she followed up with some outrageous demands that he knew she was serious. She said that before she sent the manuscript to him, there were three conditions: she wanted an advance of £500, a guaranteed first print run of 5,000 copies and the novel must be published before Christmas.

'I can't comment on those conditions until I've read the book,' said Charles.

Ursula sent the manuscript of *When the Lion Feeds* to him, Charles read it that weekend and was captivated by the first chapter. On the Monday morning, he gave the manuscript to Tim Manderson, Heinemann's sales director, who was widely read in all forms of fiction. The next day, he came into Charles's office and said, 'What a marvellous novel! We must publish it, call the agent immediately!'

He rang Ursula: 'The book is everything you said it was. We can't publish before Christmas but we'll publish in February, a much less crowded month for new fiction. As for the other two conditions, I won't offer you the £500 you suggested – the book deserves an advance of £1,000 – and your print stipulation is too modest, our first printing will be 10,000 copies!'

I think Ursula nearly fell off her chair.

Soon, a letter arrived in Salisbury from Charles, congratulating me on the novel. They were words I had been waiting to hear ever since *The Monarch of the Ilungu* – confirmation that I might yet make it as a writer. I responded by next post, telling Charles how pleased I was, and that I would visit him in England at the earliest opportunity. So began one of the most fulfilling personal and professional relationships of my life.

Publishing is a team effort and the players were in position to lead *When the Lion Feeds* out into the world.

By the time publication day was upon us, we had already reprinted a further 10,000 copies making a total of 20,000 copies in all.

As soon as contracts were signed and I received my advance, I flew to England, the first time I had visited the country I would one day call home. I stayed with Charles's family in Lindfield, under the South Downs near Brighton, forging a friendship that has lasted a lifetime.

Born in the year the Great War ended, Charles was fifteen years my senior – and a man who had seen as much of the world as I one day hoped to do. His own war had been spent in Burma, India, and on Mountbatten's far-eastern war crimes commission, a period of his life that intensified his interest in other cultures and less familiar parts of the world. He was one of that rare breed of publishers who seemed to operate by pure instinct, and, at a time when editors' tastes were the lifeblood of a publishing house, he was given licence to pursue literary excellence wherever he could find it. He was a tough publisher, extracting the best from his authors, just as he wrestled the best terms out of bookshops and foreign markets worldwide. Some said his unstinting work ethic was born after his father was bankrupted when Charles was ten; whatever it was, it had turned him into one of the canniest operators in the business. His faith in me and my work was revelatory, and his unwavering support across the decades would always anchor me.

At Lindfield, I met Charles's son Martin, who had just returned from working as a volunteer in what was then Bechuanaland, now Botswana; at the age of nineteen he had very definite ideas about Africa. We had a spirited discussion that first night, but when Charles, who would later become my literary agent, passed away, there was no chance that anyone but Martin would replace him as my agent. I also met a French publisher at Charles's house, Thérèse de Saint Phalle, who recommended *When the Lion Feeds* to Presse de la Cité in Paris, which would become my French publisher over the next few decades.

Charles and I talked from breakfast to bedtime. Patiently and enthusiastically, he shared his knowledge and wisdom with me. While we walked on the Downs he said, 'You have written one book. A good first step on the ladder. You still have a long way to go. It takes ten years for an author to establish himself. We will review your progress each year.'

He also advised me to 'write only about those things you know well.' It is because of him that I have written only about Africa. 'Do not write for your publishers or for your imagined readers. Write only for yourself.' This was something that I had learned for myself. Charles confirmed it for me. When I sit down to write the first page of a novel, I rarely give a thought to who will eventually read it. Another critical piece of advice was: 'Don't talk about your books with anybody, even me, until they are written.' Until it is written a book is merely smoke on the wind. It can be blown away by a careless word. I sit down to write my books while other aspiring authors are sometimes talking theirs away.

Finally, he said, 'Dedicate yourself to your calling, but read widely and look at the world around you, travel and live your life to the full, so that you will always have something fresh to write about.' It was advice I have taken very much to heart.

I took the advice seriously in London that winter and was determined to have a good time. After the weekend at his house, Charles invited me to the Heinemann office Christmas Party. He told me afterwards that one girl had swooned on the staircase at meeting their 'hot new author'. I didn't believe a word of it.

I walked into the room where the party was in full swing and looked across and there was this little English rose – she was just so cute. She had a peaches and cream complexion and the sweetest smile. I saw her steal a glance at me and then go back to chatting to her friends. I did the rounds, talking to the sales and publicity people, marketing executives, the production department and other important folk, and then I went up to the girl – let's call her Suzie – and her circle of colleagues. The sales manager said, 'Wilbur, this is Suzie,' and Suzie turned to me and said, 'Your novel is the most fantastic book I've ever read.' She then planted a sucker of a kiss on my lips. I'd never experienced anything like it. It was so joyous. After the party was over, she insisted we go for a dance, and of course I had no choice but to enjoy her charming company!

It was London in the swinging sixties, an uninhibited time, and girls were just as happy as men to make the first move. It was exhilarating, liberating, there was so much optimism in the air, and women had opinions, they could take you or leave you. You'd go on to a dance floor and start dancing and a girl would just sidle up and whisper in your ear. There was an innocence about it all, as if young people had been reborn and were going to change the world. I had such an amazing time in London during my first trip.

I decided to visit as many high street bookshops as I could and I started terrorising the booksellers stocking my books. I'm not sure what I really expected to find. I thought there might have been twenty or thirty journalists and as many photographers hanging on my every witty word. I thought that I would see every bookshop in London jammed with my books and posters screaming, 'A great new literary genius hits the shelves.' I thought, perhaps, even the Queen might invite me to Buckingham Palace for tea.

None of these happened. In fact, I found myself wandering from one bookshop to another looking for my book, and often I found it at the back with the children's books or still boxed-up in the store room. Sometimes I would speak to the owners of the bookshop and pester them to display it in the front window; at other times I would take the book from the shelf, hide it under my coat and put it in the window myself. I was caught doing this by one bookshop owner and he phoned my publishers and said, 'Keep that young author of yours out of my shop!' Others had phoned to complain as well. 'Pain in the neck' was one of the politer epithets.

Finally, somewhat disillusioned, I headed back to Africa. I was in the departure lounge at Heathrow Airport, sitting waiting for my plane, when, looking across the lounge, I saw a woman reading my book.

The thrill was so intense that the hair stood up on the back of my neck and I came out in a cold sweat as I watched her. She was turning the pages, and I was desperately hoping she'd burst into tears, or laughter – show some emotion! But she didn't.

I pretended to go to the bathroom and passed behind her chair, sneaked a glance at what page she was on, came back and finally I couldn't resist it anymore. I went and stood in front of her and said, 'Excuse me, madam.' She looked up and said 'Yes?' And I said, 'That's my book you're reading.' And she said, 'I'm terribly sorry, I just found it lying here,' and she thrust it into my hand.

That was my first reader, at least the first one I had met, and I came across as a stalker!

Things improved, after a fashion. A year or two later, with two or three books under my belt, I was invited to New York City to sign books at the Doubleday Bookstore. Now, the Doubleday Bookstore on Fifth Avenue was the largest bookstore in the world – twelve storeys high – as big as the Taj Hotel. I thought that was quite an honour. I accepted with a smile, flew to New York and on the chosen day I left my hotel, caught a taxi and arrived at the bookstore. I think I was expecting all the staff to be outside ready to greet me and the general manager to be standing with arm outstretched, offering to shake my hand and usher me in. But no, I was standing on the pavement, once again on my own.

I wandered into the bookstore and thought, 'What do I do now?' I saw a young lady behind the till collecting money from customers who were buying books. I joined the queue and stood there, slowly working my way to the front, and when it was my turn, she said, 'Yes sir, what can I do for you?'

I said, 'I'm here to sign books,' and she said, 'Oh, you're one of those are you; and what's your name?'

I told her, 'Wilbur Smith,' and she said, 'How do you spell Wilbur? With a U or an E?' and I said, 'U.' She looked down at her piece of paper and said, 'Yes, you're on the list. Fourth floor. Take the elevator up, turn right from the elevator and you will find your table there with your books on it. Go ahead.'

I thought, 'Well that's a warm welcome,' but I went up to the fourth floor and sure enough, there was my table with a huge pile of books, a glass of water, lots of pens – and nobody to be seen wanting to buy my books. I sat there for some considerable time. Eventually, I looked across to the other side of the huge room and there I saw another author – a well-known writer of western novels.

He was sitting at a table like mine. And like mine, his books were a towering pile – but he was signing them, frantically. Yet the room was empty, there was nobody standing in front of him getting their books signed. I thought that was very strange, so I decided to find out what was happening. I went across to him and said, 'Excuse me, who are you signing those books for?' He said, 'It doesn't matter who I'm signing them for. If I sign them, the bookstore can't send them back to my publisher and I get paid a royalty.' I said, 'Oh,' and shot back to my table and signed 300 books in something like ten minutes. I then had some time on my hands, and feeling smug and pleased with myself, I looked around and saw a whole shelf of Freddy Forsyth books. I thought, 'Now Fred is a good man,' so I did him a big favour and signed all his books.

. . .

Charles remained my publisher for many years. I trusted him implicitly, and we developed a strong and enduring friendship that eclipsed our professional relationship. When he contacted me after the publication of *The Burning Shore* in 1985 to tell me he was retiring from Heinemann after twenty-three years, everything had to change. *The Burning Shore* had been a turning point in my writing life. It was the first time I expanded my range and tested my ability by seeing the world through the eyes of a female main character, and Charles's retirement sparked another epiphany: I did not want to lose Charles, not if there was a way I could keep him. I asked if he would consider being my agent. 'Charles,' I said, 'all my energy goes into researching and writing the books. But you have always looked after my contracts and developed my overseas business and seen me through my whole writing career.' Charles thought about it for a few days, and then told me he would be happy to act as my literary agent. He set up the *Charles Pick Consultancy* precisely for this purpose. His relationships with his authors were legendary in the business, instilling mutual respect and unshakeable loyalty. He was a fantastic guard against the unscrupulous chequebook publishers who would go out to poach successful authors from other stables. And now his energy would be employed in fighting my corner.

'You must keep your authors close,' he once said, describing his philosophy. 'You must become a sort of nanny to them. You must know their marital problems. You must know their economic problems, their work problems, their blocks when they can't write some days. You become their nursemaid . . .'

Well, I didn't need a nursemaid, but Charles went from tough publisher to even tougher agent. Soon he had negotiated a lucrative new contract and moved my work to Pan Macmillan, previously my paperback publisher. In the contract, he'd outlined the number of books that would be published, their advertising budget, how the adverts would run, and so many more advantageous nuances that I'd never considered before. My head spinning, I called him up. 'Charles,' I said, 'you've been cheating me all these years!'

He laughed. 'They were good terms Wilbur, but these are even better – that's what a good agent is supposed to do.'

He had been an incredible publisher and he was an even better agent.

. . .

On the day I begin a new novel, I look into my bathroom mirror, shave the stubble from my jaw and stare into my eyes. For six months, a story will have been developing in my mind. I have done my reading. I have done my research. I know how the first ten pages will look and feel written down. As I shave, I repeat the opening to myself, over again, listening to it, tuning it. It is a little ceremony I have devised, a petition and a prayer. Where those ten pages will take me, I do not yet know, but, when I have finished shaving, I settle in my study and write them, without looking up. Only then do I set off into the unknown. Writing is a voyage of discovery. You're familiar with the port you're leaving from, the islands you intend to visit along the way, but the destination is obscured by the haze of distance.

'How do you do it, Wilbur? How do you become a writer?'

It's a question I have been asked many times over the last fifty years. At my glibbest, the answer has always been 'luck'; at my most practical, it has been that I 'sit down in front of a blank piece of paper, or a screen, and start writing.' The truth is, there is only one first step to becoming a writer: you must want to do it above everything else. Anything less than total commitment, and you will fall at the wayside, because the business of telling stories is long and lonely, and only those people willing to climb that cliff face alone will make it. If over fifty years of writing has taught me anything, it is this: the process of wresting characters and plot onto the page is at once the most soul-destroying exercise imaginable, and the most exhilarating activity life has to offer. To get to the joy of it, a writer must break through the punishing barrier of solitude that can stop the best of us, and the only reason to put yourself through that torture is if you have a story you passionately want to tell. My books have all been works of passion, right back to my abortive first attempt. They must be, because in the beginning you're writing them on stolen time, after hours or before you go to work, over weekends while the rest of humanity is carousing and having fun. Writing is invasive. It is a task that demands stamina and time. Sometimes the words flow like a river in flood, at others they trickle and have to be clawed out of the dry river bed. A writer must endure it all, and have faith that the story is good, needs to be told, entertains, and is something to which they can be proud to put their name.

Even now, I still doubt I can do it again. The thought of a marathon eight months behind a desk, forging a novel out of the pig iron of half-formed ideas clattering around my mind, the enforced separation from loved ones and friends as the process becomes a barrier between us – these are things that unnerve me as I lift my pen. Every time I declare it will be my last, but then I start another novel, and I fall in love with writing all over again. It's a compulsion, perhaps a sickness, but writing is also a way of ordering life.

Like hunting, the secret to good writing is tenacity. Without willpower and purpose, a novel will never become manifest. I assemble my books painstakingly word by word, building a narrative edifice that I hope will be appealing to enter, but often I receive letters from would-be authors saying, 'I write for three days, realise it's all nonsense, then have to go back and rewrite it.' This is the first fatal trap all writers should avoid. A writer should get it all down straight from the pen or keyboard without looking back. Spontaneous writing like this comes from the unfiltered, animal part of the brain, one's instinct, and therefore has real value. Each of my drafts is unique. Each one encapsulates a part of my life, a part of my thinking that I will never be able to revisit. When I read back old material, I can picture myself as I was then – reading Sean and Garrick Courtney, now, is to see myself as a thirty-year-old tax assessor; or *The Dark of the Sun* takes me back to the Inyanga Mountains. Novels become monuments to our former selves.

The best ideas cannot be chased down. Instead, you

must wait for them and given time they will present themselves. Often a character will emerge out of the shadows, demanding I tell their story – which is what happened with *Golden Fox* and Bella Courtney. Sometimes a character will change of their own volition, escaping my direction. I have learned not to plot a novel in detail – too rigid a plan can stifle its animating force. If you start with an ending in mind, it's possible you'll obstruct the writing by conniving the story towards that end, rather than giving the characters freedom to determine where they end up. My characters sweep me along on their journey; they are responsible for the action – the tensions between them, their private motivations, their loves, hates and jealousies, all the elements that bring life to a novel. If you know the characters well enough, the story will tell itself. As for the destination, you'll glimpse it when it's on the horizon. A novel's ending is instinctive: you let it come to you, trust it and write it down.

The true writer must find joy in words, in their music, and acknowledge their potency: 'Words are, of course, the most powerful drug used by mankind,' said Rudyard Kipling. Words can start wars, they can ignite love affairs, they can bring down civilisations. The world has been torn apart by words spoken by evil men; they are more powerful than any weapon, at once dangerous and sacred. The skilled writer can employ words to devastating effect, conjuring hope and hopelessness in equal measure. They can amaze and delight, fill your mind with strange and wonderful thoughts – or they can lay you low, make you moan and weep. A writer must respect language, cherish it, treat it with love and care, put it to work parsimoniously and with precision. Words are diamonds, the writer is the diamond cutter.

Ever since *When the Lion Feeds*, I have treated writing as my job. I keep set hours, maintaining the structure of what I am trying to create and how I create it. Some people write in fits and starts and edit and rewrite as they go along, but I have always been a gusher. My first responsibility is to get the story onto the page, and only then will I look back and edit when I can see it in context. It is the spontaneity of the first draft that appeals to me. Hemingway thought differently: 'I write one page of masterpiece to ninety-nine pages of shit. I try to put the shit in the wastebasket.' For him writing was rewriting. For me, the first draft is where the magic happens, where all the important creative decisions are made, when I'm in the thick of it with my characters, swept up in their story in the same way as my readers will hopefully be. It is the purest experience of writing a novelist can have.

Spending so long immersed in a novel's story can be a wearying endeavour, but the writer must learn to manage their own spirit. A strong spirit is a writer's most vital resource, because if he cannot give his heart to his work, then he cannot expect his readers to do so. Writing a novel demands sacrifices which can take their toll. You lose perspective and a grip on the real world. There comes a point when I step away from the page, begin to see the flaws, decry the entire rambling concoction, and declare my intention to scrap it and start again. Now, because I've done it so often, I can anticipate the warning signs, and it's time to take a week, or even a month, off. I travel, take myself out of the story, revisit reality, and return rejuvenated.

Knowing how to pace yourself is difficult for an aspiring writer. I have learnt to recognise the point of creative exhaustion and stop before I end up writing myself into a corner. I never keep on writing until I run dry. Sometimes I stop mid-sentence, so I have something to continue with the following morning. Often, I will go to bed worrying over a section of the novel, a problematic passage or a moment of transition when the plot is changing direction. I sleep on it and usually the solution appears from the mist when I look in the mirror to shave the next morning. Somehow, my subconscious has untangled the threads that my faltering waking mind could only further twist and knot.

The writing impulse is fed and nurtured by a love of reading. My passion for reading has never dimmed since those days on my father's ranch and at boarding school when books were all I had. My tastes have evolved over the years, but they remain true to the enthusiasms of that young boy colonising the school library in the Natal Midlands almost seventy years ago. Looking back, I am proud to see myself as a link in a great chain of storytellers going back to classical myth and beyond. It has often been said that every plot has already been written, that there is nothing new, and I am a firm believer that this is true. Across the years, I have drawn from classical conflicts but what every new writer must do is put a unique interpretation on the elemental plots, set them in a new age and give the protagonists fresh conflicts to resolve. Being steeped in the stories of the past is the best education a novelist can have – whether that be the *Biggles* and *Just William* books I devoured as a boy, the novels of C. S. Forester and H. Rider Haggard I consumed as a young man, the works of Hemingway, Steinbeck and Lawrence Durrell I still go back to, or the classical tales of the Bible, Greek myth and William Shakespeare.

The writer who has toiled over his story, who has turned down invitations, shunned family and friends so that he can lock himself away with imaginary characters for months on end, must have nerves of steel. He must have Kipling's 'If' as his motto, be prepared to risk it all on a game of pitch and toss, and treat triumph and disaster in exactly the same way. There are many talented writers who have weathered countless rejections before seeing their novels succeed. A writer must be thick-skinned, or else be ground down by the weight of opinion. After *When the Lion Feeds* was successful I was hailed as an 'overnight' success, but my first novel was rejected by numerous publishers! However, this is nothing compared to some other authors. Louis L'Amour was rejected two hundred times. Zane Grey was told he had no business even bothering publishers, but his books have now sold 250 million copies. *Catcher in the Rye* was rejected; *The Chronicles of Narnia* were rejected; D. H. Lawrence felt so dejected that he self-published his work in Italy before Penguin took a chance and published *Lady Chatterley's Lover*. Margaret Mitchell collected thirty-eight rejection letters for *Gone with the Wind*, and nobody dared take a risk on publishing Chinua Achebe's *Things Fall Apart*. When it was finally published, it became the most widely read book in modern African literature. J. K. Rowling's first Harry Potter novel was turned down by all the publishers in the first round of submission. 'An absurd and uninteresting fantasy which was rubbish and dull' was the verdict of a publisher on William Golding's *Lord of the Flies*, which went on to sell over fifteen million copies.

Books are as individual as people. There are no rules, no templates and no guarantees. More often than not you're inviting grief into your life if you write a novel and want to see it published. But that does not mean you mustn't try. As in every enterprise, in achieving every dream, as in the very business of life itself: do not ever give up! Fortune will favour the brave.

When I started writing, I was told by people in the industry, 'You're too late, the day of the book is gone,' so I said, 'Well that's fine, I'll just soldier on.' I've been writing for over fifty years now. I was lucky enough to miss the big wars and not get shot, but also lucky enough to grow up among the heroes who had served in them and learn from their example. I was lucky to live and write when books were an essential part of society and people were not distracted by cell phones or tablet computers. I have lucked into life continuously. I have ended up in situations which have seemed appalling at the time, disastrous even, but out of them have come another story or a deeper knowledge of human character and the ability to express myself better on paper, and so to write books which more and more people have read and continue to read.

Along the way, I have enjoyed a life that I could never have imagined. I have been privileged to meet people from all corners of the globe. I have been wherever my heart has desired and in the process my books have also taken readers to many, many places. I always say, I've started wars, I've burned down cities, and I've killed hundreds of thousands of people – but only in my imagination!

I don't have to write any more – I haven't had to financially for a long time – but I continue to do so because I derive so much pleasure from storytelling. Stephen King once, very kindly, said, 'You can get lost in Wilbur Smith's world.' Well I get lost in Wilbur Smith's world too. At one stage in my life I was really excited by danger: I flew, drove fast cars, dated faster women, hunted dangerous animals, all the activities that pushed me to the edge of the precipice. I've had tough times, bad marriages, people I loved dearly dying in my arms, burnt the midnight oil getting nowhere, but it has all, in the end, added up to a phenomenally fulfilled and wonderful life with a woman who has become my soulmate in the autumn of my days.

My goal now is to write until I turn 100, living with the same zest as I imbue the characters in my books. I want to be remembered as somebody who gave pleasure to millions and had a wonderful time doing it. I look back on my life and I don't have any regrets. Right now, in late life, as autumn leaves turn gold, burnished brown, blazing orange, I'm having so much fun. I won't stop writing until I stop breathing and even then, the lid of the coffin will creak open and a bony claw will emerge and write THE END. As Hilaire Belloc wrote: 'When I am dead, I hope it may be said: "His sins were scarlet but his books were read."'

APPENDIX

The Monarch of the Ilungu
Wilbur Smith
(twelve years old)

Dawn, grey and somber, stole softly across the terrible swamps that stood guard to the Ilungu forests. A leechuwee barked softly at the dawning day and a flight of wild ducks whistled swiftly overhead. A moorhen gave its harsh cry and a goose settled unwarily on the glittering reed-studded water – a slight splash and a startled cry as the bird disappeared in the crystal waters; a few feathers, driving slowly across the surface, marked its grave. A second later a crocodile pushed its hideous snout above the surface and then with a swirl it was gone.

Two days travel across this dreary waste and the glistening tree-tops of the Ilungu rose on the barren horizon. This was the domain of the king of the elephants, the Monarch of the Ilungu. His gnarled shafts of ivory, as thick as a man's thigh, had battered man and beast alike to shapeless pulp and had thrown to earth trees whose mightily balks would have baulked a charge of dynamite; whilst, lodged beneath his seared and furrowed hide, were six primitive arrow-heads and a hunk of lead that had left the muzzle of a Gibbs 450 high velocity rifle travelling at 3,000 yards per second; but the man who had fired it paid dearly, he had borne the whole fury of those smashing ivory shafts and pounding hoofs.

Then, for three months, the old bull lay on the brink of death, groaning horribly and sucking short gasping breaths; with only the strength in his wasted frame to drag himself down the slight slope to the water hole. At last he could stand and for three more months he stayed resting and feeding while his gaunt frame filled out and the same weariness and cunning attended his movements that had been there six months before that journey through the swamp.

Now he sallied out to find his herd, rumbling deep in his throat and grazing steadily along. He came upon them a wee bit later. It was dawn. Dew sparkled on the grass and trees; while the monkeys chattered shrilly from the branches and a lion heralded the day with a long low roar.

The herd stood in among the trees, the cows sleepily

fanning their ears back and forth and the calves noisily having breakfast. The old bull squealed his delight but the herd hesitated to come to him. He called again and this time he saw the reason for the uncertainty; another bull left the herd and slowly strode in his direction, swaying slightly from side to side – a huge bull this, with 120lb of tusk gleaming dully in the new light, his rugged grey coat scarred and torn and his eyes gleaming redly as he came on, rumbling a challenge.

The big bull hesitated; then went in, catching the youngster's tusk in his trunk and ripping it out by the roots; using this as a weapon, he beat the other to his knees.

Ten minutes later the clearing was deserted except for a ring of vultures round about and a pair of jackals who had come across the scene of carnage and now fought greedily over the battered flesh.

Half a mile away the old bull grumbled with content and led his regained herd down to the swamp.

INDEX

(the initials WS refer to Wilbur Smith)

ACKNOWLEDGEMENTS

My thanks to Kevin Ritchie for extensive sessions of memory jogging and his deep research, Robert Dinsdale for his structural ideas and Martin Fletcher for his editorial work.

Turn the page for a short story by Wilbur Smith, with an introduction below from the author.

I was working as an assessor in the tax department in what was then Southern Rhodesia. The job was a soul shrivelling grind. I wanted to find a way to break out of my cage so I tried my hand at a short story.

I had just discovered rock climbing. On the weekends we climbed the granite kopjes, which are so much a part of the Rhodesian landscape. This was a gruelling terrain in which to start. The granite walls are sheer and smooth and offer few good hand holds. It was not long before I came off. While I was swinging helplessly on the end of the rope, with a few hundred feet of open space beneath me, the plot of a story occurred to me. Fortunately my good friend Colin Butler was belaying me. He is, or rather was, an immensely powerful man, and he hauled me bodily back to the ledge from which I had taken the plunge.

I sat down to write the story a few days later. I wrote it in longhand as I was unable to type. I didn't have any high hopes or expectations for it; however a few weeks later, having submitted the story to Argosy magazine under the pseudonym Steven Lawrence, I received a letter and a cheque from Argosy that exceeded my monthly salary from the tax department by a considerable amount.

The door of my cage was at last opened. Very soon after this happy event I sat down again to write my first full length novel, *When the Lion Feeds*.

Having been writing full time for over fifty years, I believe that I'm safe in saying that I've found a method that works for me. Yes, writing is a joy, but it is also hard work. One has to be totally dedicated to the task. Once I start on a new book I work at it, every single day, for a full working day, until I am able to write 'THE END.' My advice to budding writers is to remember that to be a writer you have to stick to it month after month, and year after year!

On Flinders' Face

Dirk De Lange jammed his hand down on the hooter and blew another long blast.

'Damn him, he was supposed to be ready at four o'clock – it's half past now, almost morning.'

He wound down the car window and put his head out, twisting his face upwards to look at the one lighted window in the block of apartments above them.

'Damn it, Mike, I don't know why you couldn't have found someone else.'

The street light lit Michael's face from the side, but left his eyes in shadow. 'Who else could do it?' he asked quietly, the way he always spoke.

'Rusty or Colin – they're both strong boys.' Dirk's head was still out of the window.

'They're strong, but neither of them has the reach.

Strength isn't enough, Dirk, you know that; you've been on Flinders' Face before.'

Dirk drew his head inside and sat staring across the black bonnet of the car. Yes, he had been on Flinders' Face before and the memory of it came back to him, walking softly up his spine until it tickled under his scalp and made the hair on his forearms lift. Yes, he had been on Flinders' Face with one fist jammed into the crack in the rock and his other hand reaching out sideways, desperately, futilely clawing for a hold on the knob that was Flinders' nose. It had been too long a reach for him as it had been for everyone else who had tried to climb that mountain, and in the end he had swung his body back and held on to the crack with both hands, his breathing burning the back of his throat, the sweat running into his eyes, and fifteen hundred feet of open drop below him sucking at his heels. With a small shudder Dirk brought himself back to the present and turned to Mike.

'Well, I don't like it. It's going to be a really fouled-up climb, they always are when they start like this. I don't like it and I don't like Shep. When I go on to a mountain I like to have cheerful types with me, not a great loud-mouthed oaf.'

'You want to climb Flinders', don't you?' asked Mike.

'Of course, but –'

'Well, there's only one man who can reach across from the crack to the nose, and you know it.'

Dirk lit a cigarette to cover the fact that he hadn't an answer. He blew out smoke, jetting it against the windscreen and watching it roll back in a round cloud.

'Well, I wish he'd hurry up,' he said with less feeling.

'Here he comes.' Mike pointed with his chin at the front entrance of the building, and Dirk turned to watch Shep coming down the steps. The light was behind him and his body was a dark silhouette; an inverted pyramid of wide shoulders narrowing down to his waist. He was a huge man. The rucksack he carried in one hand looked like a schoolboy's satchel against his bulk.

'Are you Oakies in a hurry?' he asked as he opened the back door of the car and threw his rucksack on to the seat.

'Damn it all, Shep, we've been waiting half an hour,' Dirk protested.

'I was busy, I couldn't stop what I was doing.' Shep climbed into the back of the car and settled against the seat. He folded his arms across his chest and grinned cheerfully. Dirk looked at his arms; they were long and thick, ridged with muscles and coated with black hair. He wanted to tell him that the only reason they were taking him with them was those arms, but instead he demanded, 'The light's been on in your room the whole time; what were you doing? You should have had your gear packed last night.'

Shep grinned again. He had white teeth, and his jowls

were shiny from a new shave but already they were blue with beard.

'I was taking another spoonful out of the honeypot,' he said. 'We might be three or four days on the mountain and that's a long time with no honey.'

'You had a woman up there?' Dirk asked.

'Some woman,' affirmed Shep. 'I wish I could get *her* into my haversack.'

'We've got a big day on the mountain ahead of us,' said Dirk, 'and you must do that all night. What kind of shape are you going to be in?'

'Don't worry about me; when you get tired, I'll be the one that picks you up and carries you. Now let's get going.'

Dirk started the engine and slammed into gear. He pulled away from the kerb fast, and Shep transferred his attention to the back of Michael's head.

'Hullo, Mike.'

'Hullo, Shep.'

'How have you been?'

'Not too bad, thanks.'

'How's your wife?' Shep grinned. Yoni was as plump and as darkly ripe as only a young Jewess can be. 'I haven't seen her since the Mountain Club dance.'

Haven't you! Haven't you! Michael thought bitterly, but his voice was quiet as ever as he answered.

'She's fine, thanks.'

'Give her my regards, will you?'

'All right,' said Michael. 'Oh, you bastard, you dirty bastard.' His lips formed the words, but in the darkness neither of the others saw them move.

• • •

They drove out along the coast road and the sea was grey with the mist on it. The headlights were long white shafts in the mist and the wind throbbed against the car. At the twenty-five mile peg Dirk slowed and swung off on to the unmade road. The dust lifted sluggishly behind them, heavy with the dew. The night and the mist drew back as the morning light gathered strength, and Dirk switched off the headlights. The road went up another rise, and as they reached the top they saw the mountains ahead of them. Blue and ragged crested, softened by distance and the early light.

Dirk felt something start to screw up tight inside his stomach and he groped for the packet of cigarettes in his top pocket. The fear that was always his companion on the mountains was with him again – not strong yet, but unmistakably there.

He glanced sideways at Michael. Michael's lips were slightly parted and he leaned forward in the seat. Michael's eyes were so blue they were almost black. His thoughts moved in them like the shadowy shapes of fish below the surface of the sea. Dirk could seldom tell whether the shapes were sunfish or sharks, but now, looking at his eyes, Dirk could read his feelings. Michael was watching the mountains the same way a man watches the woman he loves.

Shep leaned over and tapped Dirk's arm. 'Have you got a smoke for me?' he asked.

'Where are yours?' Dirk demanded. The man irritated him. Michael had love for the mountains, Dirk had fear, but Shep had nothing, and especially not fear or love.

'I forgot to bring any,' said Shep.

'And I suppose you forgot to bring any food, the same as last time.' Dirk passed the packet of cigarettes back over his shoulder.

'The stores were closed when I knocked off work last night.' Shep laughed. 'Anyway, I knew you'd have enough.' He lit one of the cigarettes and dropped the packet over on to the front seat.

'Thanks, Professor.'

'I'm not a professor,' Dirk told him.

'What are you then?'

'I'm an architect.'

'You're a professor,' said Shep with finality. 'Architects are professors. Michael's a professor too. He's a doctor and doctors are professors – only Michael's a specialist, he specialises in women.'

Michael said nothing. He went on staring ahead, but his lips closed and the thing in his eyes changed shape.

'Cut it out, Shep,' snapped Dirk.

'Nothing wrong with that,' said Shep. 'I do the same

only I'm not a professor. I don't get paid for it.' He chuckled, drew on the cigarette, and leaned back against the maroon leather seat. The top of his head almost touched the roof of the car and his legs were too long for the space between the seats.

. . .

The road climbed out of the grassland and started twisting through the foothills. Dirk drove fast, holding the car into the curves and Michael went on looking at the mountains. They were close now, hanging over the road. Grey rock split into buttresses, collapsed into scree slopes or rearing proudly to the peaks. The gullies were choked with olive green scrub and, at one place, a waterfall dropped sheer a thousand feet – white water with spray blowing off it like smoke.

'Slow down,' said Mike. 'You'll miss the turn-off.' Dirk lifted his foot off the accelerator. 'There it is. Gently now, Dirk, or you'll knock the sump out.'

Dirk dropped into low gear and turned on to the track. Storm water had washed it out and left it cluttered with boulders. Dirk sat forward on the seat and eased the car over them, grimacing at every ominous scraping that came from under the chassis. The track ran through a wattle plantation, and the trees were in flower. Bright yellow flowers against the dark leaves. The trees were planted close together and their branches blocked out the sky; it was gloomy and clammy cold in the plantation. The road ended at a stream.

Dirk stopped the car, pulled on the handbrake, and cut the engine. His voice sounded unnaturally loud in the sudden quiet.

'The end of the line, gentlemen. What's the time?'

'Seven o'clock,' answered Shep.

'If we're going to reach the ledge below the nose before nightfall, then we'd better jump about. It's eight hours from the foot of the face to the ledge and, thanks to Shep, we're still five miles from the mountain.'

They climbed out of the car, moving stiffly from having been so long confined, and Dirk went back and opened the boot. He took out the two rucksacks and the thick coils of nylon rope, then he slammed the boot closed and locked it. He unbuckled the flap of his own rucksack, took out an old jungle hat and pulled it on. He swung the pack on to his back and shrugged his arms through the straps. He bounced from the knees, settling the pack between his shoulders, then he picked up one of the coils of rope and draped it round his neck.

'All set?' he asked the others. They went to the stream with Michael leading, and clambered down the bank. The water was tinted to the colour of Scotch whisky; it gurgled eagerly as it hurried between the boulders that choked its course. There was a pool downstream from them and Dirk could see the trout lying in the shallow brown water, fanning their tails to hold their heads into the current.

Michael had stopped at the edge of the water, and now he looked back at Dirk. They grinned at each other, neither of them had to say anything; they both understood; that shared grin had said it for them. It had asked and answered all the questions. 'Do you see the trout? Can you taste the air? Can you smell the wattle flowers and do you feel the excitement for this mountain that we are going to climb?'

'Come on, you Oakies, is this a Sunday school picnic? Let's get going,' said Shep.

They crossed the water, jumping from boulder to boulder. The plantation ended just beyond the stream, and they left it behind and went on to the first slope of the range. It was steep, pimpled with rock and covered in knee-high grass. The path ran straight up it. They leaned forward against their packs, their bodies loosening and the sweat starting to come. Every few paces Dirk lifted his eyes to the top of the slope where the path ran through a deep saddle between two small peaks. Dread and anticipation mixed in an exhilarating cocktail in Dirk's stomach – for from that notch they would be able to see the mountain.

Michael took the slope without stopping and both he and Dirk were puffing a little as they came up on to the crest. Shep was breathing easily and there was only a fine dew on his forehead. They spread out across the path, standing shoulder to shoulder with their thumbs hooked into their shoulder-straps and their woollen shirts making three bright spots of colour in the wilderness of brown grass and grey rock.

Ahead of them was Flinders' Face. Clean and smooth as an axe stroke, the wall of rock stood two thousand sheer feet up into the sky. No man had ever climbed it, but some had died trying. This mountain was a killer.

Once accustomed to the immensity of the face, the eye could discern the pattern of cracks and ledges that covered it the way the prints cover the ball of a thumb. In some of the cracks grew little pockets of bright green vegetation, looking forlorn and out of place on that perpendicular sheet of rock. Rainwater had painted yellow stains down it, and in places there were vivid patches of lichen, reds and pale blues.

They stood silently and watched it.

Oh, God! thought Dirk. If only you would give me the power to put some of that beauty into just one of my buildings – if only I too could create something so eternally alive, something possessed of such serene ferocity. Then his mind darted off in a different direction. And please God, protect me from death on this mountain today. His right hand came up to cross himself but he stopped and glanced guiltily at Michael. Michael had seen the movement and now he looked at Dirk. They did not grin this time, but the understanding was still there.

It is good to have someone like Michael to climb with, thought Dirk. I wish that Shep weren't here to spoil it.

Dirk looked at Shep and he felt a little flutter of relief.

Shep was staring at the mountain, his face was intent, and the wings of grey hair at his temples softened his otherwise brutal good looks. Shep turned his head to Dirk; there was a thoughtful, almost bewildered expression on his face, and Dirk felt a sudden rush of affection for him. Shep was feeling it too; Shep understood.

'I suppose you brought baked beans again,' said Shep.

Dirk stared at him.

'I suppose it's baked beans and tinned peaches – is that right?'

Dirk nodded, unable to speak as the first tender shoots of feeling withered.

'Hell!' said Shep disgustedly. 'Baked beans – always baked beans.' Then there was a little flicker of hope in his eyes. 'Michael, Michael man, what did you bring?'

'Beans as well,' said Michael softly. He did not look at Shep, not once the whole morning had he looked at Shep.

'Hell!' said Shep. 'The two professors with their big bank accounts, their big motor cars and their big houses on Marine Drive – but what do they eat? They eat beans! You Oakies related to horses or something? Didn't no one ever tell you that man's food is meat?'

'Come on,' said Michael, and led off towards the face.

'Beans,' said Shep, 'beans!'

They went down into the shallow valley and up the other side. They scrambled over the scree slope with the rock rolling and sliding under their feet and at last they stood at the foot of the face. They were in shadow, for the mountain filled half the sky above them, and yet it was not so terrifying when they were this close to it. Perspective had foreshortened the face. It might only have been a hundred feet high instead of two thousand.

Michael looked at his watch. 'A quarter to ten – we've made good time. We'll take a fifteen-minute breather, and then we'll go to it.'

'You Oakies tired or something?' asked Shep. 'That's what comes of eating beans all the time, saps your strength.' But he dropped his pack and sat down. 'Give us one of your smokes, Professor.'

'Don't call me that,' snapped Dirk. He took a cigarette out of the packet and tossed it to Shep, then he lay back and looked up the cliff. The clouds were blowing in from the sea, and as they disappeared over the edge of the mountain their movement gave Dirk the sensation that the cliff was falling forward on top of him. Dirk sat up again hurriedly.

'You see that flat rock there?' Shep pointed to a rock the size of a dining-room table. 'That's where we found Charlie Laurens. Did you come up that time with us to fetch him in, Michael?'

Michael shook his head without looking at him, and Shep went on reminiscently.

'He was trying to reach old Flinders' nose, and he came down to where he'd started from a damn sight quicker than he went up.' Shep laughed and drew on his cigarette.

'He was lying on his back on that rock. Not much

blood, just a little out of his mouth and nose. You'd have thought he was sleeping, except for his colour – he was as purple as a Satsuma plum all over; every inch of him. He must have burst every blood vessel in his body when he hit, and when we tried to pick him up—' Shep chuckled again—'it was like trying to pick up a plastic bag full of jelly. There wasn't a piece of bone in his body bigger than the top joint of your little finger. A fifteen-hundred foot fall sure smashes an Oakie.'

Dirk stood up abruptly.

'Let's get going, Mike.'

Michael looked at him with his blue-black eyes, and his dark hair flopping forward on to his forehead.

'I'll lead the first pitch,' he said. 'Then Shep will come next.'

He stood up and buckled the waist-strap of his rucksack. He handed his coil of rope to Dirk, took the end back from him, and tied it round his waist. Then he went to the wall and stood facing it. He touched the rock, running his hands over it to get the feel of it.

'I'm on!' he said, and started to climb. Dirk liked to watch Michael climb. He moved daintily but deceptively fast, using his legs mostly, leaning back from the rock, his body always in balance, poised above his feet, and the rope hanging down behind him like a tail, slithering after him up the face. Fifty feet up, Michael reached a shelf.

'Come on, Shep,' he called down.

Shep tied himself on to the rope and went to the face.

Then he flung himself at it, lunging for each hold, climbing with his arms and legs and his whole body, flailing his way up to where Michael waited for him on the shelf.

'Come on, Dirk,' called Michael.

Dirk swallowed the thick slime that had accumulated in his mouth. He tied on to the rope. There was a pulse beating in his ears. He went to the face, and the stone was rough and sharply harsh under his hands. He started to climb.

• • •

They went upwards all that day, climbing without packs on the tricky pitches and pulling them up afterwards on the rope. With each hour the drop beneath them was deeper, more magnetic. The sun came over the mountain and burnt on to their backs. The rock bounced the heat back on their faces and their clothing moistened with sweat.

They ate a late lunch on a ledge twelve hundred feet above the valley. They sat in a row with their backs to the rock and their feet hanging over the edge.

'How does it go from here, Michael?' asked Shep through a mouthful of tinned peaches.

'We go along this ledge for fifty feet or so, then there's an easy chimney which takes us to the bottom of the Wailing Pitch.' Michael spoke out into space.

'This Wailing Pitch is quite something, isn't it?'

'There's a nasty little overhang at the top of the chimney, but the last time I was here I left pitons in it, so it's fairly easy to get round.' Michael paused. 'However, once you're on to the Wailing Pitch – well, let's just say it deserves its name. It's where strong men cry. If you fall, you can't expect anyone to hold you – there's just not enough room at the top of the chimney for a decent belay point.'

Shep held the peach tin to his mouth and emptied it. He wiped a trickle of juice off his chin and threw the tin over the edge.

'That's where Tiny Klur and Jimmy Marsden came off, isn't it?' Shep swallowed the peaches and went on. 'I'm sorry I missed that. I couldn't get off work to come and help the boys bring them back. They tell me it was a rare old sight. They couldn't sort out who was who, so they put them both in one sack and left it to the undertaker. Give us a smoke, Professor.'

Dirk passed him the packet.

'Who's going to lead?' asked Shep.

'I will,' said Michael.

'Why not Dirkie boy here? How is it that Dirkie always has somebody up above him, holding him on a rope when the going gets tough?'

Michael turned his head and for the first time looked straight at Shep. There were sharks in his eyes.

'I don't think I like that, Shep. I think it's best you take it back.'

They stared at each other for a second, then Shep shrugged and grinned.

'I'm sorry, Professor. I'm sorry you always have to have someone holding you.' Shep stood up, picked up his pack and walked along the ledge. He moved as confidently as though he were in his own bedroom; the precipice at his right hand might not have existed. Dirk and Michael shuffled after him, leaning in towards the security of the face. Shep reached the chimney. It was a vertical slot that cut into the cliff.

'You want me to lead here, Mike?' asked Shep.

'All right.'

Shep dropped his pack and tied on. He stepped sideways into the chimney and put his back to the rock; he lifted his right foot and thrust with it against the far wall, holding himself in position; then, with his left foot doubled under him, he pushed himself upwards. His woollen shirt made a soft brushing sound against the rock. He grunted as he worked, changing legs jerkily, keeping himself jammed in the slot. Michael and Dirk stood close together on the ledge, almost touching, for there was little standing room. They stared up at Shep's bulging buttocks and driving legs.

'Mike—' Dirk's voice croaked. He stopped and cleared his throat. 'Mike, will you let me lead on the Wailing Pitch, please?'

Michael looked at him quickly, then up again at Shep.

'You shouldn't listen to that big baboon. He talks all the time, and very little of it makes sense.'

'I don't give a damn what he thinks; I want to do it for what I think.'

Michael shook his head doubtfully.

'I'll lead, Dirk, I know the pitch.'

'So do I, Mike. Please.'

Michael looked at him again, a slow searching look.

'Please, Mike.'

'All right,' said Michael.

Shep's voice came down to them, hoarse with exertion. 'Next for shaving, please.'

Dirk put his hand on Michael's arm, and squeezed slightly.

'Thanks, Mike.' Then he stepped into the rock slot.

At the top of the chimney they crowded into a small, three-sided cubbyhole of stone. There was not enough room to sit down. A chip of loose stone rolled under Dirk's boot and dropped over the edge. They stood quietly and listened to it rattle down the cliff. It fell for a long time and they never heard it hit the bottom.

Michael broke the silence. 'Are you ready, Dirk?'

The overhang of rock stuck out above their cubbyhole like the roof of a verandah. Driven into its underside was a row of four pitons which ran out to the lip of the overhang. The steel rings of the pitons hung down like meat-hooks in a butcher's shop.

'Yes, I'm ready,' said Dirk. His stomach felt as though it were full of warm olive oil. He wanted to be sick.

'Dirkie boy,' crowed Shep. 'Dirkie boy, are you going to lead?'

'Yes,' said Dirk. 'I'm going to lead.'

'We'll give you a sack all to yourself when we carry you home.' Shep was pleased with that joke, but he was the only one who laughed.

Dirk leaned out and grasped the first piton. He tested it, putting his weight on it. Then he clipped himself to it with the steel snap-ring karabiner on the sling round his waist. He took a very deep breath and swung out over the void. Fear kicked inside him as strongly as an eight-month foetus, weakening him, but he worked his way outwards, clipping on the karabiners, threading the line through the pitons and moving slowly, terribly slowly, towards the outer edge of the overhang.

'Don't look down, don't look down,' chanted his brain. He stared at the stone above his head and felt his feet swinging free. He came to the last piton, clipped on to it and then he groped blindly round the edge of the overhang. He found a hold, a pathetic little fingerhold, and he held it while he groped with his free hand for another. Then he dragged himself up and hung by his arms only. He was round the overhang and on to the Wailing Pitch. He was alone. The other two were left behind.

He had to get his feet on to the rock quickly; already his arms were tiring, starting to judder. There was another hold just above him. He loosened one hand and snatched at it, there was another hold above that, he took it with his other hand. The rock moved slowly in front of his face. He felt his boots scrape on stone and then his Tricouni bit in. His breath was coming in great, hissing gasps and his throat was dry.

'Are you all right, Dirk?' Michael's voice sounded very far away.

'All right,' he answered, and went on.

'Keep moving, keep moving,' chanted his brain. The holds were tiny flakes of stone. He was bleeding from under his fingernails. The blood left brown smears on the grey rock.

'Keep moving.' His fingers were numb and it was spreading up his arms.

'Keep moving.' His legs were shaking. He stopped, clinging with both hands and both feet.

'Go on, go on – move!' screamed his brain. But slowly his body flattened itself against the rock. This was the attitude of despair, the attitude of defeat. To lie against the rock on a climb like the Wailing Pitch was to invite death in a loud voice.

'I'm not afraid.' The wonder of it came to him in a bright rush. 'I'm going to die and I'm not afraid.'

The flake of rock under his right hand made a small metallic sound, a brittle sound.

Rotten rock, he thought, staring at it, but he was not afraid. He felt the flake move under his fingers and he lifted his eyes.

The ledge was level with the top of his head. He had not known it was so close, and suddenly there was a little more strength left in him. He let go with his right hand and flung it above his head. It caught. He sent his left hand after it, and then he wriggled his body on to the ledge, and he lay on his face. 'Dirk, Dirk – answer me – are you all right?' Michael's voice floated up to him, but distance could not blunt the edge of urgency in it.

. . .

Michael and Dirk sat close together on the ledge and looked out at the sea. The sun was setting into it. The sun was hot red but its light was a soft orange that made the mountains glow and threw the valleys into deep black contrast.

'How do you feel, Dirk?' asked Michael softly. He did not want Shep to join the conversation.

'I feel good,' said Dirk. He felt clean, all the fear was burnt out of him and he knew that he would never again be afraid on the mountains.

'You did very well.' Michael smiled his shy Jewish smile.

'Like hell, I did,' said Dirk happily.

'Like hell, he did,' agreed Shep. Shep was lying on his back and staring up at Flinders' nose. 'He was shaking so much, I thought the whole damn mountain was going to fall on us.'

Dirk laughed out loud. Not even Shep could spoil it

for him now. He had it locked away deep down inside him. Shep sat up restlessly. 'You know what I'd like?' he said.

'Don't tell us, let us guess,' murmured Dirk.

Shep stood up and went to the edge. He stood staring out over the valley, the toes of his boots stuck over the drop.

'The mountains are a good place for it. It must be the air up here that gets under their skirts.

Next week I've some leave due to me – there's a honeypot I know. Her husband's going to a conference somewhere – I think I'll bring her into the mountains and let her be really primitive with me.'

'One day, Shep, you're going to get a bullet where you don't need it,' Dirk told him.

Shep snorted scornfully.

'I'll tell you a story, Professor. When I was a kid we used to pinch apples out of an orchard that belonged to an old Army pensioner. This Oakie had a shotgun. He used to chase us. "Leave my apples," he'd shout at us. "Come back or I'll shoot." I used to pinch his apples almost every day and – you know what, Professor – he never did shoot.'

Shep chuckled. 'An apple and a cheating woman have about the same value: neither of them are worth risking the rope for. Most men know that. They shout like hell but they seldom shoot.'

Michael had gone very pale, he wasn't looking at Shep.

'If anybody messed around with my wife, I'd kill him,' said Dirk.

'Oh you would, would you?' Shep grinned. 'What do you know about killing, Dirkie boy; have you read about it in books? Did they teach you about it at the University while we were at El Alamein and Benghazi and Cassino?'

'I'd kill him,' said Dirk again.

'Sure, sure,' said Shep. 'Now why don't you open a tin of beans and we'll talk about something you understand.'

Michael woke in the grey of not yet day. He sat up and let his sleeping-bag fall to his waist. The world was gone, swallowed up in the mist. The mist was below them – a flat, white motionless sea. There was no wind, no sound, nothing but the mist and the mountain. Michael looked up at Flinders' nose. The nose was a shaft of rock that stuck out of the face. It was as thick as the body of an elephant and about twice as long. At the tip it was slightly mushroomed. Next to it, in the smooth face of the rock, ran a crack. The crack came right down to the ledge on which he sat. It was a small crack, about four inches wide. It passed tantalisingly close to the nose and petered out just above it.

There was a movement next to him and Michael looked down. Dirk was awake. He was watching.

'You want this mountain badly, don't you, Mike?'

Michael nodded.

'Yes,' he said. 'Yes, I do. Flinders' is my mountain. I was the first to reach this ledge, Tiny Klur and I. That was seven years ago, when I was still at Medical School. Tiny's dead now, Flinders' killed him. Now this mountain belongs to me.'

'You'll have it today. Shep will give it to you.'

They both looked at Shep. He slept on his back and his mouth was open. His lips vibrated with each breath and his jaws were black with young beard.

'Yes,' said Michael softly, 'he owes me that much.'

A small red ant ran up Shep's neck and on to his face. Shep's nose twitched and his lips rubbed vaguely together. He sighed and sat up. 'I'm hungry,' he said.

They ate food cold from the tins, not talking, but now and then looking up at the arrogant shaft of stone that thrust out of the face fifty feet above them. Shep laced his boots, stood up and swung his arms.

'Give me a rope.' He grinned at Michael, standing tall over him, big and hairy.

'The sun's not up yet, let's wait for it.'

'The hell with the sun, give me a rope.'

Shep tied on. He ran his fingers through his hair, brushing it back from his eyes; then he went to the crack.

'Stand aside, my children, there's man's work to do now.'

He thrust a hand into the crack and bunched his fist, swelling it so that it jammed between the stone sides. He put one booted foot into the crack, turning it sideways until it was in, then twisting it straight so it held. He stepped, jammed his other hand in higher, and walked up the face. Dirk was sitting with his back to the wall, paying out the rope over his shoulder, and Michael was watching Shep with dark-eyed intensity.

Shep climbed quickly, hand over hand, foot over foot, hanging back from the face, very big and unafraid. He came level with the nose and he stopped. They could hear his breathing and the squeak of steel-shod boots biting into rock. Shep crouched there a long time, gathering himself. Then his right hand came out of the crack and started moving out sideways across the face. It walked on its fingers like a hairy spider and Shep's body leaned sideways as it followed.

Watching that hand, Michael was breathing small but quickly and Dirk chewed his teeth together nervously. The hand stopped inches short of the nose. Shep's whole body was twisted sideways and his arms were spread as wide as a crucifix, but still his fingers had not reached the nose.

'He can't do it,' whispered Michael.

There was no movement. Two men frozen on the ledge and the third spread out on the face above them – then, with a simultaneous tingle of horror, they saw Shep's left hand start to squirm out of the crack.

'He's mad,' breathed Dirk. 'He's stark raving mad.'

Shep's left hand came free and his body lunged sideways and then stopped abruptly as his right hand hit the nose. He hung like a hammock, his hands on the nose and his feet still jammed into the crack.

'He's mad, he's mad.'

Shep's hands were moving on the rounded stone shaft, probing, exploring, and at last settling on hooked fingers. He kicked his feet loose and his body swung like a pendulum from the nose.

'He's mad,' whispered Dirk again.

Shep's arms bent, drawing his body up smoothly. His legs thrashed and he disappeared over the top.

'Oh, my God. He's done it.' said Dirk, and he fell back against the wall. His hands were shaking. They heard Shep start to laugh – roaring his jubilation out across the valley like a lion over a new kill.

'I'll go next,' said Michael softly.

Michael walked up the crack and looked across to where Shep sat astride the nose. Shep was still laughing: he had tied a loop of rope to a spur of rock in the face behind him and he had clipped his waist-sling to the loop. He laughed at Michael.

'Do you want to come across?'

'Yes,' said Michael.

'Yes, please,' Shep corrected him.

'Yes, please.'

'Give me your hand,' laughed Shep, and reached out to him.

Shep's hand was warm and damp with sweat. It fastened on Michael's wrist, and Michael could feel that the sinews of his fingers were as hard as bone. Shep plucked Michael across the gap and sat him on the shaft behind him.

'Thank you,' said Michael.

'Don't mention it, old chap.' Shep grinned over his shoulder at him. 'Now let's get Dirkie boy up here.'

Shep stood up, balancing easily on the rounded top of the nose. His back was turned to Michael and the loop of line hung down behind him, joined to his waist-sling by a karabiner.

Michael put his arm through the loop and settled it in the crook of his elbow. With his other hand he unclipped Shep's karabiner. Shep heard the click and he started to turn. Michael kicked him in the back of the knee and Shep spun sideways, his back arched. His arms windmilled and he plunged backwards off the nose.

Michael still had the tail of Shep's sling in his fist. He braced his body and broke Shep's fall. The jerk stretched him on his face across the nose. His one arm was dragged down by Shep's weight and the other was linked into the loop of nylon rope. He looked over the edge. Shep was hanging under him, turning slowly in the air. The sling was smearing the skin off Michael's fingers; he couldn't hold on much longer. He must say it quickly.

'Shep,' he whispered fiercely.

Shep twisted his face up and looked at Michael. Now at last he had fear, it was naked in his eyes. He made a clucking sound in his throat as he tried to speak, and a bubble of saliva broke from the corner of his mouth and slimed down across his cheek.

'Did you enjoy my apples, Shep?' Michael asked bitterly,

and understanding mingled with the fear in Shep's eyes. 'Did you think you could have Yoni, and my mountain as well? Did you think you could have them both?'

Michael let his fingers open slowly – too slowly. He had waited too long before letting Shep drop. Shep twisted back upon himself like a mamba held by its tail, and his bone-hard fingers closed on Michael's wrist. Then his free hand reached up deliberately and he took Michael's throat between his fingers.

'Pull me up, you bastard, or come with me to the bottom,' said Shep. The fear had faded from his eyes, and now there was triumph in its place. He hung suspended from Michael's wrist and Michael's throat. Far below them the mist was dispersing and the tops of the lesser peaks showed through it like the backs of black whales in a white sea.

'Pull me up,' Shep said again. Their faces were close together and they were panting at each other. Michael was stretched out across the nose by Shep's weight and only his arm crooked through the rope held them both from the drop.

'Michael, Michael, what's happening? Are you all right?' Dirk's shout came up to them, strident with anxiety.

'Pull me up.' There was the first hint of panic in Shep's voice. He was looking into Michael's eyes and there he saw hatred, unreasoning, suicidal hatred. Then Michael smiled. His lips peeled back and it was a smile to match the look in his eyes.

'Don't be a fool, man, we can both get out of this,' whispered Shep. 'Let me climb up you. Just lie still and let me get back on the nose. I'll never tell anybody – I swear it – no one will ever know. I give you my word – I'll never tell anyone.'

Still smiling at him, Michael straightened his arm. The loop of rope slid across his forearm and caught at his wrist and Shep started to scream. Michael let go. They fell locked together. They fell for a long time and Shep was still screaming. He screamed after the mist had swallowed them, he screamed all the way to the bottom on a high receding key that was cut off abruptly. The silence of the mountain closed in again, and in that silence Dirk crouched on the ledge paralysed with horror.

'Michael,' he said, and then again, 'Michael.'

Below him the mist undulated like a soft white belly digesting its prey. Above him Flinders' nose jutted out of the face in a rock hard orgasm of destruction.

WILBUR SMITH

Readers' Club

If you would like to hear more about my books, why not join the WILBUR SMITH READERS' CLUB by visiting www.wilbursmithbooks.com/subscribe. It only takes a few moments to sign up and we'll keep you up-to-date with all my latest news.

Watch out for the brand new Courtney Series novel . . .

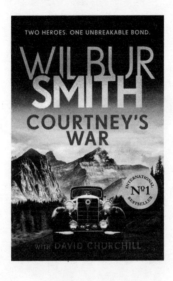

The much-anticipated sequel to the global
bestseller WAR CRY

Available now